Working in the Community: perspectives for change

"Telling the truth is always revolutionary"

Antonio Gramsci

Working in the Community: perspectives for change
is a Beautiful Daze project, published by Rod Purcell. www.rodpurcell.com

Second and revised edition 2005: ISBN 1-4116-5138-3

First edition published as a CD ROM by the Department of Adult and Continuing Education at the University of Glasgow, 2003: ISBN 0-86389-299-X

All rights reserved. No part of this publication may be reproduced or transmitted in any form or by any means, electronic or mechanical, including photocopying, recording, or any information storage or retrieval system, without permission in writing from the author.

© Rod Purcell

Printed in the USA by Lulu.com

Table of Content

About this book   1

Section A. Underlying Perspectives

    1. Why community work?   5
    2. Exploring the basics   44
    3. Global contexts   63
    4. UK context   94
    5. Theories   112
    6. Understanding the urban   170
    7. Organising for change   186

Section B. Practice Perspectives

    8. Working with groups   217
    9. Participatory practice   234
    10. Campaigning   266

Appendices   276

Resources   284

Bibliography   290

Index   307

The Seven Freedoms (United Nations Development Programme)

- Freedom from discrimination – by gender, race, ethnicity, national origin or religion

- Freedom from want – to enjoy a decent standard of living

- Freedom to develop and realise one's human potential

- Freedom from fear – of threats to personal security

- Freedom from injustice and violations of the rule of law

- Freedom of thought and speech and to participate in decision making and form associations

- Freedom for decent work – without exploitation

"Freedom is never voluntarily given by the oppressor, it must be demanded by the oppressed" Martin Luther King

About This Book

"We live, it is suggested, in new times: dominated by globalisation; shaped by the new information technologies; culturally postmodern; a world of uncertainty and risk; sceptical of the old enlightenment faiths; new times in need of new ethics; politics in search of ideas beyond left and right". (Driver & Martell 1998)

"If there is no struggle there is no progress". Frederick Douglass

This book is for all those working in the community. This may be as *an unpaid worker, volunteer, community activist, student* or as a *community work professional* or any other worker who is involved with community groups as part of their job. This may include *health workers, adult educators, youth workers, planners, architects, housing officers, environmental workers* and a wide range of other activities. The book also provides underpinning knowledge for students on a range of community, social and youth work courses.

The book is mainly concerned with practice in the UK. However, due to the global perspectives under discussion it will also be of interest to a wider readership in other countries. The book promotes the view that the UK is so firmly integrated into the world economy that we have to take a comparative global view to development issues. It is not as Peter Lilley then Secretary of State for Social Security proclaimed after the World Summit for Social Development in Copenhagen, that development was only for poor countries. We need to recognise that the world has become a very small space and what happens in British cities, housing estates and rural communities is no longer just a local matter. In turn current economic and social policy is largely a response to these global issues. It is these policies and the local effect of global economics that greatly affect the quality of life in British communities. To this end it is not just a matter *of thinking global and acting local*. It is also about *thinking global to understand the local*.

This book offers a number of distinct points of view. It is underpinned by a belief that community work is an activity driven by values, needs and rights. Its purpose is to promote community empowerment for the improvement of sustainable quality of life in communities. Working in the community should be about enabling a shift in the balance of power. Success can only come through participatory, liberating and transformatory practice. To be able to do this we need to understand a wide range of theories, processes and practice skills. It also acknowledges that in Britain we have much to learn from practice in other countries and critiques of development practice

The book is in two linked sections. In the first section, chapters 2 to 7 we explore a range of underlying perspectives that provide a value and theoretical background to practice. In the second section, chapters 8 to 10, we discuss practice perspectives and the integration of theory to practice. These chapters can be read sequentially or independently as required.

In more detail:

> In **chapter 1** we ask the question 'why community work'. What does community work methods, properly implemented, offer deprived communities? We explore this question through the use of case studies. The chapter goes onto to take a brief look at the development of community work in Britain over the 150 years. We then contrast this history with what we term the 'secret history of protest'. Does real change only come from agitation outside of the established political system? The chapter ends with a discussion of current trends within the community work field and the challenges and contradiction that are currently being worked out.
>
> In **chapter 2** we explore a range of basic perspectives which we can use to inform our work. We consider the importance of holding clear personal values to inform practice. We go on to explore the concepts of equality, needs, rights and democracy.

Chapter 3 looks at the condition of the world at the start of the new millennium. We explore the failure of the current world development model. Particular reference is made to the effects of globalisation and the development of what is termed the information age The chapter goes on to look at some key global issues; women, urbanisation, poverty and sustainability.

In **chapter 4** we discuss how these global developments have affected the UK. Firstly, we review the Thatcher years and the continuing New Labour Agenda. We explore the current social policy around modernising the economy, welfare reform, poverty, social inclusion and lifelong learning.

Chapter 5 takes at look at competing theoretical ideas that attempt to explain the world. We briefly introduce the concepts of socialism, Marxism, capitalism and feminism. The chapter reviews some of the current debates around liberalism and libertarians, communitarianism and the new right and the modernist v postmodernist debate. The importance of the ideas of Gramsci and Freire are discussed alongside theories of the state.

The majority of people now live in urban communities and community workers need a sophisticated understanding of urban social processes. **Chapter 6** explores the nature of community, the core ideas of urban social life and provides case studies on urban festivals and street life to amplify the themes.

Chapter 7 starts with a discussion towards developing a revised model of community work practice that encompasses ideas from the forgoing chapters. We then consider the use of participatory methods, organisational strategies and power to build powerful community organisations. And in the light of this reflect on community leadership, participation, building networks and coalitions.

In **chapter 8** we look at a number of basic participatory issues for working with groups. This include, understanding the purpose of community groups, the workers role and an overview of the multi dimension nature of the groups themselves.

In **chapter 9** we start to consider the issues and techniques for putting the above ideas into practice. We look at participatory models for identifying needs, planning intervention in communities and evaluation

Chapter 10 is concerned with exploring the basic methods of establishing a running a community based campaign.

Each of these chapters starts with an outline of the content. At the end a summary reviews the major points made in the chapter. Suggestions are given for specific reading relating to the main points in the chapter. Sources quoted in the chapter and listed in the bibliography will also be useful. Internet links are proving to be increasingly valuable and these are listed both in the text and in the reference section at the end of the book.

1

Underlying Perspectives: Why community work?

We have managed to make the celebration of diversity our mode of resistance" Vandana Shiva

"Development requires democracy, the genuine empowerment of the people". Aung San Suu Kyi

Aims of this chapter

In this chapter we ask the question 'why community work'. What does community work methods, properly enacted, offer deprived communities? We explore this question through the use of case studies. The chapter goes onto to take a brief look at the development of community work in Britain over the 150 years. We then contrast this history with what we term the 'secret history of protest'. Does real change only come from agitation outside of the established political system? The chapter ends with a discussion of current trends within the community work field and the challenges and contradiction that are currently being worked out.

What the community development approach can do for communities

Work in the community takes place under a number of guises with a diverse range of purposes. A review of community focussed publications reveals literally hundreds of definitions. A mass of terms, such as community action, community development, community education and community organising commonly appear often with contradictory statements.

The report on Monitoring and Evaluation of Community Development in Northern Ireland (Barr, Hashagen, Purcell 1996) surveyed these definitions and identified common themes for working in the community. In reality it is seldom that all the following themes will appear in a single piece of work. However, the more that these themes are applied to practice, the more likely that focussed development work is taking place. The themes are:

- Combating social exclusion, poverty and disadvantage, and promoting full citizenship
- Anti-discriminatory action in relation to factors such as race, disability, age, gender, sexual orientation
- Commitment to community led, collective, democratic processes of action
- Empowerment and participation
- Preventative action
- Problem focussed adult learning
- Commitment to partnerships between common interest groups and between government and citizens
- Public issues and public policies
- A range of actions from self help to campaigns

The report called activity on these themes community development and this book will do the same. This is a more radical definition of community development that many of the others which historically have defined community development as a strategy to sustain the status quo. This reworked definition makes clear that the purpose of working in the community is to promote social change, to facilitate empowerment and enhance sustainable quality of life, and that a range of activities from promoting self help to working with government bodies to oppositional campaigning are all legitimate depending upon the situation. As we shall see such activity takes place in the context of a defined set of values and rights as well as ideological and political contexts.

At its best therefore, community development can make major contributions to improving the quality of life in communities. Using community development practice in the West of Scotland as an example, the following case studies (from Barr, Drysdale, Purcell, Ross 1995) summarise a range of good community development practice that has produced tangible achievements. As we shall see later even the best products can fall far short of their potential.

The Aveyron Project is a parents group which campaigned to establish sophisticated carer controlled service responding to a significant need. Formed in 1988 the group submitted a 5 year Urban Programme application in 1990 for a day care centre with a capital cost of £420,000 and recurring revenue costs of £150,000 per annum. The centre opened in 1993 and worked closely with the Social Work Department. The project illustrates the contribution of community development work to community care provision.

The project provides a direct service to 5 profoundly learning disabled adults, a day time respite care service for families, community education about earning disability fostered through local community participation and a focus for mutual support and action among carers of profoundly learning disabled adults. The project had many benefits, which included:

- a high quality service to a neglected client group
- a service directly accountable to and managed by carers
- enhancement of the participation of carers in the planning community care
- establishment of collaborative networks to more reflect and respond to a community need
- greater community understanding of the needs of profoundly learning disabled people including volunteer involvement
- growth of individual skill and knowledge of both service and providers
- through all of these the fulfillment of Statutory requirement under the 1984 Mental Health Act, 1990 National Health and Community Care Act and 1968 Social Work (Scotland) Act

The role of community work was highly valued by the group. The community worker initially supported the investigation and analysis of need. From this analysis a range of assistance to the group developed. For example, helping the group to develop, establishing priorities, organising, campaigning and negotiating. The worker also assisted in providing training to support the development of necessary knowledge and skills for the group, and become the managers of the service.

Barrhead Single Parents Project. Lone parents are more at risk of poverty and its consequent pressures than any other social group. This Urban Programme project, established by the Social Work Department in 1991, employed a community development approach to lone parents to meet their own needs. Over a hundred women and their children have used the project which has active links with the SWD Area Team, health services, housing agencies Women's Aid, One Plus, money advice.

The project provided community and group work support and counseling, advice services on debt and benefits, a contact point for single parents and a base for organising new activities and services. There have been many beneficial outcomes:

- Social workers report reduced involvement in child cane.
- a strong Single Parents Support Group has been formed and now largely determines the direction of the project
- a new community controlled, Urban Programme funded Women's Centre, employing 9 fulltime local staff grew from a women's group formed in the project. It ran training for employment a drop in café, crèche facilities, after school care, self defence classes, confidence building and assertiveness training, established links with Women's Aid, medical and money advice services.
- a Young Mothers Group developed in conjunction with the local Youth Action Project to provide support for teenage parents
- two women from the crèche, supported by Renfrewshire Enterprise, established a local after school care business.
- a project drama group performed regularly at local venues.
- health issues have been addressed
- group holidays, theatre visits and children's outings were regularly organised.

- training events were delivered (e.g. machine knitting, reducing stress, assertiveness. committee skills, returning to work, child care)
- local women attended events and conferences (Women and Poverty, Domestic Violence, After School Care Child Care)
- single parents said their confidence, skill and self esteem had been raised

The role of community work has been to support the obvious capacity of single parents to take action on their needs.

Crew 31 Health, Drama and Public Participation. Crew 31 was a community drama group, supported by Motherwell Community Health Project. The project raised awareness and fostered community participation in health issues. The group was made up of young people frequently at risk from living in a disadvantaged housing scheme. It had significant benefits for those directly involved and illustrated the potential of arts initiatives as a component of wider community development and education in the field of health. The activities of Crew 31 have included:

- involving local young people in health and drama training programmes
- contributing to the development and presentation of a local community health profile
- drama performances at health fairs, the local Arts Liaison Committee and other events
- creation of a health video: 'Boabs Big Breakfast'
- photographic displays for public health events
- individual and collective growth of skill, confidence empowerment, leadership and social responsibility among group members
- liberation of community creativity and imagination an innovative and effective, community led, means of expressing views about health
- partnership between public authorities and the community on health issues including contributing to the development of a community health strategy with the

Area Liaison Committee and other agencies raising of health awareness in the community development of long term vision of a better community
- effective collaboration with other agencies particularly the local Further Education College and Social Work Arts and Culture team

The community work role stimulated the creation of the group and supported its continued activity through sharing and passing on responsibility and skills, providing guidance, developing leadership potential: assisting with administration, publicity and funding application: securing access to community assistance.

Hands On Women's Community Business. This project demonstrated the role of community workers in generating community enterprise, in this case focused on equal opportunity and community care. Hands On was formed in 1993. It was a community business providing training services to disabled and black and ethnic minority women to create employment opportunities and high quality services for community care client groups. The project applied for Urban Programme funding and received European Social Fund money to train 15 people in 1994 (all of whom are unemployed) and 30 people in 1995. The 1995 training budget was £ £170.000

The project provided training for disadvantaged groups in social care skills, access for trainees to the employment market, the basis for direct, and contracted, service development in community care by a local community organization. The were substantial beneficial outcomes:

- training and employment for disadvantaged groups in an area of high unemployment
- a service developed and managed by ethnic minority and disabled women
- skill development to support the establishment of more effective community care services for ethnic minorities
- involvement of disabled people as providers rather than consumers of care
- collaborative relationships between social work education housing and other agencies

- partnership with other local community organisations
- fulfillment of objectives of the Regional Council Social Strategy in relation to community care, enterprise and regeneration.
- the enhancement of equal opportunities

The community workers role had been varied. The worker helped the group to come together and organize, promote and sustain equal opportunity and anti discriminatory principles, develop the skills and knowledge of the group, support negotiation with other agencies, help build links with the Social Work Department, assist in the preparation and presentation of funding applications, help sustain momentum and enthusiasm.

Lilybank Tenants Forum successfully established an effective organisation to represent community interest in one of Glasgow's most disadvantaged and stigmatised areas. The Forum has:

- built a credible organisation with strong local support
- had a key influence on major housing investment in the area
- stimulated and supported: a Credit Union, a Food Co-op, women's group for a monitoring group for a sheltered housing complex, local employment initiatives, development of community based adult education (with over 100 participants).
- led the process through which approximately 30 local people have been trained in crèche work (over half are now employed)
- contributed centrally to creating more positive perception of the area

Beneficial outcomes are wide-ranging and include:

- influence over public policy through democratic processes for a severely disadvantaged and previously excluded community
- development of community infrastructure to sustain the resulting investment

- more positive relationships between communities.
- a local Initiative structure with community leadership, well placed to propel long-term change
- the basis for strong community involvement in economic as well as social regeneration.

The role of the community worker has enabled the establishment of the group. In addition the worker supported group members to increase their confidence and skills, assisted informal learning by group members as they have engaged with agencies and addressed complex issues, helped the group to think through tactics and strategies, passed on knowledge of structures, policies and legislation and helped the forum to access more specialist support; made the group aware of opportunities and hidden local issues such as requirements for special needs housing. In this example good community work practice has unlocked the capacities of a community often dismissed as to blame for its own difficulties

The above examples reflect the traditional UK local authority approach to promoting community work. The following examples (from Purcell 2005) illustrate more radical practice built around a Freirian approach.

Photo-voice is an international organisation that works in local communities. It originated in Ann Arbour, Michigan, where homeless street people were given disposable cameras to record their world (Wang 1998). From the pictures conversations and people's life stories were developed, the photographs acting as codes in the Freirian sense. The resulting exhibition was used to make the issues around the 'invisible homeless' a visible and hot issue to be tackled. In this process the homeless people themselves moved from being objects in need of welfare provisions to subjects exploring and promoting their own agenda. The learning included a basic understanding of photography, the ethics of photographing 'people in need', developing knowledge about local power systems, to the range of social and confidence building skills required to complete the project. Photo-voice projects have been run in Australia on sexual health issues, homeless people in London, HIV+ women in Congo, street children in Vietnam and refugees in Nepal.

Neighbourhood Houses are an approach that have developed in Australia from the 1970s. A particular house, quoted by Foley (1999), delivers a wide range of activities for women including adult education, playgroups, a consumer and tenancy programme, community and environmental projects, discussion and self help groups. Foley identified the following outcomes arising from involvement in house activities; a place for companionship and support, learning through participation leading to new personal knowledge, skills and self confidence, learning through conflict (both interpersonal conflict and community action) and critical learning through exploring and working on women's issues. He suggests that the house operates as a 'liberated space' within which women can reflect upon experience (again being subjects in control of their learning rather than objects to be taught predetermined knowledge), able to theorise the position of women within Australian society and to plan and take action on identified issues.

The **Adult Learning Project** is based in Edinburgh. The project aims is to implement in an inner city, working class community, the principles and practices of Freire alongside a Gramscian analysis. Galloway describes the projects objectives as *"a commitment to politicise the curriculum, construct learning programmes grounded in the struggle for cultural equality, develop the use of dialogical learning methods and build an authentic relationship between learning and cultural action"* (1999: 226). Initially, project workers and local residents undertook co-investigations to explore critical issues around politics, gender and ethnicity, the inner city environment and culture. From this information new learning programmes were developed. Galloway describes these programmes as making a link between *"the cognitive and affective domains of learning... to create a basis for counter hegemony"* (1999: 233). In practice a range of learning programmes on politics, history, Scots and Gaelic language explored how power and dominant culture operated in the local community.

These learning programmes led to a range of local actions. For example, the history groups both wrote and performed plays celebrating radical movements and individuals from Scotland's past. The democracy groups actively campaigned on local issues around school closure, traffic and on wider issues such as water privatisation. The music groups promoted tradition Scottish song and organised performances. As a direct result of the critical insight gained from the learning programmes, many individuals implemented major changes to their lives and created 'spin-off' organisations.

Development of community work in the UK

Since the establishment of the first human settlements there has always been activity to improve community life. An illustration of this is the following quote from Lao Tsu written around 700bc.

> *Go to the people*
> *Live with them*
> *Learn from them*
> *Love them*
> *Start with what they know*
> *Build with what they have*
>
> *But with the best leaders*
> *When the work is done*
> *The task accomplished*
> *The people will say*
> *We have done this ourselves*

However, it is only during the nineteenth century that we can identify interventions that appear to be a precursor to modern community development. The first activities were firmly rooted in Victorian philanthropy with a mission to either provide charitable assistance to the deserving poor as in the case of the Charity Organisation Society. Or to more generally improve the living and working conditions of the poor who were seen to have the same worth as the rich. This latter view was promoted through the University Settlements of which Toynbee Hall in London was the most famous. By the end of the century there were 30 settlements based on the Toynbee Hall model. As Popple (1995) points out, these community work innovators were upper and middle class reformers rather than state functionaries or political revolutionaries. They worked to reduced conflict from the urban poor and promoted reformist programmes.

The Inter War period saw a growth in government funded expansion in community work. The 1936 Housing Act and the 1937 Physical Training and Recreation Act enabled the funding of community centres in the new housing estates. A range of new organisations including the Community Centres Association and the National Council for Social Service supported these centres. In the latter case the programme was designed to counter the work of the National Unemployed Workers Movement. The NUWM movement being seen as dangerously political, in contrast to the social and recreational activities being promoted through the community centres.

In the post war period the community centre movement continued alongside a number of key reformist pieces of legislation and the development of the welfare state. The most famous, the 1944 Education Act (1945 in Scotland) led eventually to the creation of the Youth and Community Service in England. In Scotland the same process saw the creation of the Community Education Service after the Alexander Report in 1975

The social and recreation agendas of these activities were clearly stated by government. The Ministry of Education booklet entitled Community Centres, defined their purpose as being:

> *"(a place where) neighbours come together on an equal footing to enjoy social, recreational and educational activities as members of groups following particular hobbies or on the basis of their common needs or interests in the same locality"*

This view is in keeping with the colonial legacy of community development. In the late 1940's and 1950's the Colonial Office had followed a policy of using workers to apply community development methods. Firstly, these officers worked to incorporate the existing ruling class into the colonial administration. Secondly, they helped prepare the administration systems for independence. There were undoubtedly reformist gains made for the local populations through these activities. However, the motivation behind this was to keep alive the link to the Commonwealth, prevent the spread of communism and protect the interests of British capital.

Many ex-colonial workers returned to the UK and worked in community centres bringing their techniques with them. Batten (1967) made a criticism of this model of practice. He said:

> *"the community worker does not attempt to decide for people or to lead, guide or persuade them to accept any of his (sic) own conclusions about what is good for them. He tries to get them to decide for themselves what their needs are, what if anything they are willing to do to meet them, and how they can best organise, plan and act to carry their project through"*

This was seen as libertarian and radical in its time. However, the non-directive approach as it became known can be criticised for failing to catalyse action. It confuses decision making by the community organisation with the job of the worker to raise issues for discussion. As we shall see in chapter 5, the work of Freire with the stress on facilitating a critical understanding on ones social condition or the American community organising model provide a more dynamic approach. Freire in particular becoming increasingly influential as his ideas become more available from the 1970's onwards.

The late 1960's were a watershed time for community activity in the UK. The Gulbenkian Foundation (1968) undertook a review of community work. Their report commented that community work was essentially:

> *"concerned with affecting the course of social change through the two processes of analysing social situations and forming relationships with different groups to bring about desirable change ... In short community work is a means of giving life to local democracy"*

This view acknowledges the importance of social change but then places it within a restricted environment. The report identified three main strands of practice: neighbourhood projects, inter-agency work and research linked to social planning. It is from this document that the characteristic of much of today's practice has developed.

Following on closely to Gulbenkian, came the Educational Priority Areas Act (1968) to promote affirmative action in selected deprived communities, and the Skeffington Report (1969) on People and Planning which recommended the appointment of community development officers to help weak groups make their case to local authorities.

The Seebohm Report on the Personal Social Services (1968) was even more influential. The report led to the creation of the integrated social services departments (social work in Scotland). In this integrated model community work was seen as a method of intervention that *"promoted a sense of community amongst those where it did not exist and for strengthening of identity and activity"*. This thread of social work practice developed through to the Barclay Report of 1982 that proposed the introduction of community social work. In many ways this report marked the high point of community works involvement with social work. There were some exceptions. In Scotland for example, Strathclyde Regional Council then the largest local authority in Europe, was by the late 1980's employing around 200 neighbourhood based community workers as part of its social strategy to counteract multiple deprivation. As a result of budget cuts throughout the 1990's this number of workers was drastically curtailed.

1968 was a landmark year in other respects. Enoch Powell's an ex conservative minister made his infamous 'River of Blood' speech predicting violence on the streets of English cities in response to continuing immigration. Evidence became increasingly available which demonstrated the high level poverty in Britain. In response the Government announced the creation of the National Community Development Project (CDP's). The project was, like much of British social policy, following on from developments in the USA.

In the USA in the early 1960 a series of area based anti poverty programmes were developed. Examples of this include the Community Action Programmes for Juvenile Delinquency and the Model Cities Programme that promoted community action and local participation. The rationale behind these projects was that social and economic problems were not caused by fundamental structural problems in the economy, society or political system. Rather they were products of local circumstances that could be solved through localised small scale intervention. The Home Office briefing to the CDP's reflected this American view and described the projects as:

> *"A modest attempt at action and research into the better understanding and more comprehensive tackling of social need... through closer co-ordination of central and local, official and unofficial effort, informed and stimulated by citizen initiative and involvement"*

There were 12 CDP's based in Coventry, Liverpool, Southwark, Glyncorrwg, Bately, Birmingham, Canning Town, Cumbria, Newcastle, Oldham, Paisley and North Shields. Each project had a generous budget and comprised an action and a research team. The researchers would identify the local social problems, the community work team would then swing into action to solve them whilst the researchers evaluation different methods of intervention.

The CDP's were never unified in their objectives, practice and analysis. As Green and Chapman (1990) point out the CDP's also exhibited a number of weaknesses in practice and theory. Like many projects at the time they ignored gender and race issues. They tried and failed to link community activity to trade unionism, and their analysis of community did not develop into a viable practice theory. Most critical of all was their failure to build political support enabling the government to eventually curtail the projects.

However, the CDP's did produce a number of influential documents that transformed the understanding of community problems and what intervention could achieve. The report, Costs of Industrial Change (1977a) identified how the specific management decisions of multi national companies could have a profound effect on local communities, and that unemployment and poverty in a community could be the direct result of an international company restructuring to increase its profit. This analysis is more relevant than ever, as we shall see in the discussion on globalisation Whatever Happened to Council Housing (1976) identified that the conditions on many estates were due to government decision concerning housing policy and the housing market, rather than the fault of tenants. Gilding the Ghetto (1977b) analysed the area based social policy approaches and argued that it was simply a diversion from the class nature of economic and social change.

Over twenty years after the publication of the key CDP reports it can feel that many of the lessons have not been learnt. The government continues with its preference for area based initiatives through the English Single Regeneration Budgets and Scottish Social Inclusion Partnerships and Community Planning. Such approach is based essentially on a pathological analysis of poverty and deprivation. In one sense this is understandable for government in that is unlikely to produce a structural critique of capitalism. On the other hand to perpetuate the area based approach, in the face of the evidence that such strategies fail to address the fundamental structural issues, is to say the least disappointing.

During the 1970's and 80's community work in Britain was subjected to three main trends: the impact of feminism and race, co-option by the state and reduction in funding.

The impact of the feminist movement during the late 1960's began to have a major impact on community work practice from the early 1970's. In many ways feminism has reshaped both the community work agenda and modes of practice. The increasing social confidence of women became reflected in the more active participation of women in community groups, the identification of local issues concerning women (e.g. caring and reproduction) as well as the recognition that women bear the brunt of dealing with housing and poverty issues. Feminist analysis began to challenge male assumptions of practice. Gender relationship, the use of power within groups and the understanding that the personal is political confronted and eventually changed the patriarchal approach of many white male workers.

If the arrival of feminism and the need to take on board a gender perspective shook the world view of the stereotypical white male community worker, the need to incorporate race issues caused him to be fundamentally stirred. The changes that immigration from Africa and the Indian sub continent imposed on British, especially English cities are hard to understand, without first hand experience. I vividly remember growing up in Southall, West London during the late 1950 and 1960's. New people arrived, shops changed hands, the local cinema began to show Asian films and the town slowly developed a new style and vibrancy of its own.

Not everyone welcomed this change. I also remember fascists holding meetings on Saturday morning in the high street and racist marches through the town. Enoch Powell's speech in 1968 expressing his fear that English cities would flow with 'Rivers of Blood' caused by inter-racial violence, reflected the views on a significant minority of the UK population. As an active expression of these views institutional and informal racism actively discriminated against the new communities.

Some community workers actively engaged with these issues, others saw the race question as a sub division of the class system, whilst some simply ignored it entirely. Slowly work around racial issues grew due a variety of factors including the continuing growth of new communities, the campaign against the apartheid system in South Africa and the need to resist the resurgence of fascism. This came to a head in 1979 when the Metropolitan Police, protecting a Nation Front meeting in Southall, rioted and killed Blair Peach a member of the Anti Nazi League.

Over the next ten years white community workers, faced by the critique of their practice from their Black and Asian colleagues, increasingly took on board race issues and the importance of making themselves and community work appropriate and accessible to the new communities. The new Community Relations Councils steadily developed a variety of grass roots activities and many Black / Asian only groups were created to help build and defend their communities.

Particularly in the major English cities current practice is now firmly underpinned with gender and race perspectives; and to a lesser extent other oppressions around sexuality and disability. This has lead to a greater stress on the process of work. Good practice today is not just about achieving your goal, it is essentially about the inclusiveness and sensitivity by which the work has been developed. As women and Black workers pointed out to their white male colleagues the personal is political. It is not enough to just organise in a community to obtain a result. Of equal importance is how you go about it. Specific oppressions around race, gender, disability and sexuality need to be openly addressed. Roles within groups (who holds the power), the use of language and respect for diverse opinions are central to an empowerment process. For many white and male workers these questions posed a fundamental challenge to their world view and how they operated in groups.

The 1970's also brought other changes. The Comprehensive Community Programme in1974 and the Housing Action Areas lead to the growth of social planning with community workers employed in effect as intermediaries between authorities and the local community. The economic crises of the decade and the arrival of the Conservative government in 1979 also set in train funding cuts for public services and community work employment and crucially the closure of many community and resource centres from which community activity could be undertaken.

The result of these trends was that community work lost it way. Waddington (1983) in a classic article commenting on the disorientation of many workers said; "t*he plain fact is that many community activities, as we originally conceived them, have simply lost their point. Our current predicament is that we are no longer collectively quite sure of what we are trying to do or how to do it".* Barr's (1991) study of community workers identified much radical rhetoric amongst generally conservative practice and confusion of purpose and reinforces Waddington's point.

In fact community work has spent much of the past two decades trying to catch up with social and economic changes that that been driven through as a result of globalisation or as policy objectives of the New Right. The community work profession turned inward during this time with a number of protracted and largely unresolved debates. These included fierce arguments about whether council housing should be defended or would the new housing associations give tenants a better deal, was community care a legitimate area for practice.

During the early 1990's community work was out of favour with national government. With the Prime Minister Margaret Thatcher proclaiming *'there is no such thing as society'* and cuts in social expenditure, interest in and the employment levels of, community workers began to fall. But by the mid 1990's community work staged some sort of revival. In part this has been through its intermediary role in the Single Regeneration Budget funded programmes in England, the partnerships in Scotland and the Peace and Reconciliation money in Northern Ireland. Surprisingly, or perhaps an indication of the de politicisation of community work since the CDP's, even the Conservative Government warmed to community work. In 1996 in a speech delivered to an invited audience at Toynbee Hall. Virginia Bottomley then Secretary of State for National Heritage said: *"apply lesson one of any community development handbook, start from where you are. The national debate should focus on how to help people to improve the conditions of their lives".* She went on to quote T H Green *"Action by the state to enable its citizens to grow in freedom; freedom in the positive sense ... the liberation of the powers of all men equally for the contribution to a common good"* and concluded *"freedom to contribute to your own community in the way you choose is vital. Community groups and those who support them help to make this happen"*

The coming to power of New Labour in 1997 with a commitment to a social policy framework built around social inclusion and partnership approaches has led to a rise in the number of community work posts. This new funding has moved employment in community work away from the local authority employed generic worker, to specialist posts employed in the voluntary sector, in health and increasingly in the new partnerships themselves.

Although, it is easy to identify individual successful projects and examples of innovative practice, there is also a lot of anecdotal evidence that overall community based work often fails to deliver much of value. Reflecting on twenty five years of practice as a volunteer, paid worker, trainer and academic, it appears to me that community work practice is often seriously undermined by a lack of vision, analysis, purpose and creativity. It is also caught in a dilemma.

Community workers say clearly that they are committed to challenging oppression, for social change and social justice. The numerous definitions of community work are testament to these beliefs. However, community workers are funded (usually indirectly) by the state. There are barriers, both real and self imposed, which inhibit the range of activities and issues that community workers can engage with. Sometimes this is due to fear for one's job and project funding. At others times this is the effect of hegemony on how we think and act. This history of community work practice is mostly conservative. The prime example of radical action ended both in failure through a doomed confrontation on policy with the Home Office and an inability to develop a model of practice that fitted the structural analysis produced by the CDP's

These observations are supported by research activities. I have been involved in two significant studies of practice in Scotland. These have been published as Learning for Change (Barr, Hashagen, Purcell) and Strong Community Effective Government Volume 2 (Barr, Drysdale, Purcell, Ross). These publications include case studies selected by the field as examples of excellent practice. Much of the practice described is indeed excellent. However, the weaknesses outlined below are also apparent in many places. The disturbing fact is the poor quality of much of the work put forward as demonstrating excellent practice contained fundamental weaknesses.

In particular, I think current practice in the UK can be generally criticised on five counts:

1. Poor application of basic concepts and techniques
2. Absence of a viable practice theory
3. Dominance of the social planning approach
4. Insularity and the failure to learn from the experience of others
5. Inadequate training in essential knowledge and key skills

Many workers in the community are often unable to properly define and utilise a number of key concepts and processes. Community involvement and participation has become either a token policy requirement or a routine exercise without any real understanding of how or why it is important to do this. Key concepts such as empowerment, participation and sustainability are poorly defined. This has led many practitioners to reject the concepts entirely. In addition, practice often fails to apply basic techniques to properly identify community needs, effectively organise, plan or learn from experience.

As an occupation, we suffer from a lack of a coherent practice theory. Most community based workers have a potted understanding of how practice has developed in the UK. This provides a route map of where we have come from. But the map is blank when it comes to informing the way forward. In the absence of our own coherent practice theory we either adapt, with various degrees of success, theory from other professions. Or, and this is worse, give up on theory altogether and simply react to circumstances as we encounter them. An ex tutor of mine described this as 'mindless activism'. To appear to be busy is not the same as being effective.

In the UK at present practice often is driven by social planning agendas. This may be through the Single Regeneration Budgets and Social Inclusion Partnerships, Community Planning or via the planning mechanisms of individual service agencies. This is not to say that partnerships and social planning are undesirable per se. As Craig and Mayo (1995) comment: *"the current global context ... points to the increasing importance of appropriate 'top-down' planning and strategic intervention"*. Effective social planning is of course essential for the improved targeting and delivery of services. The involvement of the community is important for planners to identify agendas, check out the appropriateness of plans and evaluate service performance.

However, there are limitations to the effectiveness of this approach. Often the 'community' is only given token involvement in these processes, despite rhetoric to the contrary. Crucially, for a community to be anywhere near equal players in the planning process it needs to be equipped with the appropriate skills, knowledge, leadership and have its own autonomous and powerful organisations. Sometimes the community's interests may not coincide with the social planners and oppositional action may be required.

It is possible for partnerships to facilitate the development of communities according to locally identified needs and priorities. Hughes and Carmichael (1998) explore such an experience in Belfast. The critical factors here appear to be the *"sense of ownership and the extent of empowerment and a breadth of participation not previously experienced"*. This was the product of long term and intensive work to build community strength and may also be a product of the unique, in the UK context, Northern Ireland experience. Sadly, such positive outcomes are not often repeated in mainland partnerships.

Unfortunately, partnerships due to the inherent conservatism of many workers and organisations, are usually the mechanism for the public sector to keep control of both the regeneration process and define the limit of community based activity (Cockburn 1978). The contradiction is that the majority of workers are employed by the state in various ways but at the same time recognise that local communities may have interests against the state. This 'in and against the state' debate has been a feature of UK practice since the 1970's. It is unresolved and will probably remain so.

We also suffer from a limited perspective to inform practice. I work in the West of Scotland, and it appears that for some workers the rest of Scotland, let alone the UK do not exist as a resource to help understand how to improve their practice. It is as if the people living on British housing estates are somehow immune from the global social, economic, environmental and political developments that are rapidly reshaping the world. Experience shows that a thoughtful analysis and adaptation of North American and developing world practice experience can be of immense value. As an extrapolation of this point I believe that it is impossible to understand what is happening in communities without an appreciation of the globalisation process which, like it or not, affects all of us.

Saul Alinsky the great American community organiser often said that his staff had to be extraordinary people. This point is also reflected in the Learning for Change study, which suggests that the critical factor in the success of development work is the skill, knowledge and vision of the key players. Alinsky believed that his community organisers had to deeply believe in the core values of democracy and rights and had to be able to apply sophisticated interpersonal skills, an understanding of strategy and tactics, commitment, honesty and flexibility to their work. To this we can usefully add a working knowledge of politics, economics, sociology and psychology. In addition an understanding of culture and cultural analysis is essential.

These skills have to be taught, and as a generalisation, I think we fail to do this. Workers talk about the importance of building the capacity of the community and the importance of promoting active citizenship. However, training and support to his end, even for professional workers, is often limited and of variable quality. Community leadership, which in many countries is seen as a key component for development is relegated to a minor concern in the UK. A cynic might say that the community is not supposed to develop its own leadership; it is simply required to fit better into the status quo power systems and existing hierarchies. My last point therefore, is that focussed and rigorous training in essential knowledge and key skills is the basic component for improved practice.

Good practice requires the combination of planning, strategy, tactics depending on needs, objectives and local circumstances. Community work in the UK needs to re-evaluate its purpose and methods in the context of the impact of global trends. We need also to learn the lessons of the past and from overseas.

The secret history of protest

Running alongside philanthropy and intervention by paid workers, there is a tradition of radical, sometimes political and class motivated action driven by working class activists. This is the secret history of protest, organisation and change. The media seldom refers to it, as working people organising themselves for change is always perceived to be a threat to the established order. Much of the exciting, well organised and creative work in the UK is to be found here. And many community workers and community based organisation can learn a lot about tactics and organisation from these experiences.

It is sad but true that if you wan to promote effective social change you don't call the local authority community worker or contact the local partnership. With some exceptions, where were they during the minors strike, the poll tax, and environmental protests? This poses a critical question; is community work really is about promoting change.

In much of British history there is a deep tradition of self organised protest. We can cite examples of the Diggers of the English civil war of the 17th century who briefly established a proto communist community before being crushed by Cromwell's army. Digger philosophy as written by Gerrard Winstanley in *The Law of Freedom in a Platform* (1652) provided one of the intellectual bases for socialism. At the same time the Levellers, had a similar political programme: written by John Lilburne and called *The Foundations of Freedom, or an Agreement of the People,* it was presented to Parliament in 1649. The Levellers had three main demands: the existence of certain inalterable rights of man beyond the jurisdiction of any government, the idea that governmental authority can only be derived from the people, and the doctrine of separation of powers between law makers and those who imposed the law.

E. P Thompson,s magnificent *The Making of the English Working Class* (1978) tells the story of national and local protest, including the Chartists, as communities struggled to redirect the industrial revolution to better reflect their needs. The word Chartist being derived from the People's Charter produced by William Lovett and Francis Place and the London Working Men's Association, from the widespread dissatisfaction with the Reform Act of 1832 and the Poor Law Amendment Act of 1834, legislation that workingmen considered discriminatory. The Charter demanded universal male suffrage, annual elections and abolition of property qualifications for MP's. When the House of Commons rejected these demands, the association launched a nationwide campaign in support of its programme, and around 1,250,000 people signed a petition to Parliament requesting that the charter be made law. Direct action, a failed general strike and insurrection followed.

In the early 20th century the socialist activities on the infamous Red Clydeside was the clearest expression of the fragmented movement towards establishing grass roots working class power. This included the rent strike of 1915, disputes in the munitions factories and the reading of the Riot Act backed by tanks in George Square, Glasgow. Throughout the century notable examples of grass roots protest and organisation include:

- Resistance to Home Secretary Churchill sending troops to the South Wales Coalfield to suppress 'unrest' during the general strike,
- in 1932 the mass trespass on Kinder Scout to promote the right to roam,
- the battle of Cable Street in 1936 to stop Oswald's fascists marching through the East End of London,
- the Aldermaston marches against the H bomb which in turn leads to the Greenham Common and the Peace Camps
- the squatters movement in London
- the anti Vietnam war protests
- growth of the women's movement
- gay and lesbian movement
- anti nazi / anti racist actions
- the 1984 miners strike
- Poll tax campaigns in the early 1990's
- environmental protests of the 1980's and 90's

McKay (1996) claims that in Britain the development of this tradition has led to an increasing number of people living what is called 'DIY lifestyles'. These are lifestyles, for the inherent nature of the movement is of diversity that reflects the desire to create alternative cultures to mainstream society and capitalist ethos. It is also often about working to change society not simply escaping from it. In doing so it builds upon a number of trends including the ethics of the 1960's and the beliefs explored in Theodore Roszak's *Making of a Counter Culture*, opposition to the Vietnam war, the feminist ideal that the personal is political, identity politics, the 1970's strand that community work was a social movement and not just a job, Punks, New Age Travellers, and current dance culture. None of this is new, rather it is the increasing tempo with which each new generation both repeats and adapts the rebelliousness of the past that is significant.

This loose association of ideology and practice has manifested itself in a number of forms including early CND marches, peace camps and peace convoys, environmental protests via the Dongas Tribe and Free Watsonia, free festivals, Fairs of Albion, raves, animal rights actions, opposition to the Criminal Justice Act of 1994, creating Temporary Autonomous Zones free of state control, campaigns to reclaim the land, Reclaim the Streets and anti capitalism / anti globalisation actions. McKay sums up the changes in these cultural movements as:

> 1960's Be reasonable: demand the impossible
> 1970's Reality's a substitute for utopia
> 1980's Fight war not wars, destroy power not people
> 1990's Go and commit a senseless act of beauty

These slogans illustrate that the first objective is to free yourself from the consumerism of capitalism, to be able to think of others and be able to commit *random acts of kindness and senseless acts of beauty*. For many people this is sufficient as they believe such a lifestyle puts you beyond politics. For others changing yourself leads to working to change society. Direct action is the organisational model: that is putting yourself on the front line for causes in which you believe. McKay quotes the following illustrative passage from the political theory magazine Aufhben.

> *"by adopting direct action as a form of politics, we .. look to ourselves as a source of change ... Therefore the key to the political significance of the campaign lies less in the immediate aims of stopping the road and in the immediate costs we have incurred for capital and the state, and more in our creation of a climate of autonomy, disobedience and*

> *resistance... Thus, this life of permanent struggle is simultaneously a negative act (stopping the road) and a positive pointer to the kind of social relation that could be ... a community of resistance"*

This is the politically sophisticated version of contemporary political and social opposition to the established state. The majority of people who see themselves in an oppositional culture may have a vaguer political analysis and operate more on an emotional level for causes, the environment and oppressed groups and against exploitation and consumerism. This emotional drive for lifestyle and social change is in itself highly significant.

Obviously, these counter cultural movements have no appeal to traditional left wing political activists and offer little to the governments attempt to link everyone into the mainstream through partnerships. By definition counter cultural groups are socially excluded. Although this is from choice, it is an option that does not appear in government policy documents and falls outside its communitarian conservative approach to impose a normative view of rights and responsibilities. However, it is this loose collection of ideologies and activities that have given community action in the UK its creative edge and dynamism

In addition to major disputes and cultures of resistance, there is an unwritten history of local campaigns run by local people, with no support from professional workers, fighting for their essential interests. Often, these campaigns have tried, with mixed success, to link community organisations to trade unions. It has been the dream of the radical left to unite workers and residents *'who together will never be defeated'*. The 1984 miners strike with the range of support groups and activity is perhaps the closest this has come to reality. However, the bureaucracy of the trade union movement has never favoured supporting community action.

Castells (1977) has explored social movements such as these. He suggests that the state has to provide education, housing, welfare and transport as private capital is incapable of doing so. Although, it is interesting to note that the current Private Finance Initiative (PFI) is designed to make the provision of welfare profitable for the private sector. To a limited extent therefore, the state will tolerate such protests as long as it can be seen in terms of campaigning within the framework of pluralist democracy. However, once the degree of protest appears to seriously threaten established interest then the full force of the state will be deployed as necessary. The aggressive use of policing and restrictions on travel during the miners strike is one example.

Another example was the Criminal Justice Act of 1994. Home Secretary Michael Howard described the act: *"new powers will be at (police) disposal for dealing with public order such as raves, gatherings of new age travellers and mass trespass which can be a blight for individuals and local communities"* (quoted in McKay 1996). The civil rights group Liberty argues that the act breaches both the European Convention on Human Rights (ECHR) and the United Nations International Convention on Civil and Political Rights (ICCPR).

The act is a potential threat to any significant form of protest. And to many people a gross attack on the British sense of fair play. It is also an attempt to outlaw cultural diversity. However, the act succeeded in uniting diverse groups, initially in protest against the act. Once these links were made they have been sustained for new campaigns. New Labour abstained in the vote on the legislation, although since coming to office has continued the repressive trend with a raft of laws that extend the power of the state (for example Curfew and Anti Social Behaviour Orders).

In the new century the opposition to Globalisation and the World Trade Organisation looks like giving the current oppositional movements a harder political edge. Perhaps in our increasingly organised, yet post modernist society, there is a need for diverse cultures of resistance to confront 'normality' and develop alternative realities for the rest of us to explore. The 2005 Live 8 campaign for debt relief sits both alongside and in contrast with the militant anti globalisation protests.

As society changes, so does the field and nature of protest. Naomi Klein (2000) in her book, *No Logo*, explores the effects of globalisation on mass culture. In particular she explores the social and environmental realities around consumerisation of global brand goods. Branding through marketing is not just advertising. It is about tapping into peoples needs and feelings. In a post modern world life, claims Klein, can feel empty and pointless. Buying branded goods can make you feel better because emotionally Nike trainers link you with the success of Michael Jordan, Benneton clothes will link you to the wonders of the world and Calvin Klein will make you smell sexy.

If you wear a Rolex watch then by definition your life is successful. Consuming major brands will meet your innermost needs.

Too far fetched? Renzo Rossi owner of Diesel Jeans said *"The Diesel concept is everything. It's the way to live, its the way to wear, its the way to something"* (quoted in Klein 2000). This process is becoming so deeply rooted in our consciousness that an increasing number of young people are working for free (as interns, on work experience, etc) in high branded companies, just to be part of the experience.

The Internet and e-commerce are increasingly prime tools for such brand expansion. As Klein notes of the worlds biggest book seller, Amazon.com, *"It is on-line that the purest brands are being built; liberated from the real world burdens of stores and product manufacturing, these brands are free to soar, less as the disseminators of goods or services than as collective hallucinations"*

The current opposition to this latest form of consumerism and capitalism comes from the various networks of cultural resistance groups. That is, as we have seen, activist groups mainly on the margin of society. Klein's expectation is that this resistance will spread to the mainstream of society as the effects on employment, inequality and exploitation become more apparent. Klein writes;

> *"As more people discover the brand name secrets of the global logo web, their outrage will fuel the next big political movement, a vast wave of opposition squarely targeting transitional corporations, particularly those with very high brand name recognition"*

With this awareness comes a deeper understanding of the realities of the world and how it affects us locally. For example links are made between the sweatshops of the developing world and the casualisation of employment in the developed world. Questions are being posed about the replacement of citizenship with consumerisation. Just as the opposition to the Poll Tax, animal rights and roads protests have activated many non political people, the reaction to global brands and transitional consumerism may have an unpredictable effect on the communities in which we work. It is interesting to note this shift in protest from political to economic targets; a reflection perhaps of the decline in the power of the nation state relative to transnational corporations.

With this change in focus come new forms of community action. Building on the experience of the 1960's Pranksters, the Situationalists in the Paris uprising of 1968 and even Dada of the 1930's, 'culture jamming' is the parodying of advertisements or the hijacking of billboards with a more potent message. Pictures of corpses attached to cigarette advertisements, for example. And as you would expect the Internet is a prime source for such actions (see for example Adbusters at www.adbusters.org and Undercurrents at www.undercurrents.org).

On the one hand such 'playful' actions might appear simply a meaningless postmodernist gesture. On the other hand their proponents argue that in an information age where image is more important than substance, the counter image has a direct political effect. Actions such as these are about the use of '*memes*'. The word comes from biologist Richard Dawkins (1989) and refers to packets of cultural information: songs, beliefs, trends, that pass through the population similar to the way genes reproduce through a species. Powerful memes create cultural change, from contraceptive pills, to pokemon, to ecstasy, to mobile phones, to txting. According to Adbusters, and many others:

> *"Meme warfare is growing ever more intense. The next revolution will be, as media guru Marshall McLuhan predicted, "a guerrilla information war." It will be fought in the streets with signs, slogans, banners and graffiti, but it will be won in newspapers, on the radio, on TV and in cyberspace. It will be a dirty, no-holds-barred propaganda war of competing worldviews and alternative visions of the future".*

On a more direct action level is the Reclaim the Streets movements (www.urban75.com/Action/reclaim2.html). Here loosely organised groups of people occupy streets, roads and intersections to immobilise traffic and to act out counter culture and environmental protests and to party. This is about reclaiming public space and filling it with a living, if temporary, display of an alternative society.

These actions have spread and of late have been linked to global actions against the World Bank, IMF and the World Trade Organisation. Although, it appears that recent actions, for example Prague 2000, have been in part taken over by groups intent on violence, at the police, corporations and perhaps generally at anyone. Opinions vary as to why this is. Some see state directed agent provocateurs at work, others see working class frustrations boiling over, whilst a third view is that it simple right wing drunken thugs out for fight. As non violence is at the heart of Reclaim the Streets its future as a radical movement may be seriously undermined.

This refocusing of protest from traditional political targets to transnational corporations can be surprisingly successful. Ultimately, governments can, and do, use force to resist protest and sustain their power. Corporations have to retain mass public goodwill or else their sales plummet. Despite their increasing global power, corporations can also be surprisingly vulnerable and an easier target than a national government. Shell capitulated to Greenpeace over the proposed sinking of the Brent Spar oil platform in the North Atlantic. And Nike has moved to reform its activities after the exposure of its sweat shops in Asia.

Conflicts that break out in these areas can be used to politicise the contradictions of capitalist society. By focusing on the activities of transnational corporations and their international support agencies, protests can illustrate the links between environmental destruction, poverty and denial of human rights. They also expose the weakness of traditional politics and nation states in the face of global economic power. How far it is possible to link the geographical and issue diversity of these protests into powerful national and global alliances for change is subject to debate. There is no doubt however, that the rich vein of community protest will continue.

Current trends

As we noted above, community work underwent a minor revival during the period of the Major administration that has continued under New Labour. As we argue in chapter 4, an international perspective drives UK social policy development. Although, it is not consistently followed through, there are themes running across government policies to regenerate communities and counteract social exclusion that are based on the idea of building local community capacity, promoting social capital, supporting social entrepreneurs and leadership. Much of this, especially the promotion of social capital comes from the attempt to formulate the Third Way. These policies are of tremendous importance for community workers who will have the task of supporting such policies.

This trend has accelerated since the coming to power of New Labour. Sadly, this has less to do with the work of community workers themselves and more to do with the need for front line workers to deliver social planning initiatives built around government led regeneration and social inclusion strategies. Effective social planning requires the consent and some involvement of local communities. Partnership is the main game in town and who other than community workers, or those with community development skills, are going to organise the community to this end. The question for community workers is where do we go from here?

Agents of Social Planning

Social Planning can defined as *"the assessment of community needs and problems and the systematic planning of strategies for meeting them ... this may involve participative mechanisms like community health councils, planning enquiries and public meetings ... it is intended that such enquiries and consultations will elicit priorities amongst problems and suggest preferred solutions"* Thomas (1983).

For many writers on community the social planning role of community workers is the core activity. This book argues that this is not so. Whilst there has always been the tension of community workers operating both 'in and against the state' (See the London Edinburgh Weekend Return Group 1980) and often carrying a social planning role, community workers have usually defined their core task as supporting autonomous organisations to identify and develop their own independent agenda

Community work therefore, should be about assisting communities to identify their own needs and organise effectively to those ends. Often this activity will lead to community organisations engaging with social planners in some kind of partnership arrangement. However, this should be undertaken from a position of community strength and with the community's own agenda.

However, community workers are increasingly being used to act as intermediaries between social planning organisations and local communities. Or expected to take the planners message and organise the community around it. This is often undertaken in the name of participation and partnership (these terms are explored in more detail in chapter 7). Such developments are leading to a fundamental shift in the nature of the community work occupation.

Increasingly, social planners working in the climate of social inclusion are looking towards promoting participation as a way of consumer testing and legitimising their activities. An ever increasing numbers of community, neighbourhood and client focused fora, and other organisational structures are being established with whom planners can liaise. Numerous examples can be cited. Community fora linked to regeneration, SRB and Social Inclusion Partnership boards, community planning and community care fora are just some of the most common forms of 'induced' participation. Existing community work jobs are being redefined for this work and many new jobs created to this end.

This is often a good thing. The new fora often play an essential role in enabling the views of local people to be heard and acted upon. However, in many cases they are sadly a tokenistic attempt at consultation as people are encouraged to 'participate' to meet the statutory requirement of social planners. In some situations participation is simply used as a cover to manipulate a community to a pre-determined end. For example the community of St Mary's in Southampton as described by George Monbiot in his book Captive State.

It appears therefore, that increasingly the social planning role provides the employment for the majority of community workers and associated jobs. The mapping study of community development workers in the UK (CDF 2004) reported that 71% of respondents were involved in social inclusion work, 55% on regeneration and that 60% worked with local partnerships. As long as the social policy thread around social inclusion and regeneration continues, this trend will continue to develop.

The good news is that this means a steady growth in community development type jobs. The bad news is that these jobs will often be time limited and linked to specific funding packages. They will have defined job titles and briefs linked to client groups such community care, detached youth work, the long term unemployed, and undertaking work on health and mental health issues, environmental activity, capacity building, developing active citizenship and supporting leadership training, etc. Increasingly, these jobs will be based in voluntary and community organisations as the responsibilities of local authorities diminish.

The generic community worker, who roamed their neighbourhood looking for issues to develop, will become an increasing rare species. Boundaries will be placed around these jobs under some kind of pluralistic heading, which sees developing community partnership with welfare agencies as the core purpose. Although, much of the current work may continue to address personal empowerment issues, albeit in very mainstream ways, and generate some limited response for positive action,

The problem is that needs are often identified by social planners, community organisations are built and supported around the planners agenda, participation is limited and often on the planners terms. Extending the independent political influence of the community is not on the agenda. Worryingly, community workers tend to limit their activities according to what they think their employers will allow (Barr 1991). In this way they can often police themselves and create a self-enforced boundary around their activity.

To be employed for such work, community workers will increasingly be expected to hold qualifications, although the range of acceptable qualifications will increase. The new Lifelong Learning Sector Skills Council will introduce a range of occupational standards for community-based adult learning, community development work, community learning and development and youth work. These standards will be approved by employers organisations as meeting the functional needs of the jobs. Occupational competency, whether demonstrated through S/NVQ's or professionally endorsed university degree courses will be the norm for employment. Workers will also be expected to demonstrate their effectiveness through improved evaluations of practice.

Social Entrepreneurship

Running in parallel to the above social planning model is social entrepreneurship. On the one hand government is promoting participatory structures under its regeneration and social policy initiatives. On the other hand it also supports the idea that these structures usually fail. Recent work by Demos (a policy think tank) and Paul Brickell (2000) argue that the traditional structures used by social planners to engage the community have failed and that new radical approaches are required to free local creativity. Specifically the usual methods of community involvement are criticised as:

- failing to effectively engage people
- stifling creativity and local initiative
- promoting the idea of dependency upon public bodies
- are often dominated by 'professional' community activists who have limited accountability
- deskill and disable local people by expecting then to understand and respond to complex issues with inadequate support

Instead it is argued, successful regeneration comes not through bureaucratic structures, but through mobilising the creativity and resourcefulness of people on the margin. Anyone committed to the principles of community development will agree with this. However, where we part company is that rather than collectivise and build autonomous organisations around local issues, social entrepreneurship gives reign to the idea of the creative individual who will cut through red tape and bring their individual skills to play, pulling the local community along behind them.

In his very first speech after becoming Prime Minister, Tony Blair gave his support to this individualised approach. He said that we should all *"back social entrepreneurs, those people who bring to social problems the same enterprise and imagination that business entrepreneurs bring to wealth creation"*. Social entrepreneurs usually work with local community organisations. It is their self-definition as expert and leader that offends the principles of community development.

In social entrepreneur theory there is no difference between a social entrepreneur and a commercial one. The skills and personal attributes are the same. Only the purpose is different, i.e. to meet social needs rather than simply generate profit. Social entrepreneurs therefore are likely to be the following:

- They are people whose creativity and drive open up new possibilities in education, health, the environment and other areas of human need. Just as business entrepreneurs lead innovation in commerce, social entrepreneurs drive social change.

- Social entrepreneurs see opportunities, and act by identifying under-used resources - people, buildings and equipment - employing them to satisfy unmet social needs.

- Social entrepreneurs tend to come from out side the mainstream bureaucratic institutions and often find themselves at odds with public sector agencies.

- They tend to have a 'can do' attitude, overcoming significant obstacles.

- A social entrepreneur could be a businessperson whose business has a social benefit dimension.

The idea of social entrepreneurship, like so many UK social policies, comes from North America. In the USA, the National Center for Social Entrepreneurs was founded in 1985. The Center serves a wide range of clients throughout the United States and abroad. It claims that in the market economy voluntary and community organisations are expected to become more customer driven and financially accountable. The skills of entrepreneurship therefore become essential to the non profit sector as this enables them to match their skills and assets with marketplace opportunities. In addition the adoption of entrepreneurship skills assists organisation to sharpen the focus of their operation, to increase their impact and effectiveness and to generate surplus income. This revenue allows the organisation to develop services independent of funding agencies.

In the UK, business and national voluntary organisations are picking up on the idea of social entrepreneurs. A key initiative in this area is the School for Social Entrepreneurs in London. The School recruits students *"with high levels of energy and persistence and a tendency to relish uncertainty, change and new ideas"*. Students are placed in community settings and encouraged to work through and implement their ideas. Information on the School is available at www.sse.org.uk. In Scotland there is a similar initiative (details at http://senscot.spl21.net/)

These initiatives are widely supported by business such as Marks and Spencer and large voluntary agencies. Perhaps this reflects the more business orientated approach that has been adopted by national voluntary agencies, in response to the promotion of the contract culture in social welfare. Social entrepreneurship though, may also lead to the diversion of energy of community organisation to making revenue generation the main focus. This may also allow funding bodies to cut back or redirect their funding so there is no net gain to the community.

The idea of releasing individual and community potential cannot be faulted. It is true that much community development work is hindered by both the bureaucratic practices of local authorities and by the mindset of many officials. Communities need people with skills, vision, creativity, drive and the ability to cut through red tape. The sad thing is that in the early 1970's it was thought that community workers might be these people. How many people link community workers with these attributes today? Community workers ability to respond this way is increasingly marginalised through their shift into the servicing role of the planning agenda.

From a community development perspective therefore, social entrepreneurship is problematic. The focus of social entrepreneurship is individualistic rather than collective. In the USA the market culture is much stronger in the non-profit sector and organisations take more readily to entrepreneurial ideas. In the UK it is more likely that social entrepreneurs will be operating as individuals bought in for specific activities.

As we explore below, the core values of community development are to develop collective experience and facilitate people to work together to provide community driven solutions. The danger is that social entrepreneurship will provide *for* communities rather than enable communities to *learn and provide for themselves*. This would be essentially disempowering when a key purpose of community development is to facilitate empowerment. AS we have noted the objective of community development is not just to enhance the quality of life in communities but to value the process of how it is done.

Given the level of political and increasing financial support there is likely to be a growth of people acting as social entrepreneurs.

This may manifest itself in a number of ways. Firstly, as individuals moving into a community with a 'bright idea' around which they try and build support. Secondly, as people recruited by, for example, partnership boards to get things going. Or individuals directly recruited by local community organisations themselves. All of these approaches can be seen as implied criticism of community workers and their failure to get the job done. If social entrepreneurship rapidly takes off then mainstream community workers may end of being defined solely in the social planning support role. Of course creative and energetic community workers may decide to recast themselves as social entrepreneurs as a way of breaking free from bureaucratic constraints.

community-development.com

This will be coming soon to a computer near you. It is based on a mixture of ideas from REFLECT learning circles used to teach literacy in the developing world, convivial tools and deschooling from Ivan Illich, freelance consultancy and e-commerce. An example of this is being promoted by Frank Odasz who describes himself as 'carpenter, college professor, dude rancher and lone eagle' and can be found at http://lone-eagles.com/comdev.htm

The idea is that the Internet makes knowledge and skills development available anywhere. Whilst it is true that the many socially excluded people do not have their own Internet access, community organisation do. Research by CINNI in Northern Ireland and by the author in Scotland (Purcell 1997) demonstrates that community organisations are aware of the potential of the Internet, far more so than paid community workers.

Freelance workers, or lone eagles in North American e-commerce speak, will offer training courses, consultancy and information available on demand over the Internet. This will of course cost money, but less than existing professional fees, due to the expansion of the market and reduced overheads. Expertise from anywhere in the world can be delivered to your community. This increases choice and skills from just having to rely on local workers.

More interestingly perhaps, community organisations themselves can network together to build bigger alliances for better campaigns and develop their own skill sharing and training. To some degree this will make local paid workers irrelevant and provide more flexible and community driven capacity building programmes possible. This may help shift the balance of power in local partnerships to the communities favour.

This approach will tend to be favoured by the social entrepreneurs and community activists rather than those who prefer the security of mainstream employment. However, as the social economy becomes more market driven the potential for growth in this area is unlimited. It is possible to speculate that in a future fully marketised social sector all community development activity may be contracted out.

No doubt this, like any attempt to guess the future, will turn out to be wide of the mark. However, it is important to think about where community development is going and to try and shape its direction. Otherwise one day we may look around and wonder what happened to the occupation which we thought held so much promise for promoting empowerment, social justice and freedom.

Summary

In this chapter we have covered the following points:

- Effective community work is based upon responding to a number of defined themes around anti oppressive practice, empowerment strategies, etc.
- Community work can make positive contributions to empowering individuals and improving the quality of life in both geographical communities and communities of interest on a variety of issues. For example housing, employment, area development, etc
- Community work has a diverse history stretching back to Victorian times. Over the past 150 years the definition and focus of community work has changed substantially
- Current community work practice has a number of ingrained weaknesses that inhibit effective work
- For effective practice it is essential to understand structural issues, gender and race dimensions

- Social change often comes from grass roots protest. Community work has often failed to support and respond to these movements
- Increasing movements for change have a global related focus that recognises the growing power of corporations and the declining power of the state
- The community work profession is expanding. However, the nature of the work appears to be shifting towards a social planning role
- There is increasing political support for social entrpreneurship approaches to working in the community

Further Reading

For an in depth look at community work practice using Scottish case studies try Alan Barr, Robert Hamilton and Rod Purcell's **Learning for Change,** (London, CDF 1996)

David Thomas in **The Making of Community Work**, (London, George Allen and Unwin 1993) explores in an easy to read way, the history of community work. Keith Popple in **Analysing Community Work,** (Buckingham, OUP 1996) does so with a more current and analytical focus.

For a detailed exploration of the non directive approach see Batten, **The Non Directive Approach in Group and Community Work,** (London, Oxford University Press 1967). Martin Loney explores the CDP's **in Communities Against Government: The British Community Development Project 1968-78,** (London, Heineman 1985)

The secret history of protest in covered by George McKay in **Senseless Acts of Beauty; cultures of resistance since the sixties,** (London, Verso 1996). To look at classic USA experience using a totally different approach see Saul Alinsky: **Reveille for Radicals,** (New York, Vintage Books 1969) and **Rules for Radicals**, (New York, Random House 1971)

For a discussion on feminism and community work see Dominelli **Women and Community Action,** (Birmingham, Venture Press 1990) and Barker **Recapturing Sisterhood: A Critical Look at Process in Feminist Organising and Community Work,** (Critical Social Policy 16). Also Butler and Whitlam, **Feminist Group Work; Self Identity and Change**, (London, Sage 1989)

To explore community work with Black and Asian communities see Jan **Ellis Women and Community Action,** (Birmingham, Venture Press 1989). Another view is given by the Newham Monitoring Project **Forging a Black Community - Asian and Afro Carribean struggles in Newham** (NMP/CARF 1991). Also Sivanandan **Communities of Resistance; Writing on Black Struggles for Socialism**, (London, Virago 1990)

2

Underlying Perspectives: Exploring the Basics

"If civilization is to advance at all in the future, it must be through the help of women, women freed of their political shackles, women with full power to work their will in society. It was rapidly becoming clear to my mind that men regarded women as a servant class in the community, and that women were going to remain in the servant class until they lifted themselves out of it". Emmeline Pankhurst

Aims of this chapter

This chapter explores a range of basic perspectives which we can use to inform our work. Firstly, we consider the importance of holding clear personal values to inform practice. We go on to explore the concepts of equality, needs, rights and democracy.

Values for practice

All human activity is affected by the values of the people involved. In working in the community it is essential that we are clear about our own values and how they affect our practice. Thompson (1998) suggests that in working for change there are four key aspects of society that we need to understand.

> 1. The contemporary social order is characterised by a range of social divisions (class, race, gender, age, disability and so on) that both embody and engender inequality, discrimination and oppression

2. These inequalities and ideologies that support and sustain them are generally taken for granted and subtly influence our actions and attitudes.

3. Unless we develop an understanding of inequality and the ideologies underpinning it, we are likely not only to fail to address discrimination and oppression, but also to reinforce or even exacerbate them

4. Issues of equality must therefore be central to human services work. To offer health, social welfare or related services without taking into account inequality is a very risky undertaking indeed. Good intentions and kind-hearted actions can, and often do, cause a great deal of damage if they are not premised on an understanding of, and sensitivity to, the inequalities that already exist and the potential for making them worse.

The importance of values in underpinning work in the community is recognised by the UK Government. For example the Northern Ireland Voluntary Activity Unit (1996) defined community development as being; *"directed at particular people who feel excluded from society. It consists of a set of methods which can broaden vision and capacity for social change, and approaches, including consultation, advocacy and relationships with local groups. It is a way of working, informed by certain principles which seek to encourage communities – to tackle for themselves the problems which they face and identify to be important .. to empower them to change things by developing their own skills, knowledge and experience .. the way in which such change is achieved is crucial and so both the task and process is important"*.

Throughout the various definitions of community development four key values are usually present. Firstly, the importance of collectivisation; that is bringing people together to work on common problems and create new community based organisations. Thereby, as C Wright Mills wrote in the Sociological Imagination (1959), make *private troubles a public issue*. Secondly, recognising that a learning process takes places for local people to develop skills, knowledge and confidence to tackle issues. Thirdly, to confront discrimination and oppression and promote equality and social justice. Fourthly, to increase meaningful participation in the public area and promote the ideals and practices of participatory democracy.

Equality

To work effectively in the community must mean that we are committed to a belief in equality. Like many terms we will come across it needs to be closely defined before it becomes meaningful. We need to recognise that the concept of equality is ideological. As we shall see later many belief systems explicitly reject the idea of equality as being either impractical or undesirable.

At one level equality can be seen in terms of fairness of opportunity. Hence equal opportunity policies and legislation that protects individuals from discrimination based usually on gender or race. This is a limited and conservative position because it individualises public issues and ignores the wider economic, social and cultural forces that cases the discrimination in the first place. At a higher level equality is concerned with protecting fundamental rights to which every human being is entitled. We explore the nature of rights in the next section.

Inequality operates through discrimination in a number of diverse ways at a various levels in society. It can operate through marginalisation of minority groups or individuals thought to be undesirable in some way. This may be through stigmatisation where negative attributes are generalised and placed on an entire class of person. Or it may be through simply ignoring people's presence or needs. Thompson (1998) describes the various levels of discrimination as:

- *Economic* – unequal distribution of income leading to poverty and social depravation. Operates at a macro level
- *Social* – unequal status in terms of race, class and gender. Operates at a macro level
- *Political* – unequal access to power. Operates at a macro level

- *Ideological* – inequality being controlled through manipulation of ideas and information. Operates at a cultural level
- *Psychological* – where expectations are held on how members of particular groups should behave. Operates at a personal level.
- *Ethical* – the best protection against inequality is a belief that it is wrong.

Discrimination is usually based around six areas: class, race, gender, age, disability, and sexuality. Often people are subjected to multiple discrimination. In the UK a number of acts of parliament have been passed to challenge discrimination. Notable examples are: Race Relations Acts 1965, 1968, 1976, Equal Pay Act 1970, Sex Discrimination Act 1975, Welsh Language Act 1993 and the Disability Discrimination Act 1995. Community workers should take steps to inform themselves of the content of this legislation so they can help inform community groups of relevant legal position.

Class is another contested term. For example Marx defined class in terms of the personal relationship to the means of production. He sees class conflict as the critical factor in promoting economic and social change. In contrast Weber defines class in terms of market position within an existing socio-economic structure. Without entering into debate on definitions, it is still clear that a low class position is not just about low income and poverty. It is also about the inability to lead a 'normal' lifestyle; it has negative effects on self esteem, insecurity, reduced access to services, poor educational opportunities and ill health. The signs of poverty, for example poor clothing and appearance, can lead directly to stigmatisation and marginalisation. We discuss poverty in Britain below.

In contrast to the common assumption racial categories are socially, not biologically, constructed. Dividing people into artificial socially constructed categories is a way of making sense of the world and reducing the complexity of life to a simple 'them and us' criterion. Most of us have prejudice about people who are different from us. Prejudice is based on not understanding or valuing people who are different to 'us' in some way. These differences may be related to culture, religion, dress, sexuality or race.

Racism is what happens when prejudice is linked to the application of power. It follows therefore, that in the UK racism is produced by white people against Black and Asians, as white people hold power in society and Black people do not. It is not acceptable to claim, as many do, that racism is a product of the number of Black people in a given community. That in communities where there are few Black people there is no racism. What is missing in this situation is the opportunity for racist beliefs of white people to be acted out.

There are many instances of outright racism, although most of these are now illegal in the UK: for example refusing access to a service, housing or employment on the grounds of colour or race. However, most racism operates more informally at a cultural and interpersonal level. This ranges from the 'joke' to verbal abuse in the street, to the greater likelihood of Black and Asian people being treated unequally for housing and employment and with a greater incidence of arrest, imprisonment and being detained in mental hospitals. We must be clear that simply ignoring racism is to condone it. Community workers need to develop a range of techniques for challenging racism wherever it occurs. Whether this happens in community groups or the workplace it still has to confronted

In response to inequality a number of strategies have been developed. Multiculturalism was fashionable in the 1980's as a cultural approach to racism. This approach celebrates difference and diversity of cultures and seeks to bring different cultural groups together for shared activities. This strategy tends towards preaching to the converted and does little to address individual attitudes towards discrimination or challenge wider social forms of discrimination.

Many workers argue (for example Dominelli 1998) that a more robust response is anti-discriminatory practice that specifically seeks to create patterns of work, policies and procedures to counteract discriminatory attitude and behaviour. Its strength is it attempts to ensure that institutions act correctly to combat discrimination. Recently anti-oppressive practice has come into vogue. This is a step on from anti-discrimination, where action is taken to analyse and respond to structural discrimination.

Like racism, discrimination based on gender follows similar marginalisation, stereotyping and invisibility patterns. The same biological difference argument is also applied, but gender roles are socially constructed. A society's view of what women should and should not do is based on culture and changes over time. We only have to compare countries where women fulfil roles as aircraft pilots and civil engineers to some Middle Eastern countries where women are not allowed even to drive a car for evidence of this.

As we see in chapter 5 many feminists argue that all societies have some degree of patriarchal power where men use their dominant position to formally or informally discriminate against women. This manifests itself in a number of ways: through domestic and sexual violence, harassment, low pay and poor promotion prospects. Women also have the responsibility for the majority of domestic work and caring, both for children and relatives.

In 1996 the UK the Office of National Statistics produced the following figures illustrating pay and employment inequality. The figures demonstrate that regardless of the type of employment women on average earn only 2/3 of male income. Partly this is due to women not gaining promotion through lesser opportunity for training or the informal discrimination of the 'glass ceiling'. It also reflects that in many areas women are still paid less than men for equivalent work

	Weekly earnings Manual	Weekly earning Non manual
Females	195.2	302.4
Males	301.3	464.5
Differential	106.1	162.1
Female earnings as % of male earnings	65	65

Similar patterns of discrimination are found in respect to age and disability. The 'value' placed on an elderly person varies from respect for their years, the contribution they have made to society and their wisdom to assumptions of worthlessness. Again these assumptions are socially constructed.

In many ways issues around sexuality expose the most blatant discrimination. The debate in the UK during the early part of 2000 over the proposed repeal of Clause 28 of the Local Government Act (1990) which made it illegal for local authorities to promote homosexuality is an illustration. While some people opposed to repeal spoke in terms of protecting children, others in the tabloid press promoted the myth of schools about to give gay sex lessons, and some church leaders were open in their views and described gays as perverts. Views on this matter are clearly culturally and ideologically based. However, this does not legitimise active discrimination against minority groups within a society.

Thompson (1998) provides a clear overview of these issues. He sees the oppression and discrimination operating as concentric circles with the individual at the centre.

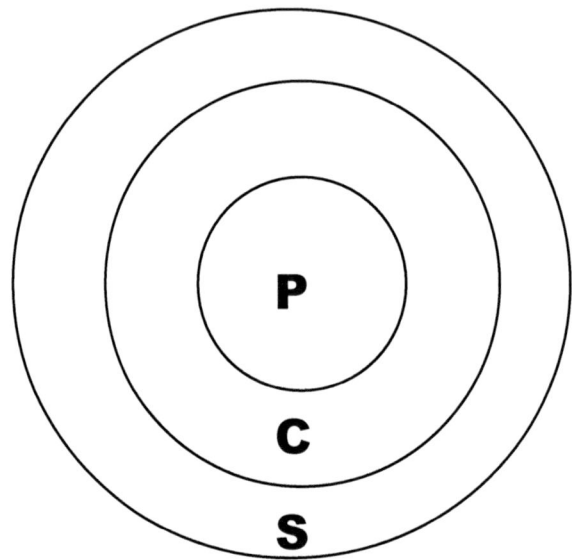

The **P** level concerns the individual. This is where discrimination is usually experienced and enacted. However, on its own it cannot provide an adequate explanation as peoples actions are often determined by cultural influences. This is Level **C** in the diagram. As Thompson points out: *"a significant feature of culture is the way in which members of a particular cultural group become so immersed in its patterns, assumptions and values that they do not even notice they are there - they become part of the 'taken for grantedness of everyday life'"*

The structural level **S** is where the wider social, political and economic dimensions generally come into play. The unifying factor here is the unequal distribution of power. After all you can only oppress or discriminate against someone if you have a degree of power (formal or informal) over them. White people impose racism on black people, men impose gender discrimination on women, and heterosexuals impose sexual discrimination on homosexuals. Culture, social, economic and political institutions are used as the means for such actions.

The community worker's role is to both oppose discrimination and to open up discussion to explore its social construction. This leads us onto consideration of needs, rights and democracy.

Needs

Community workers claim that the purpose of development activity is to meet people's needs. Unfortunately, identifying needs is a more complex process than may be first thought.

There is the difference between what people *need* for the basis of a quality life and their *wants* in terms of non-necessities or luxuries. In economic terms needs do not exist. Economists only respond to wants as expressed through purchasing power. And as we know the poor and excluded have very little economic power or ability to express their needs or wants. This situation is of considerable importance for community work. Usually, the middle class members of a community are the most vocal and organised. Because most of their basic needs have been met they tend to argue for their wants. For example, a new sports hall or landscaping improvements. If community workers are not careful they can easily respond to these wants, at the expense of ignoring the more urgent situation of excluded people who have little opportunity to voice their needs.

So what are people's needs? Firstly, it is important to avoid the trap of letting 'experts' define people's needs. This has been described by Illich (1997) as *"the condition of post-modern man and his universe has become, according to this view, so complex that only the most highly specialized experts can function as the priesthood capable of understanding and defining needs today"*.

The principles of community work concern assisting people to express their felt needs. However, it is important to have some understanding of what these needs may be. Reviewing work undertaken in South America, Max-Neef (1989) suggests the concept of what has now become known as the 'Wheel of Fundamental Human Needs'.

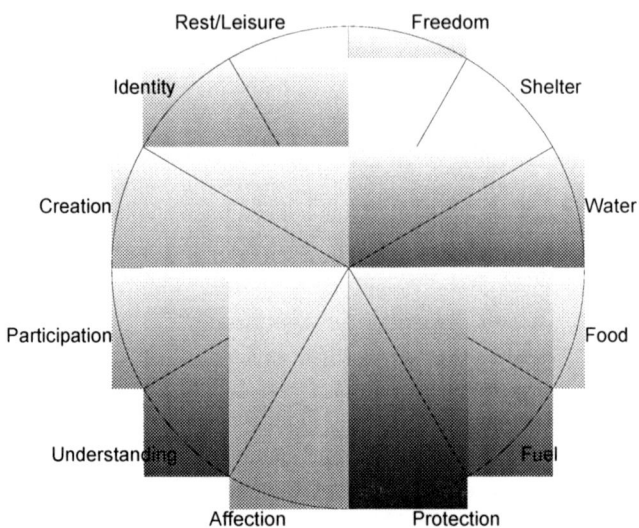

The Wheel illustrated above identifies the 12 basic needs of any individual, family or community. If the basic needs of a community are not met over the medium term then violence, crime and apathy are likely to result. Often we blame the victims for this behaviour instead of seeing the cause of the problems through unmet need. The wheel is therefore useful for enabling people to explore their particular set of needs and the interrelationship between them. As such the Wheel becomes a tool for self-determination and development. It is does, however, not provide a list for the development worker to tick off according to his or her own understanding of local needs.

Maslow (1943) provides another perspective on needs. He has produced a Hierarchy of Human Needs that recognises some needs are more urgent than others.

Least urgent	**Personal Growth**	Recreation, education for personal pleasure
	Self Respect	Growing personal empowerment and expanding boundaries of activity
	Love and Belonging	Mutual support, social and community activities
	Safety	Personal security
Most urgent	**Physical Needs**	Food, water, shelter, clothing, medicine

For a truly fulfilling quality of life all aspects of these needs must be met. So it can be misguided to spend development time on trying to promote recreational activities when the basic needs of shelter and clothing are being ignored. Creative development work should seek to ensure that the most urgent needs are being met whilst taking the opportunity to work at other levels. For example a housing campaign seeking to meet basic needs of warm, wind and water tight accommodation can be linked to building a community organisation which promotes feelings of belonging and self respect and which starts to promote personal growth.

Rights

Traditionally in the UK Human Rights are usually presented by the media as only concerning physical abuse and torture in other countries. By implication the message given is that human rights are nothing really to do with society in the UK. This is simply inaccurate. Mary Robinson, the UN High Commission said in 1997 at The Romanes Lecture in Oxford, *"my own approach to human rights is based on an inner sense of justice. Perhaps because I am from Ireland and have my roots in a past struggle for freedom"*. Robinson went on to say *"poverty is a violation of numerous human rights"* and added that she is committed to *"treating economic and social rights with the same priority as civil and political rights. They must be treated as interdependent and indivisible if either set is to be realised".*

The concept of human rights has a long history in European thought. Magna Carta in 1215 set down a number of rights under feudalism and gave protection from excessive government abuses. Although limited in its provisions, Magna Carta is seen as creating the basis of English constitutional liberties. This is illustrated by the clause *"No freeman shall be taken and imprisoned or disseised or exiled or in any way destroyed, nor shall we go upon him nor send upon him, except by the lawful judgement of his peers and by the law of the land."*

European philosophers claimed rights were 'natural' because they were intrinsic to being human, rather than granted through nationality or religion. These principles were reflected in the U.S. Declaration of Independence which said: *We hold these truths to be self-evident; that all men are created equal, that they are endowed by their creator with certain unalienable rights, that among these are life, liberty and the pursuit of happiness.* This statement was echoed in 1789 with the French Revolutionaries 'Declaration of the Rights of Man'

During the 19th the concept of natural rights gradually fell out of favour to be replaced by the idea of universal rights. Based on the writings of Thomas Paine with the Rights of Man (1998), John Stuart Mill in Essays On Liberty (1989), and Henry David Thoreau (see Myerson 1995). It was Thoreau who first used the term, 'human rights' in his treatise Civil Disobedience. This work outlining non violent direct action against unjust government has been extremely influential on individuals as different as Leo Tolstoy, Mahatma Gandhi, and Martin Luther King as well as much direct action in the UK.

The Universal Declaration of Human Rights was formulated by, the then new, United Nations in 1948. Dominated by the victors of the 1939 – 45 war and concerned with the abuses of fascism the document focussed on what are called 'first generation rights'. That is the right not to be tortured or imprisoned without due process of law. Many countries were not satisfied with the document and in 1950's a range of 'third generation rights' concerned with self determination and development were added. These new rights included the International Covenants on Civil and Political Rights on Economic, Social and Cultural Rights.

Despite these additions, the definition and extent of Human Rights remained a contested area. In 1989 the UN General Assembly adopted the Convention on the Rights of the Child. Four years later the first UN Summit on Human Rights for 25 years was held in Vienna. This meeting acknowledge the gender bias in the original declaration which subsumed women under the generic class of 'man'. The Conference resolved that 'the human rights of women and the girl child are inalienable, integral and indivisible'.

The 1998 Oslo report on Human Development and Human Rights concluded that *"human development can be seen as practically synonymous with human rights... the two perspectives focus on the same ends (human life and human dignity) .. on the same processes and key characteristics (people-centred, participatory, equitable, non-discriminatory and empowering)"*. It is this broad concept of universal rights that help us make sense of many of the values discussed above and help us put them into practice.

Human Rights have at last been incorporated into UK legislation. The Human Rights Act 1998 sets out to integrate parts of the European Convention on Human Rights into UK law. In the introduction to the Act Prime Minister Tony Blair commented *"It will enhance the awareness of human rights in our society. And it stands alongside our decision to put the promotion of human rights at the forefront of our foreign policy"*. Unfortunately, the Act only covers the basic 'first generation rights' but makes no comment on the economic or social rights. Despite these limitations the act will have significant impact on a number of contested areas including: benefits, discrimination, education, employment, family life, health, housing, immigration, policing and privacy.

It is easy to be cynical about human rights. Western governments have a long track record of supporting military regimes that actively suppress human rights. Poverty and gender issues are routinely ignored through the official support for business and profit. Some developing countries argue that the notion of personal freedom is a western concept that is irrelevant to the need to organise poor countries to combat famine and poverty. There is debate that the rights of women are in conflict with the culture of Islam.

For example Jiang Zemin then president of China said in comparing rights in the USA to China, *"the two countries differ in social system, ideology, historical tradition and cultural background, the two countries have different means and ways in realising human rights and fundamental freedoms"* (China Daily 28/12/1995). It is also argued that China has a cultural tradition of obedience to authority, collectivism and family which, it is claimed in Chinese government circles, is opposed to the 'western' ideals of individual freedom and tolerance of political dissent.

Are rights therefore, variable according to local culture, a western conspiracy to impose liberal capitalist norms on developing nations or a universal safeguard? Although the concept of rights is a product of western thought, Xiaorong Li (1998) argues that the cultural argument is bogus because the fundamentals of human rights protect rather than restrain cultural expression. Reduced to the core principles universal human rights are based on:

- Individual and collective security under the law
- Common access to essential conditions for physical and mental development
- The right and duty to work – freely chosen
- Participation in the planning and working of political institutions
- Freedom of association and contract
- Freedom of expression, conscience, belief, assembly and from legally acceptable self development.

In reality cultural arguments have been used to justify political repression. In China's case this includes the suppression of political protest in Tiannamen Square, religious persecution of Buddhism in Tibet and Islam in Singiang. Ayton-Shenker writing for the United Nations (1995) commented that: *"human rights are the birthright of every person. If a state dismisses universal human rights on the basis of cultural relativism, then rights would be denied to the persons living under that State's authority. The denial or abuse of human rights is wrong, regardless of the violators culture"*.

Across the world the human rights situation is variable. The following table identifies the degree to which various conventions have been ratified.

Convention	Countries which have ratified or acceded	Countries not yet ratified or acceded
Prevention and punishment of genocide	120	72
Convention of the status of refugees	125	67
Economic, social and cultural rights	135	57
Civil and political rights	136	56
Elimination of discrimination against women	153	39
Convention against torture	102	90
Rights of the child	190	2

(Source: New Internationalist 1999)

Clearly the Human Rights agenda has many outstanding issues. The United States has not ratified treaties on the rights of the child, women, or economic, social and cultural rights. Objectors to the convention on torture include Indonesia, Nigeria, Sudan and Belgium. According to the United Nations Development Programme one in five women are subject to violence either outside or within the home, but only a minority of countries have enacted protective legislation despite ratification of the UN convention. For example only 44 countries have laws against domestic violence, 17 countries have made marital rape a criminal offence and just 27 countries have sexual harassment laws.

Notwithstanding this, the broader concepts of Human Rights provide both an agenda and mechanism for development work. The following is a summary of the core rights as outlined by UN Conventions. Further details are available on the Internet at the Human Rights Web; www.hrweb.org.

The Covenant on Civil and Political Rights include:

- The right to legal recourse when rights have been violated, even if the violator was acting in an official capacity
- The right to life
- The liberty and the freedom of movement
- The right to equality before the law
- The right to privacy
- Freedom of thought, conscience and religion
- Freedom of opinion and expression
- Freedom of assembly and association

The Covenant on Economic, Social and Cultural Rights describes the basic rights of individuals and nations which include:

- Self determination
- Wages sufficient to support a minimum standard of living
- Equal pay for equal work
- Equal opportunity for advancement
- The formation of trade unions
- Freedom to strike
- Paid or otherwise maternity leave
- Free primary education and accessible education at all levels
- Protection for intellectual property
- Forbids the exploitation of children

The Convention on the Rights of the Child makes provision for civil rights, freedom from degrading treatment or punishment, protection from abuse or neglect, basic health and welfare, access to education and adequate leisure and recreation

Workers can use these rights to provide a justification for taking collective action, a starting point for helping people reflect on their lives and planning campaigns, a check list on the actions of government agencies, a challenge for a more open and democratic society, and to resist those (for example as we shall see, communitarians) who argue that we have too many rights.

Democracy

There are two basic forms of democracy: representative and participative. Representative democracy is the basis of government in most western societies. Under this system citizens elect their representatives to govern them for a set period of time, at a local and / or national level. In contrast participative democracy seeks to extend the democratic process to a level where citizens are essentially self governing.

Barber (1984) argues that true participatory democracy is based upon the adoption of fundamental changes in how a country is governed. The balance of power should be invested in the citizens rather than 'entrusted' to elected representative who usually follow a party line in their decision making. Barber suggests the following reforms:

- Extensive decentralisation of decision making to neighbourhood assemblies
- Civic information service
- Informal lay justice system
- More use of referenda
- Electronic balloting
- Election to office by lottery
- Universal citizen public service
- Workplace democracy

This is the radical view of participatory democracy. Other writers suggest a middle road of elected representatives with workplace and neighbourhood councils or associations as part of a wider civil society.

Community workers generally support moves towards participatory democracy. John Baker in his address to the 1996 AGM of the Irish Community Workers Co-operative (1997) made the case under four principles: equality, self determination, community and self development. Baker links equality to participatory democracy in three ways. Firstly, it enables a more equal distribution of power amongst the population. Secondly, it counteracts unequal status and divisions in society. Thirdly, it is the only way the powerless and oppressed can obtain social changes in their favour. Baker goes onto argue that citizens can only be empowered if they are in control of their own lives. People are collectively involved with others at various levels in society: through the workplace, neighbourhood, interest groups, as well as at national level. Participatory democracy is a way of ensuring that the collective decision making is democratic as possible. The community itself is strengthened by such a process. Everyone is more involved and becomes committed to actively making the community a better place to live. Finally, participatory democracy promotes the acquisition of skills and knowledge necessary to be actively involved. As a result individuals become more confident and able.

The counter argument is that there are a number of practical difficulties with making participatory democracy function properly. The first problem is the time it takes to make it work. Representatives are elected to save the majority having to worry about the complexities of, and making time for, decision making. In any case do citizens really want become this involved with government? To spend time understanding the issues and learning the skills means less time to be with families and following leisure activities. More worryingly do not people mostly respond to self interest? Under a participatory democracy the majority could simply impose discriminatory measure on unpopular minorities. Finally, it assumes that everyone has equal resources with which argue their point of view. The rich and powerful will always have more resources and will therefore get their way regardless of other views.

For the community worker the issue is how to extend democracy. There a various approaches that can make participatory democracy work at local level. Citizen councils, neighbourhood forums, workplace councils, proportional voting, making representatives directly accountable to their electorate are amongst a number of approaches that can be tried. The point is not about prescribing a system of democracy but encouraging people to engage in debate about how institutions that govern their lives can be made accountable. There will be different solutions for each place and context.

The challenge for those active in the community is therefore to hold onto, and apply, a number of key perspectives. Firstly, the worker must have a clear understanding of what community work can achieve - a vision of how the local community can be a better place to live. Secondly, the worker needs to ensure that the value positions outlined above are central to their practice, and that they work in a way that also promotes equality, openness, accountability and local democracy. Thirdly the worker has to enable local people to reflect on their experience, understand their rights and explore their hope to identify their own needs.

Community workers therefore have a responsibility to actively challenge oppression and discrimination in all its forms. Often this is uncomfortable and difficult. In some case it may result in withdrawing from a group because of their oppressive attitude and actions towards, say women or ethic minorities. So be it, as it can never be acceptable to collude with oppression.

Furthermore, simply organising people to meet the agenda of planners and other professionals is also not acceptable. Despite what we might wish to believe in the UK, many people do not know and do not receive their rights, their needs are unheard or decided by others. Democratic processes are often less than transparent or fully accountable than is claimed. The role of the community worker is to promote change and these principles outline the basic terrain of the struggle.

Summary

In this chapter we have explored:

- That all human activity is affected by the values of those involved
- Differences in values often lead to discrimination and oppression
- Effective community work requires a commitment to promoting equality
- Equality issues operate at economic, social, political ideological and psychological levels.
- To promote equality requires awareness and understanding of class, race, gender, disability and sexuality
- Community workers need to effectively identify the needs of communities and recognise the hierarchy of needs
- The concept of human rights informs practice

- We need to understand and work with both representative and participative democracy
- Community work is essentially about challenging oppression and this challenge must be met as required

Further Reading

Neil Thompsons **Promoting Equality** (Basingstoke, Macmillan 1998) is the essential guide to exploring values issues.

In more detail racism is discussed by Brahan et al in **Racism and Anti Racism** Buckingham, OUP 1994). American activists Angea Davis writes on **Women, Race and Class** (London, Womens Press to be published during 2001). Issues around women are discussed by Sheila Rowbotham in **Hidden from History,** (London, Pluto Press 1970) and **Dreams and Dilemmas** London, Virago 1983)

Bradshaw discusses the idea of need in his classic article **The Concept of Social Need**, (New Society, 30 March 1972). Another view is expressed by Ivan Illich in **Needs** in Sachs W, **The Development Dictionary** (London, Zed Books 1997)

The extensive reports on Human Rights can be accessed through the United Nations website at www.unhchr.ch/ Benjamin Barber explores the relationship between citizen participation and democracy in **Strong Democracy** (University of California Press 1985)

3

Underlying Perspectives: Global Contexts

"The future has arrived. It just isn't equally distributed".
William Gibson

Aims of this chapter

This chapter looks at the condition of the world early in the 21st century. We explore the failure of the current world development model. Particular reference is made to the effects of globalisation and the development of what is termed the information age We then consider some key global issues; women, urbanisation, poverty, and sustainability.

Global overview

At the time of writing (summer 2005) over 1 billion people live on less than $1 per day. World development, alongside climate change (and the two factors are symbiotically linked) present the major challenges for the world. All 191 countries represented at the United Nations have agreed the Millennium Development Goals. For each goal one or more targets have been set, most for 2015, using 1990 as a benchmark. The table in appendix 3 outlines the goals, the current world situation and on current trends when the goals may be achieved.

Live 8 provides an example of what this means in practice for an individual country: Zambia. It was one of sub-Saharan Africa's wealthiest countries, but is now one of its poorest and least developed. The living standards of Zambians are in rapid decline and the country is now lower placed on the human development index (HDI) than in 1975.

With a life expectancy of just 33 years, Zambians die earlier than people anywhere else in the world. The Zambian Ministry of Health expects half the population will die of AIDS. Roughly half the teachers trained every year die of the disease. The Zambian government is crippled by the massive debt recalled by international financial institutions. Debt repayments are making it impossible to respond to the health, educational and economic challenges facing Zambians.

In 2004, Zambia used 7.35% of its Gross Domestic Product (GDP) ($377 million) repaying its debt. It spends twice as much repaying its debt as it does on education. Zambian students struggle to learn in classes containing on average 70 pupils. Zambia has endeavoured to meet the debt relief conditions and has privatised public utilities, removed subsidies, deregulated its markets and opened its doors to foreign imports. In spite of these efforts, by 2003 Zambia's debt had been reduced by only 5%. The failure to cancel Zambia's debt in full is having catastrophic consequences for poor Zambians. Current trends suggest not only that Zambia will be unable to meet most of the Millennium Development Goals (MDGs), but also that it gets further from them as time goes on.

The failure of traditional development

Most people agree that aid to help developing countries is a good thing. However, in many ways development has failed. In contrast to the radical activists motto of *random acts of kindness senseless acts of beauty* we could re-title much of world development as *random acts of self interest senseless acts of policy.*

Before the 1939-45 war the idea of development was concerned with economic growth in colonies in the interest of the home country. The end of the war saw the move away from political colonisation. This change was driven partly by the costs of the war and also by the desire of the USA to break up the British, French and Dutch colonial empires and open them for American business. The key date is 20 January 1949 when President Truman said in his Inaugural Address:

> *"We must embark on a bold new programme for making the benefits of our scientific advances and industrial progressed*

available for the improvement and growth of underdeveloped areas.

The old imperialism – exploitation for foreign profit – has no place in our plans. What we envisage is a programme of development based on the concepts of democratic fair dealing"

The 1950'and 60's were seen as the 'golden age' of world development. The USA through the International Monetary Fund (IMF) and World Bank provided much financial assistance to developing countries. Partly this was due to a desire to buy political support and allegiance against the Soviet Block. Western multi national companies invested heavily in the developing world. Often production was shifted from Europe or North America to developing countries due to the cheaper labour costs. Developing world cities expanded as people moved from the countryside looking for work.

Developing countries themselves responded in a variety of ways. Some governments invested heavily to build domestic industry (e.g. South Korea) others diverted tax revenues and international loans to build massive armed forces (e.g. Pakistan), whilst others engaged in conspicuous consumption (e.g. Middle East oil states). A fourth group tried to promote their own form of socialism with expenditure on welfare, health and education services (e.g. Tanzania). In many countries domestic subsistence farming was reorganised to provide crops for export. This led in some cases to food shortages and basic supplies having to be imported. Traditional labour intensive methods of agriculture were replaced by larger scale and mechanised farming. This resulted in more people leaving the countryside to seek work in the urban shanty towns. As we shall see below these changes are now causing seriously social, economic and environmental problems.

Overall, the goal was for modernisation and industrialisation that would raise living standards. Indeed, the whole development idea was a modernist concept that industrially led policies would lead to progress for humanity and the inequality between the western and developing countries would be reduced. The global market for multinational companies and profits would be increased. Wealth would not be equally distributed between countries or within countries. However, wealth would 'trickle down' and over time everyone would benefit. There were a number of growth success stories, for example, Singapore, Taiwan, South Korea and Hong Kong. However, many countries especially in Africa and parts of Asia did not do so well.

In 1973 the oil producing countries (OPEC) imposed a fourfold increase in the price of oil. This action led to a net flow of money from western economies to the oil states. The resulting economic chaos in the west, even though short lived, had profound effects for development. Interest rates were increased pushing many countries that had borrowed to finance industrialisation into massive debt. The demand in the west for the raw materials and cash crops produced by developing countries fell, thus reducing their exports and income.

Increasing debt led to many countries being unable to pay their international loans. The IMF provides support funding to these countries in return for agreeing to the adoption of a Structural Adjustment Policy (SAP). This is essentially the imposition of neo liberal capitalist orthodoxy, which means

- Tighter financial control by the government
- Devaluation of the currency, which leads to increased exports and more expensive imports
- Elimination of subsidies on food and services
- Reduced state spending on health education and welfare.
- Reduction on controls over business and investment and privatisation of state industries

The net result of these changes is to protect the banking interests of the west and make domestic markets more accessible for transnational corporations. The cost of these changes is felt by the poor through higher unemployment, loss of income, reduced services, and increase in prices of basic goods. The argument in favour of SAP's is that there is no alternative and that the economy will eventually grow with wealth trickling down to the poor. In the long run therefore, SAP's are in everyone interest. In the short run the poor have to suffer.

Even for countries where development has been deemed to be successful e.g. Brazil and Indonesia), it has been bought at the expense of high external debt. And these debts remain a critical problem. Many countries are unable to meet the payments on the interest let alone repay the sum borrowed. The following table shows a selection of countries debt relative to their export income. It is the money received from exports that pays for the repayment of international loans.

Country	Internat'l Debt $ billion	Debt as % of export income
Brazil	219	40
Chile	47	32
Ethiopia	3	42
Indonesia	141	37
Mexico	149	35
Peru	30	35
Sierra Leone	1.5	52

(Source: CIA)

Many people now think the basic concept of development is fatally flawed. It is clear that the developing world economies cannot all industrialise to the same extent as the west. Finite natural resources, environmental degradation and vast urbanisation mean this is not only undesirable but also impossible. The rapid industrialisation of China and India, driven by the consumption of fossil fuels, is a major threat along with the USA to attempts to reduce global warming. It is argued therefore that the goal of development must change from simple measures of economic growth to poverty reduction and sustainable improvements in the quality of life.

Sachs (1997) comments that *"from the start, developments hidden agenda was nothing else than the westernisation of the world"*. He goes onto argue that this imposition of a cultural and economic view of what is progress has been at the expense of diversity and difference in the world. *"In this view, Tuaregs, Zapotecos or Rajisthanis are not seen as living diverse and non-comparable ways of human existence, but as somehow lacking in terms of what has been achieved by the advanced countries. Consequently, catching up was declared to be their historic task"*. Development has been a failed modernist project. What is required is a more diverse and flexible post modernism response to inequality and poverty. The UDP support this view and the latest Human Development Report argues that cultural liberty and diversity underpins effective development (UNDP 2004).

The Mexican Zapatista leader Subcomandante Marcos develops this theme. Quoted by John Berger in the Guardian (20 November 1999) Marcos sees the world engaged in a struggle between the poor and the power centres: that of international finance where the only imperative is to expand market penetration and profit. Commenting on the fragmented nature of the world, Marcos argues that it is like a jigsaw where only a few pieces are currently visible.

£ The first piece of the world jigsaw is the concentration of wealth in fewer hands and the increase of poverty and hopelessness

△ The second piece is a triangle representing a lie. Heralded as progress, it is the extension of the barbarism caused by the industrial revolution that proceeds unchecked by ethics or principle,

○ This is the circle of enforced emigration where millions of people have to leave their homes to seek a living.

□ This piece is a mirror reflecting the relationship between commerce and international crime.

⬠ The pentagon represents the loss of national independence. The role of nation states has been reduced to protecting the interests of business and policing the poor.

✺ This piece represents the break down of international frontiers and the fragmentation of countries (Yugoslavia, USSR)

⌂ The final piece is the pockets of resistance developing against the new economic order. What they have in common is the defence of the poor and the redundant and protection of human values. However, given the fragmented nature of the world they cannot form a united programme of opposition.

These pieces only provide a partial view of the world that is broken and fragmented. An overall understanding of the world is impossible and the pieces can only be in conflict with each other. Marcos concludes by acknowledging the need to find a non capitalist way forward, whilst rejecting any authoritarian single solution. He recognises the need to respect and build on diversity by saying "*It is necessary to build a new world, a world capable of containing many worlds, capable of containing all worlds*"

Globalisation

There is no doubt that the world is both a very unequal place and is changing fast. Wherever we are in the world we are not immune from these changes. Whether we live in the UK, Africa, Asia or North America we cannot understand how the local economy operates, explain levels and nature of unemployment, have insight into social processes and culture if we do not have a basic appreciation of how the world is changing and its local effects. As Craig and Mayo commented (1998) *"Community development is often thought of as an essentially local approach to problem solving. With the globalisation of the economy and the emergence of transnational organisations concerned with social and/or economic issues. Community development needs to rethink its approach to incorporate a global dimension"*. In short we need to understand the process of globalisation

During the 1980's and 1990's the process of globalisation and trade liberalisation has increased. Where I live in the West of Scotland, the main local private sector employers are an American transnational manufacturer of consumer goods and the Whiskey industry. Although the latter is Scottish based its market, and consequently local employment, is heavily dependent upon sales to the US and other overseas countries.

Recently, on a working trip to Pakistan the late night discussion with workers from local NGO's were broken off to collect pizza from Islamabad Pizza Hut. While we waited I was invited to select music from their extensive collection of British and American artists (mostly pirate copies from Singapore) or to pick a satellite channel on the TV. During another trip to Jordan I found myself in

McDonalds, sited conveniently in downtown Amman next to the Roman ruins. At the next table local Jordanian children played with Disney figures from their Happy Meal while their father in full Bedouin dress conducted a conversation on a mobile phone made in Finland. Most bizarre of all was spending the night in a hotel at 13,000 feet on the Tibetan Plateau. Outside the hotel compound in the nearby Tibetan village the remnants of tradition culture struggles to survive. Inside the hotel a mixture or Asian and western races watched satellite TV from Beijing, with glossy light entertainment shows and commercials advertising BMW's, hi tech electrical goods and the latest fashions. This economic and social integration of the world is what globalisation means.

The driving forces behind globalisation are twofold: the continued 'liberalisation' of economies and trade, and the improvements in communication, especially the digital revolution. Liberalisation of the world economy is about privatising nationalised industries, reducing controls on the free movement of money and capital between countries. It also concerns the removal of trade barriers between countries. The General Agreement on Tariffs and Trade (GATT) and its successor the World Trade Organisation (WTO) have progressively negotiated the removal of trade barriers. The liberal argument is of course, that increased trade creates wealth which will trickle down from the rich nation to the poor. Although the wealth of countries (excluding sub Saharan Africa) has increased due to trade liberalisation the gulf between rich and poor continues to increase.

The alternative point of view argues that trade liberalisation has removed the protection of fragile developing economies from domination by transnational corporations (TNC's). Writing in the Observer (21 November 1999) Barry Coates the Director of the World Development movement commented that *"the UK Government in particular has been practising its powers of spin to present free trade as the panacea that will solve all the world ills"*. He suggests that the WTO is not concerned with assisting developing countries to expand their domestic economies for the good of their people. Rather he claims *"Its (WTO) mandate is not to create sound international rules but to dismantle any rules that impede trade, elevating it above the protection of workers, consumers and the environment"*. The anti globalisation demonstrations from Seattle at the 1999 WTO conference onwards demonstrated both the growing discontent against the effects of trade liberalisation and the ability of diverse groups; trade unions, environmentalists, NGO's and ethnic groups to combine in a loose coalition of protest. However, there is increasing support for the view that it is trade restrictions that are compounding underdevelopment in poorer countries. What is required is fairer trade not restrictions on trade.

Parallel to trade liberalisation the International Monetary Fund (IMF) and the World Bank have been pushing free trade and mainstream capitalist programmes in return for loans to developing countries. The IMF was originally set up to prevent world economic recession. It does this through imposing an economic orthodoxy on recipient countries. Once in economic trouble the IMF requires a debtor country to adopt a Structural Adjustment Programme (SAP) in exchange for support funds. SAP's usually require that debt repayment is of prime importance and often this is financed through reduction in state welfare, health and education programmes. At the same time recipient countries are expected to reduce their regulation of the economy, trade and inward investment. This allows TNC's to invest more freely. The result is sometimes economic growth, sometimes not. However, the reduction in welfare expenditure almost always leads to worsening of conditions for the poor. This is seen as a necessary consequence for development. A similar programme was imposed on the UK in 1977 when a balance of payments crisis forced the then Labour government to seek IMF support. The resulting cuts in public expenditure contributed to Labour's election defeat in 1979.

The role of the World Bank is to finance economic development. Although, almost all countries are members, the richer countries have greater representation. In effect the World Bank is controlled by the rich western economies. Again, a capitalist orthodoxy underpins the working of the Bank. Since the 1990's it has begun to see poverty reduction as a key target as well as traditional economic growth. It has also slowly moved away from large capital projects towards smaller and more environmentally sustainable developments.

Overall the world economy has grown significantly as a result of the trade liberalisation policies. In development terms, it has been a failure as the gap between rich and poor has increased. In 1960 the western economies were 20 times richer than the developing economies. By 1980 they were 46 times richer. The chart below illustrates the gains and losses from trade liberalisation to the end of 1999.

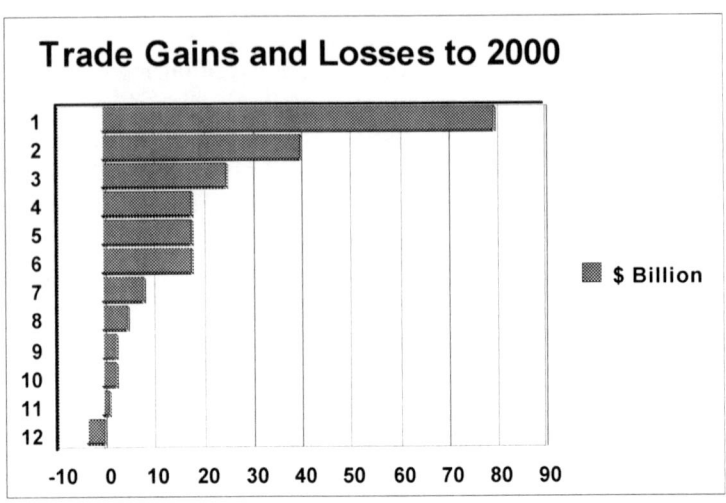

1. EU	2. China	3. Japan
4. USA	5 Upper Income Asia	6 Other Industrialised Countries
7. Latin America	8. India	9. Eastern Europe and former USSR
10. Low Income Asia	11. Other	12. Africa

(Source: New Internationalist)

In the 1999 Human Development Report the UNDP explored the nature of globalisation. The report, whilst acknowledging that globalisation is not a new process pointed out the quantitative change currently affecting the world:

- New markets—foreign exchange and capital markets linked globally, operating 24 hours a day, with dealings at a distance in real time.

- New tools—Internet links, cellular phones, media networks.

- New actors—the World Trade Organisation (WTO) with authority over national governments, the multinational corporations with more economic power than many states, the global networks of non-governmental organi-
- zations (NGO's) and other groups that transcend national boundaries.

- New rules—multilateral agreements on trade, services and intellectual property, backed by strong enforcement mechanisms and more binding for national governments, reducing the scope for national policy.

The UNDP report goes on to show that in 1999, 80 countries have per capita incomes lower than in 1990, mostly in sub-Saharan Africa and the ex-Soviet Union. The world's richest 200 people now own assets worth more than $1 trillion. The top three have a combined income in excess of that owned by the 600 million poorest people. The process of globalisation is increasing the concentration of wealth and ownership in fewer hands. The top 500 transnational corporations control 66% of world trade, whilst the top 10 TNC's have an income in excess of the GDP of the poorest 100 countries. This concentration of economic power threatens to undermine the position of nation states. For example, the world largest corporation General Electric was worth $341 billion in 2004 (Wall Street Journal). Second was Exon Mobil at $301bn and Microsoft third at $294bn. Vodaphone comes 13th at $155bn and Coca Cola at 24th $108bn. In contrast the GDP of Belgium is $349bn, Denmark $243bn and South Africa $212bn.

In theory the economic power of the TNC's is based in the nine most industrialised countries (see table below). However, the rationale of TNC's is to develop market share, to expand and to maximise medium term profits. The location of these companies is a product of their history. No nation state, with perhaps the exception of the USA is able to challenge to power of TNC's. Globalisation as a process is beyond the control of any one country and arguably, beyond the control of any grouping of countries.

Country	Number of top 200 TNC's
Japan	62
USA	53
Germany	23
France	19
Britain	11
Switzerland	8
South Korea	6
Italy	5
Netherlands	4

(Source: New Internationalist 1999)

The UNDP outlines a number of threats to human security caused by the workings of globalisation:

- *Financial volatility and economic insecurity* - the recent financial turmoil in East Asian led to 13 million people losing their jobs and cuts in health and education budgets. Real wages declined by around 50% in Indonesia. After a financial crisis it generally takes three years for real wages to recover and several years for employment levels.
- *Job and income insecurity* – in both poor and wealthy countries unemployment is caused through TNC's restructuring their operations. In order to remain competitive many countries (including the UK in the 1980's and 90's) have weakened workers rights making dismissal of employees easier for companies. Many new jobs are on short term and/or part basis.
- *Health insecurity* – HIV/AIDS remains a major problem with 33 million people affected. This number is growing by 6 million a year. Most badly hit are nine African countries where life expectancy is projected to decline by 17 years by 2010. Infections in Eastern Europe, the ex Soviet Union and India are also increasing rapidly. In addition income insecurity and poverty exacerbate health problems.

- *Cultural insecurity* – the expansion of global media, especially through satellite TV, brings the image of the western way of life and demand for consumer goods. Traditional cultures are increasingly undervalued and ejected by the young in favour of the media promoted view of the world.
- *Personal insecurity* – increased international trade and deregulation has opened opportunities for organised crime. Illegal trade in weapons, drugs, counterfeit goods and women is increasing. The drug trade is estimated to account for 8% of total world trade. Over 500,000 women a year are 'imported' to Western Europe for sexual exploitation. International organised crime is estimated to be worth $1.5 trillion. In a number of countries organised crime is effect in control of the government.
- *Environmental insecurity* – the environment is faced by threats from two directions. TNC's are increasingly exploiting the world's natural resources. Poor people living on the margin are also forced to use scare resources and diminishing forest land to survive.
- *Political and community insecurity* – faced by economic and social instability, often the result of globalisations itself, an increasing number of countries are subjected to civil war. This instability is fuelled by the international availability of weapons and organised crime which uses such conflicts to exploit their interests.
- A further factor is the inequality of *access to knowledge*. As the world moves swiftly to a knowledge and e-commerce driven economy many countries are being left behind.

The United Nations Report and Human Development and Human Rights (1998) sums up these changes: *"The traditional view of human rights focusing solely on state obligation is now outdated. The economic policies of the industrialised countries and.. transnational corporations, financial institutions, currency speculators, hedge fund managers and other have contributed to great economic instability and grave human and social upheavals".* Globalisation therefore, has led to vastly increased profits for transnational corporation at the expense of the worlds poor and the undermining of the power of nation states.

The Information Age

The second strand to these developments has been the rapid growth of digital technology and the resulting improvements in communication. Peter Drucker (1994) and others argue that the world is entering into a new phase. Drucker calls this 'The Age of Transformation'. Until the early 1990's the world economy was based on access to raw materials, capital for development, technology to improve manufacturing and skilled labour. In contrast, Drucker sees the future of the world economy and society being based on the power of knowledge.

Economies and businesses will be based increasingly on the successful marketing of knowledge and information. As knowledge is easily transferable, especially with the rapid growth of the Internet, success will come from flexible and effective competitive strategies. There will no longer be poor countries, in the sense that they did not have the capital to develop business. There will only be 'ignorant' countries. The same will be true of companies, industries, organisations, *communities and individuals.* The key to success is to acquire knowledge and make it productive through flexible management techniques. The social, economic and cultural change catalysed by this development cannot be underestimated. In Bangladesh for example, a major driver of development is the mobile phone. The GrameenPhone Company, a subdivision of the micro finance Grameen Bank has provided mobile phones to 90,000 women in 50,000 villages leading to an average extra income of $700 per year through selling local phone services.

Kenichi Ohmae (1996) has followed through this theme on a macro scale and suggests that the information age will lead to the decline of the nation state. Instead of national allegiance, economic self interest will be to regional groupings. Ohmae contrasts this development with the modernist industrial age of the 19th and 20th centuries.

Industrial Age 19th - 20th Century	Information Age Late 20th and early 21st Century
Society and economy based upon: • nation state governments • national sovereignty • strong control of centralised forces • sensitive to borders • favouring a domestic capital and protects domestic companies • aiming for one state prosperity through development of exports • Government initiatives • change occurs gradually over decades **Winners:** Germany Japan UK USA	**Society and economy based upon:** • private capital and information • citizen sovereignty • autonomous networks of private enterprises • inherently borderless • welcoming foreign capital and companies • aiming for regional prosperity • entrepreneurial initiatives • change occurs suddenly over months or years **Winners:** Hong Kong / Shenzen Singapore / Johor / Bantam Southern China (Peal River) Southern India (Bangalore) North Mexico / SW USA Silicon Valley New Zealand Northen Italy NW USA

(Based on Ohmae 1996)

These changes reflect the discussion below on the nature of postmodern society. For our purposes there are two key dynamics are at work here. One is the ability to instantaneously communicate and trade globally, which makes the countries of origin and destination almost irrelevant. The second is to counteract the alienating effect of globalisation through trying to find relevance and meaning in ones locality or community of interest. Community workers can contribute to the second but only if they recognise the changing nature of society.

This insight is of profound importance for community workers. Perhaps the future for developing communities in both the social and economic sphere is through improving and effectively applying the community's essential knowledge. Traditionally, development workers have concentrated on the process of building organisation and the teaching of basic skills. We seldom consider in much detail what the community, and the active individuals within it need to know and how can they learn it. This suggests more importance should be placed on the approach of Freire and Illich's learning webs to assist people to understand and contribute to their community.

Global Issues

This section explores a number of current critical issues in the world: the position of women, urbanisation, poverty, population growth, fresh water and environmental sustainability. Although separated by geography, religion and culture the poor of the world also experience many similarities

Poverty

The Universal Declaration of Human Rights sates in article 25.1:

> *"Everyone has the right to a standard of living adequate for the health and wellbeing of himself and of his family, including food, clothing, housing and medical care and necessary social services, and the right to security in the event of unemployment, sickness, disability, widowhood, old age or the lack of livelihood in circumstances beyond his control"*

Overlooking the sexist language of the time, this definition defines the benchmark below which no country should allow its citizens to fall. Poverty therefore, is not just about money. Mari Marcel-Thekaekara visited Glasgow after working for ten years in India. Writing in the Guardian (26 February 1999) she commented:

"We were told that Easterhouse housing estate in Glasgow is considered Europe's worst slum. We thought this was ludicrous – these people had assured housing, electricity, hot and cold water, refrigerators, gas or electric cooking ranges. By Indian standards this was middle class luxury. At the back of my mind, I could see anaemic, emaciated Adivasi women carrying water in pots from half a kilometre away; huts without electricity and women searching for firewood everyday, thankful if they had a kilo of rice to feed their families.

Suddenly we were hit by the reality of the poverty surrounding us in Glasgow. Most of the men hadn't had a job in 20 years. They were dispirited, depressed, often alcoholic. .. Emotionally and mentally they were far worse off than the poor where we worked in India, even though the physical trappings of poverty were less stark"

There are two types of poverty: absolute and relative. Absolute poverty is not having sufficient income to pay for the basics to sustain life. Relative poverty is socially constructed and is measured by not being able to live according to social norms. The Adivasi suffer from absolute poverty. In Easterhouse it is relative poverty that causes the damage. The Adivasi themselves describe wealth in terms of their 'community, children, unity, culture and the forest'. The loss of culture and traditional environment is also a cause of relative poverty.

Even on the biases of absolute poverty the figures are depressing. The World Bank (1996) defines poverty as people living on less than $1 per day. In 2004 the estimate was around 1 billion people and a further 2 billion live on less than $2 per day. With the gross inequalities of wealth within countries relative poverty figures are higher. In all countries wealth is distributed unequally. Indeed in the UK inequality increased significantly during the Conservative administrations between 1979 and 1997, and USA is one of the most unequal societies in the developed world. However, the pattern of inequality varies significantly between countries. The following table compares the share of national income between the poorest 20% or the population and the richest 20%: generally, the poorer the country the greater the inequality of wealth.

Country	Poorest 20%	Richest 20%
Sierra Leone	1.1	63.4
Guinea-Bissau	2.1	58.9
Panama	2.3	60.4
Brazil	2.5	64.2
Niger	2.6	53.3
South Africa	2.9	64.8
Austria	10.4	33.3
Sweden	9.6	40.2

There can be no doubt about the growing inequalities in the world. The following figures, using United Nations data, illustrate how poverty and inequality have widespread effects on health and the quality of life. The table below compares the gross domestic income in dollars divided by the population to give an average income per head. This is the usual method for showing the wealth of a country. Note that this method says nothing about the distribution of wealth within a county or the buying power of a dollar between countries given different domestic prices.

Country (bottom 5)	GDP per capita in $ for 2004	Country (top 5)	GDP per capita in $ for 2004
Somalia	600	Luxembourg	58,900
Gaza Strip	600	United States	40,100
Sierra Leone	600	Guernsey	40,000
Malawi	600	Norway	40,000
East Timor	400	British Virgin Islands	38,500

The UK is at 19th place with $29,600. In the United States the Federal Government estimates that 12.7% of the population live in poverty. Poverty in the USA is defined as a family of four living on less than $18,800 per year ($4,700 per capita). In some urban areas, for example Chicago, the figure rises to 50%. Poverty is also distributed unequally between racial groups. Black Americans have a poverty rate of 26% whilst amongst Hispanics it is 25.6%

The second indicator is infant mortality during the first year of life for every 1000 live births. This indicator is used to illustrate the levels of poverty in countries. Poverty is usually the major cause of child death, due to the resulting poor diet and vulnerability to disease. It is also a reasonable indicator of the adequacy of health care. In the worst ranking country, Angola 187 out of every 1000 babies born die before their first birthday. In Afghanistan it is 163 deaths, in Sierra Leone 162 and Liberia 161. By contrast Singapore has the lowest infant mortality rate of 2.3 per 1000 live births. The United Kingdom rate is 5.6 and the USA is at 6.2.

Changing the perspective slightly we can look at life expectancy at birth. This gives an overview of poverty, health and welfare services. The figures do not show the distribution of life expectancy within countries in terms of gender or between rich and poor. Life expectancy for the very poor in these countries will be significantly less than the average. Note the bottom five countries are African and this is due to a mix of HIV / Aids and the effects of civil war. The UK's figure is 78 years and the United States 77 years.

County (bottom 5)	Life Expectancy at Birth 1995	Country (top 5)	Life Expectancy at Birth 1995
Liberia	38 years	Andorra	83 years
Angola	38 years	Macau	82 years
Lesotho	34 years	San Marino	81 years
Botswana	33 years	Singapore	81 years
Swaziland	33 years	Hong Kong	81 years

The final indicator is access to fresh water. This is a key determinant of a healthy life and an indicator of poverty. In the top 33 countries 100% of the population have access to safe water. In

Madagascar it is only 10% of the population. For the Central African Republic it is 12%, Uganda has 15% access, Ethiopia 18% and Somalia 21 %. Overall, 27 countries cannot ensure fresh water supplies to the majority of their population.

The United Nations Development Programme has created the Human Development Index (HDI) to give an overview of the level of development between countries. The HDI is made up from statistics covering life expectancy, educational attainment and income. The details can be accessed in the Human Development Global reports at :

http://hdr.undp.org/reports/global/2004/pdf/hdr04_HDI.pdf

There is considerable debate how to respond to poverty. Suggestions range from radical change to welfare and self help schemes. The table in appendix 4 summarises the four main responses to alleviating poverty

Urbanisation

At the end of the 20th century around 50% of the world's population were living in urban areas. By 2025 this is expected to increase to almost 70%. Urbanisation is caused by development as people move off the land where agriculture is being mechanised, and move to cities where industrial development is taking place. In doing so the ability of urban administrations to expand public services is often overwhelmed. This becomes especially acute in countries subject to IMF structural adjustment. As a result urbanisation leads to increasing poverty, homelessness, pollution, deficiencies in sanitation and fresh water supply, and decline in health and educational services.

Rank	Cities 2005	Pop (m)
1	Tokyo	34
2	Mexico	22
3	Seoul	22
4	New York	21
5	Sao Paulo	20
6	Mumbai	19
7	Los Angeles	17

8	Jakata	16
9	Osaka	16
10	Calcutta	15
	Total Urban pop	3 billion

(Source: United Nations)

In the developed world high incomes allow individuals to provide for themselves. This level of income also enables cities to develop a tax base to finance public services. In the developing world the annual income for many is less than $200 thus making both self help and local tax solutions impossible. The following table of government expenditure per person illustrates the problem (UNDP 1996).

Regional grouping of cities	**$ per person**
Sub-Saharan Africa	16.6
South Asia	15.0
East Asia	72.5
South America	48.4
Eastern Europe, North Africa, Middle East	86.2
Western Europe, North America, Australia	656.0

On the other hand urbanisation leads to economic growth through increased industrialisation, increased productivity, easier provision of education for the middle classes and upwardly mobile sectors of the working class. The global pattern therefore is likely to be continued in the growing cities with a rich elite, an increasingly wealthy professional class, a working class covering the manufacturing and service sector with poverty concentrated amongst a growing underclass subsisting on casual employment.

Most cities, including developed world cities, have antiquated water supply and sewage systems. It is the poor areas of the city which are most likely to be without adequate fresh water supply. In 1986 the World Health Organisation estimated that 26,000 people a day die as a result of drinking polluted water. Overall, the World Bank (1996) estimates that 1.5 billion people do not have access to fresh water and 1.8 billion to sanitation. As city populations increase the supply of potable water is becoming a critical issue. To prevent disease capital expenditure on these systems is a priority.

The urban poor need access to cheap and reliable public transport to enable them to access employment. In many developing world cities public transport suffers from under investment and severe overcrowding. The increasing use of cars and taxis leads to severe air pollution.

UNDP estimates that world wide 500 million people are either homeless or living in severely sub standard accommodation. With poor housing there is the increased likelihood of ill health and extra barriers to education. With limited city finance self help schemes may be the only way to develop affordable low cost housing

Women

Although women comprise more than 50% of the world's population, they are largely excluded from decision making in community and social affairs. Discrimination both informal and institutional affects women. This discrimination is world wide and is not limited only to developing countries. Such discrimination is reflected by lower wages, less access to the better jobs, longer working hours (for paid and unpaid work), lower educational provision, poorer health, as victims of violence, from cultural, ethnic or religious practices. For example in India only 38% of girls receive secondary education, women earn 21% of men's income and hold just 7% of parliamentary seats. In Morocco the figures are 32%, 28% and 1%. For Bolivia it is 34%, 27% and 6%. In the developed world the figures for the USA are 97%, 41% and 11%, and for the UK 95%, 35% and 8% (New Internationalist).

The United Nations declared 1975-85 as the Decade for Women. The gains made during this time were limited but it did achieve a critical focus on the global position of women. In 1995 the United Nations held the Fourth World Conference on Women in Beijing. The Platform for Action adopted by the conference was based on the recognition of the central role women have to play in development and that for this potential to be realised the empowerment of women is of central importance.

Being subject to universal discrimination means that women and girls should be the primary focus of development activity. Ironically, it is women who usually provide the core of any developmental opportunity. Women hold multiple roles as homemakers, caretakers of children and the elderly, breadwinners both within and outside the home. Because women are likely to be more concerned with the welfare of children they often take a longer term view than men of development and value financial restraint and education.

In June 2000 the UN held a follow up conference from Beijing (Beijing + 5) to review progress on the development of women. An international working group, Women Watch (www.un.org/womenwatch) identified the following issues for review.

- Violence towards women
- Economic inequality of women
- Increasing women's role in environmental sustainability
- Greater involvement of women in power and decision making
- Securing and promoting women's health
- Ending poverty for women
- Reducing the effects of armed conflict on women
- Achieving educational equality
- Addressing the presentation of women in the media
- Empowering female children
- Claiming women's human rights

This agenda for the development of the position of women and girls is applicable on a global basis. It should be integrated into our work wherever we may practice

Sustainability

The Rio World Commission on Environment and Development in 1992 defined sustainability as *"that which meets the needs of the present without compromising the ability of future generations to meet their own needs"*. Attended and endorsed by 178 governments this view stands in contrast to traditional enlightenment and modernist position of exploiting nature for human needs. Such a position has been characteristic of both capitalist and Marxist views of development.

Due to the opposition of the transnational corporations and some western governments the products of the Rio conference were limited. It agreed a climate treaty, set of Forest Principles and a biodiversity treaty (which the USA refused to sign as it conflicted with its economic interest). The conference also agreed the action programme called Agenda 21, which outlines in over 500 pages, what sustainable development means. This document has been used in diverse ways to influence economic and social development. Agenda 21 has made sustainability issues a mainstream concern. Unfortunately, its meaning can also be interpreted in so many ways that it can often appear to offer something to everyone, when in fact it is little more than rhetoric.

Unsurprisingly, exploitation rather than conservation of nature remains the position of the majority of transnational corporations. Jeremy Leggatt in the Carbon War (1999) chronicles, from his personal experience, how transnational corporations have attempted to reduce the effect of international treaties on reducing the effect of greenhouses gasses to protect their profits. This is a fascinating case study of the political role of transnational corporations and how their search for profits can override not only national, but also international agendas. It is argued that the influence of such corporations explains the refusal of the United States to sign up to the 1997 Kyoto Protocol for limiting carbon emissions to limit the effects of climate change.

Max McGraw, Professor of Sustainable Enterprise sums up the global issues by identifying what he terms 'global signals of human-caused unsustainability' (Financial Times 13 December 1999).

Swelling population
- 3.6bn more people by 2050
- Rising international migration
- Shortage of family planning
- 250m child labourers
- Rapid unplanned urbanisation
- Resurgent infectious diseases

Persistent deprivation
- 850m adults illiterate
- 2.7bn lacking sanitation
- 1.4bn in poverty
- 1.3bn without clean water
- 1bn lacking adequate shelter
- 840m malnourished

Social disintegration
- 1.2bn un/underemployed
- Increasing inequality
- Gender bias
- Political repression
- Inequality based conflict
- Increasing family breakdown

Threatened biology
- Freshwater ecosystem decline
- Global deforestation
- Wetland / coral reef loss
- Habitat fragmentation / loss
- Loss of biological diversity
- Cross boarder bio invasions

Altered biogeochemistry
- Ozone depletion
- Global climate disruption
- Global nitrogen overload
- Compound build up
- Hydrological cycle change
- Accumulating nuclear waste

Declining renewable resources
- Freshwater scarcity
- Soil erosion/ degradation
- Collapse of fisheries
- Rangeland degradation
- Cereal yield stagnation
- Spreading desertification

Sustainability now has to be an integral part of any development activity. At Istanbul in 1996 a follow up UN Conference was held on Human Settlements (Habitat II). In preparation for this event international NGO's came together to produce a paper on Sustainable Communities and Societies. Following a position of arguing from fundamental rights the NGO's declared that *"all peoples have a right to live in dignity as members of sustainable communities within sustainable societies .. this right also implies the responsibility of all peoples to actively participate in the work of building such a society"*. A number of essential principles were developed to guide such development activity:

Central concepts
- Interconnectedness and interdependence of all issues
- Recognition of the right to sustainable communities and societies
- Implementation of universally recognised human rights
- Healthy ecosystems
- Gender equality

Sustainable livelihoods
- Redefinition of work
- Sustainable production and consumption
- Socially responsible business practices
- Empowerment

Social sustainability
- Inclusiveness, pluralism and participatory decision making
- Justice and equity
- Decentralisation of power, wealth and decision making
- Co-operation as the basis of economic, political and social relationships
- Education, including girls and women
- Mechanisms for conflict resolution

Sustainable culture
- Preservation of local culture
- Promotion of cultural and social diversity
- Recognition of local knowledge systems

Sustainable economics
- Redefinition of prosperity and how we measure it
- Identify the real social and environmental costs
- Access to shelter and alleviation of poverty
- Access to credit and finance including women and the poor

Physical sustainability
- Recognition of ecological limits
- Emphasis on renewable resources
- Natural resource planning
- Sustainable energy and water systems
- Human scale developments
- Renewable and recyclable materials
- Promotion of biodiversity

These principles are applicable to all communities. If we are serious about promoting sustainability as a central concept of our work, then these principles should both inform, and provide a check on what we do. The world is now far too integrated for us to be able to just work in our own communities and assume we are immune from outside influences. Of course, each locality has its own unique characteristics, but it will also have its own share of problems that are common to others as well as potentially benefiting for the experience of other communities.

As the diagram below illustrates, community workers needs an awareness of global developments and an understanding of sustainability: of how economic and social trends around globalisation, urbanisation, unemployment, poverty, the position of women and the resulting national and local political responses may be acting on the community. The next chapter explores how these trends have influenced developments in the UK

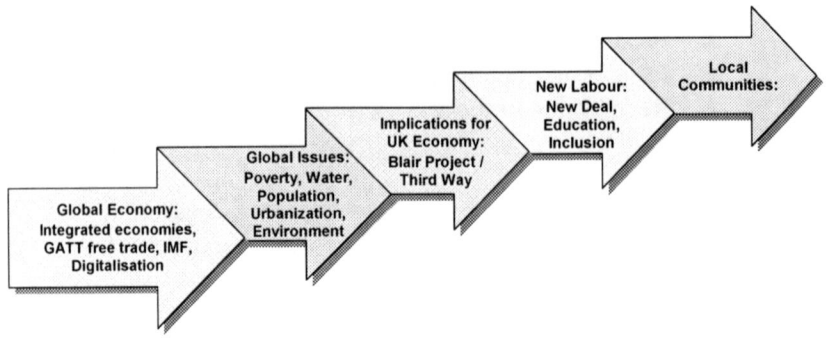

With the growth of the Internet it is now easy and essential for community workers and community groups to keep in touch with what is happening across the world. It is also increasingly possible to make links with and learn from the experience of other communities.

Summary

This chapter has covered the following points:

- The traditional approach to development has failed
- Development is governed by the needs of the main industrial countries and transnational corporations through the World Trade Organisation, World Bank and the IMF
- There is a growing movement for a more equitable development strategy
- The process of globalisation is imposing major changes across the world
- Through globalisation the richer part of the world is growing richer and inequality is increasing
- The 'information age' based around new technology is accelerating the pace of globalisation

- A number of global issues around poverty, health, urbanisation are reaching crisis point,
- Women provide a key to future development
- Sustainability issues must be embedded in all development activity
- Understanding the local is based on understanding the global

Further Reading

The **United Nation Human Development Reports** provide analysis and commentary of the social condition of the world.. They are available on line at http://www.undp.org/. For current debate on sustainability see the United nations Framework Convention on Climate Change at http://www.unfccc.int/

A fuller critical discussion of development can be found in Sachs **The Development Dictionary** (London, Zed Books 1997). Naomi Klein give a current view of the effects of global capitalism in No Logo (London Flamingo 2000)

It is also important to consider the experience of individuals and communities and not simply deal with statistics. After all it is easy to become lost in global trends and numbers and forget that behind the numbers are real people. Throughout the world millions of families are trying to make a living and bring up their children in the face of poverty and oppression. Sometimes the problems are generated by national government, by local bureaucracy or corruption, sometimes by the workings of transnational corporation and financial institutions or the effect of IMF structural adjustment policies.

Palagummi Sainath an Indian journalist explores in **Everyone Loves a Good Drought** (1999), the reality of life for the poor in his country and the negative effects of development and government failures on their lives. He describes how inefficiency and corruption diverts much of the aid money away from the poor. Even worse he explores the 'socialism for the rich - capitalism for the poor' scenario where aid money subsidises the rich at the expense of the poor. For example India trains 14,000 doctors a year, mostly from middle class families, many of whom emigrate to work in the west. At the same time only 8,000 nurses on whom the burden of basic primary health care is placed are trained. Considerable sums are spent on education. However the 15 to 19 years olds from the top 20% of households have completed on average 10 years of schooling. For the bottom 40% of households the same age group averages less than 1 year of schooling.

Also in India between 1951 and 1990 over 26 million people were displaced off their land to make way for development projects in mining, irrigation and manufacturing. The majority of the displaced have not received compensation, adequate rehousing or employment. Arundhati Roy in **The Cost of Living** (London, Flamingo1999) undertakes a critical analysis of the Narmada dam development in India. She argues that large scale development projects are used by government s as a means of social control for the poor and profit for the establishment.

Slavenka Drakulic in **Café Europa: life after communism,** (London, Abacus 1996) explores the reality of life for people living in the ex-communist countries of Western Europe. She illustrates that although the regimes have been liberalised to varying degree, the mind set of many remains that of fear and self repression.

John Pilger in a number of books, **Distant Voices**, (London, Vinatge), **Heroes** (London, Pan) and **Hidden Agendas** (London, Vintage) tells the individual stories of families in Australia, Britain and developing countries. What these stories show is that despite geographical and cultural differences the issues and struggles that face ordinary people across the world have many similarities.

Nick Danziger in **Danzigers Brtiain,** (London, Flamingo, 1997) takes the reader on a journey of the dispossessed in modern Britain. Danziger comments that: "*I was to discover there are many types of poverty, and one startling difference, the excluded and marginalised people of British cities are in many ways less able to deal with relationships and circumstances than the shanty town dwellers in Third World countries*".

In **The Ends of the Earth,** (Papermac 1997) Robert Kaplan reported on his travels through Africa, the Middle East, Iran, Central Asia, the Indian subcontinent and Indochina. He gives vivid description of life in many countries and concludes:

> *We are not in control. As societies grow more populous and complex, the idea that a global elite like the UN can engineer reality from above is just absurd as the idea that political scientists can reduce any of this to a science. As the tax base of the West stagnates and populations climb in the third world, foreign aid will make even less of a difference in coming decades .. People will either solve or alleviate their problems at the local level. .or they wont."*

Middleton in **Kalashnikovs and Zombie Cucumbers: travels in Mozambique** (London, Phoenix 1994) echoes this theme in his writings on Mozambique. He explores the effects of colonialism and western sponsored civil war on this African Country. He also contrasts the successes and failures of NGO's to effectively offer meaningful aid and development assistance.

4

Underlying Perspectives: UK Context

"We are the party of the individual because we are the party of the community". Tony Blair

You have the right to food money
Providing of course you
Don't mind a little
Investigation, humiliation
And if you cross your fingers
Rehabilitation
The Clash

Aims of this chapter

In this chapter we review the Thatcher years and the current New Labour Agenda. We explore the current social policy around modernising the economy, welfare reform, poverty, social inclusion and lifelong learning

The Thatcher years

From 1945 until 1979 there was a consensus across much of the western world that social democratic policies would lead to a rise in living standards for all. Economic growth would provide increasing funds for social expenditure. Pressure groups could operate in a pluralist framework that would allow them to obtain funding for their self defined needs.

By the late 1970's it was clear that the British economy was in serious decline. The post war boom had foundered with the crisis produced by the rise in oil prices in the early years of the 1970's. The economy was characterised by low levels of profits, productivity and investment. Inevitably this was causing the steady loss of export markets and increased penetration by imports. In this weak financial position government finances were only maintained through inflationary policies. These trends were compounded by the world recession. The effects of the International Monetary Funds structural adjustment programme were causing unemployment to rise and to cuts in government expenditure. In this context the social consensus fell apart leading to industrial conflict and the election in 1979 of a new government with a New Right agenda

The incoming government sought to reverse the decline in the economy by freeing the economy of the controls of collectivism and allowing the market to decide the allocation of resources. This would entail massive structural reorganisations as unprofitable organisations went bankrupt to be followed by the creation of new more market oriented new businesses. For this to happen the government thought it had to do two things. Firstly to reduce its control over economic and social life to ensure businesses and families became more self reliant. This would be achieved through a whole raft of policies based on the provision of sound monetary policy, reliance on supply side economics for regenerating the economy. This means reducing labour costs and increasing the opportunities for making profits, privatisation of services, restraints on local government activity and financing as well as social policy initiatives in education and welfare. Secondly, to become stronger in key areas of policy implementation including managing industrial and social unrest.

For example, in the 1980 budget regional aid was slashed, the Parker Morris council housing standards were abolished, council rents increased and grants to local authorities reduced. Rate capping was introduced for those local authorities that were seen to be profligate. The Greater London Council was abolished along with the six metropolitan councils who refused to tow the government's line.

The miners strike of 1984-5 showed the determination of the government to win whatever the costs (estimated at £2.5 billion to the national economy). This was a major defeat for working class organisations and had a significant knock on effect for other forms of organising. If the miners union could not win what hope was there for small community organisations? The one hopeful sign was the spontaneous creation of women's support groups for the miners that reflected the growing impact of the feminist movement.

Running parallel to the shift of state services (electricity, gas, telephones) to privatised bodies, the government, after the 1987 election, embarked on the reconstruction of the public sector according to market principles. Economists of the New Right were challenging the structure of the public sector where administration rather than market criteria were the dominant factor in resource allocation. The economists argued that market solutions will always provide superior results to the current forms of public provision. Allocating resources through markets would provide least cost services that were distributed according to need and avoid 'distortions' arising from lobbying by effective pressure groups.

Inherent in this approach was the principle of scraping universal services and benefits as well as reducing the negative effects arising from the 'culture of welfare dependency'. Instead individuals would be forced into active self help financial prudence and bidding for services through the market. These ideas are derived from Hayek (1960, see also Barry 1979) and other members of the Austrian School of economists. These views came together in what the government called 'new public management'. Essentially this was a set of ideas for managing public institutions on the basis of internal markets, contracting out, tendering and financial incentives. This policy development manifested itself in the 1988 Education Reform Act. 1989 Next Steps report on the Civil Service, the Working for Patients white paper on the NHS and the move to competitive tendering for local authority services.

These new proposals lead to further cuts in state benefits and government expenditure to allow for tax cuts prior to the next election. The first serious attempt at this was through the introduction of Income Support in the mid 1980's. One effect of these policies has been the removal of many local government functions to unelected bodies that are little influenced by community based pressure groups. Increasingly, local government services were subject to competitive tendering. Value for money became the main criteria not what the community thinks of the level and quality of service.

As a result a market economy was being created in the provision of social welfare. Local authorities increasingly become enablers who purchased services from a range of private, voluntary and possibly community bodies. The reorganisation of local government was a further step in this direction. The context of the relationship between community organisations and local government was fundamentally changed. It is essential to realise that as a result local authorities are less involved in directly delivering services and in offering grants to community organisations. The future relationship continues to move steadily towards community organisations acting as service providers and tending for local authority contracts in competition with an expanding private sector.

By the end time of the Conservative governments defeat in 1997 poverty in the UK had increased from their first election win in 1979. The following table illustrates the current levels of poverty by the following characteristics by personal, economic and family status.

	Total number (m)	Proportion Poor (%)	Number in Poverty (m)
Adult women	22.2	24	5.3
Children	13.0	35	4.5
Adult men	21.1	20	4.2
Elderly	9.8	31	3.0
Lone parent family	4.3	63	2.9
Unemployed	4.6	78	2.3
All		25	14.1

(Source: Department of Social Security 1998)

According the DSS statistics between 1979 and 1997 the number of individuals in poverty, defined as living below 50% of average income after living costs, rose from 5 million to over 14 million. Over 8 million people were dependent upon income support and job seekers allowances.

What is also important is how income is distributed amongst social groups and between communities. The average annual household income in the Top 5 postcode being around 10 times that of the bottom 5 postcode areas. The top four areas are in London: Temple, Blackfriars, Barbican and Belgravia with the fifth in Berkshire; Gerrards Cross. The Bottom five are outside of the South East of England in Bootle, Leicester, Middlesborough, Belfast and Birkenhead.

By the end of the Conservative government the rich had become richer and the poor, poorer. But the economy had not effectively become stronger. The problems of short term planning and under investments remained. The Conservative Party had, perhaps, too many vested interests to allow it to fundamentally modernise Britain. John Grey (1996), a leading New Labour thinker sums up the legacy of Thatcherism as:

> *"Thatcherism was a modernising project with profound and irreversible consequences for political life in Britain. The question cannot be: how are the remains of social democracy to be salvaged from the ruins of Thatcherism? But instead: what is Thatcherism's successor".*

This takes us onto a discussion of New Labour and the Third Way

New Labour and the Third Way

It is becoming increasingly recognised that in the present global economic and social environment neither governments nor the market can solve the current world problems explored above. In the USA the Democratic Leadership Council (1996) argued that in the information age citizens have realised that the strong centralised and bureaucratic government does not work. The promises that the government will solve economic and social problems have not been delivered. Neither do people want the radical conservative agenda of dismantling government and handing services over to the private sector. People want, according to opinion polls, good quality, free or cheap public services.

Therefore, says the Democratic Leadership Council, a Third Way of government needs to be found. This has to be a new progressive form of government that is the servant, not the master of the people. It also has to be a form of government that will act as a catalyst for regenerating citizenship and communities. This Third Way should be built on the principles of American democracy: equality of opportunity, mutual responsibility, and self government. Such a view is very similar to the ideas of communitarianism explored below. This definition of the third way focuses on responsibility rather than rights, and the idealisation of the correctness and normality of mainstream American ideals and culture.

The Third Way has been described contradictorily by its critics, as the last stand of modernism, post modernist socialism or just a variant of late modern capitalism. But whatever the theoretical base the Third Way has gained significant political support from a wide range of political parties, organisations, academics and policy makers. It dominates the agenda of most of Europe's social democratic parties. Tony Blair has incorporated the ideals of the Third Way into New Labour policy and is seen as the leading light for its political development in the UK.

Anthony Giddens (1999) Director of the London School of Economics is often seen to be the main European theorist for the Third Way. He argues that the old idea that the 'left' in politics was about social change and the 'right' was for retaining the status quo is no longer valid. Under the Thatcher administration the Conservative party was pursuing a radical agenda to free the economy from state control, reduce the power of trade unions and local government and push back public spending and public services. The New Labour administration is morally very conservative in its adherence to personal responsibility and communitarian concepts. Furthermore, old class driven perspectives have been replaced by what he terms, 'life politics'. These concern issues of personal identity (race, sexual orientation), environmental conditions, quality of life for communities and the nature of civil society in general.

Giddens argues that the effects of globalisation have caused these political changes. He identifies six policy elements that he believes can enable countries to respond positively to globalisation:

- The development of dynamic governments which will actively assist public affairs without controlling it.

- Reconstructing civil society through involving more people in community affairs.
- Developing a new mixed economy based on a balance between regulation and deregulation. To allow economic freedom and diversity whilst protecting consumers and social groups.
- Reconstruction of the welfare state. A programme that recognises that the old welfare state did not really protect the vulnerable, reduce inequality and failed to acknowledge the importance of individual freedom and initiative.
- Ecological modernisation; that is economic development within a sustainable environment.
- Democratisation of government responses to globalisation.

In the same vein, Blair explored the political beliefs that underpin the economic and social policies of New Labour. In his Fabian Society pamphlet, The Third Way: New Politics for the New Century, (1998). Blair describes the Third Way as:

> *"a modernised social democracy, passionate in its commitment to social justice and the goals of the centre left, but flexible, innovative and forward looking in the means to achieve them. It is founded on the values which have guided progressive politics for more than a century – democracy, liberty, justice, mutual obligation and internationalism. But it is a Third Way because it moves decisively beyond an old left preoccupied by state control, high taxation and producer interests, and a new right treating public investment .. as evil to be undone "* (The Independent 21 September 1998).

In this article Blair explicitly rejects the old left and their programme for state control as a failed ideology. He argues that politically we need to take the best of social democracy and liberalism. This can also be seen as an implicit rejection of socialism per se as a failed system and recognition that capitalism is inevitable but in need of revision and a human face. For this reason New Labour is increasing seen as a post Thatcherite approach rather than a return to a socialist programme.

Blair also acknowledges that we are inextricably linked into the global economy and that all policies, including education and social policies need to deliver economic benefits. In the global economy no country is really in charge of its own affairs. Attempts to manage the economy are doomed because individual countries cannot control the financial markets or transnational corporations. All a government can do is improve the 'supply side' of the economy. This means making the country attractive to investors through low inflation and low interest rates with skilled and flexible labour.

Furthermore, everyone has a duty to be part of this mission. Welfare reform, which puts people back to work, and where excluded communities are made productive are part of the grand vision. This reflects the winning Clinton slogan for the 1992 presidential election of *'It's the economy, stupid'*. The basis of political success is giving as many people as possible an improved standard of living and a stake in the mainstream of society. Everything else on the government's agenda is subverted to this end. This view is endorsed by Peter Drucker, who writing on the transformatory effects of the information age, commented:

> *"Every country and every industry will have to learn that the first question is not – is this measure desirable? But – what will be the impact on the country's, or the industry's competitive position in the world economy? The impact on one's competitive position in the world economy should not necessarily be the main factor in a decision. But to make a decision without considering it has become irresponsible."*
> Drucker (1994)

In Blair's view the old UK/USA model of the economy has failed due to under investment and the demand for short term profits (Hutton 1995). Blair argues that we need to create a new variant of the (capitalist) economy which adapts the best of the Japanese and German models (see capitalism section in the next chapter).

> *"The creation of the economy where we are inventing and producing goods and services of quality needs the engagement of the whole country. It must become a matter of national purpose and national pride. We need to build a*

> *relationship of trust not just within the firm but within the society. ... It is a stakeholder economy in which opportunity is available to all, advancement is through merit and from which no group or class is set apart or excluded".* (Tony Blair speech in Singapore, quoted in Driver and Martell 1998)

The concept of stakeholding is crucial. It is based on the idea of equality or opportunity and that we all in one society together. To be wealthy is good as long as the wealth has been earned. This and the open desire to make capitalism work better allows New Labour to develop a comfortable relationship with businesses.

Stakeholding rejects notions of class system and income equality. It rejects the idea of using progressive taxation to redistribute wealth from rich to poor. The poor and the excluded can get themselves out of poverty through education and work. Government has a role here to not only assist this process but also will change the welfare system to push people into living up to their responsibilities.

If New Labour is against high taxation and believes that everyone, who is able, should be in employment. It is inevitable that the welfare state will be subject to scrutiny and change. It is important not to romanticise the welfare state. Le Grand (1982) showed convincing that, despite myths to the contrary, welfare state expenditure goes significantly to the middle classes, especially in terms of education and health. Overall, the welfare state in its current form has only a slight effect on redistributing wealth as the majority of its expenditure is self financing from social insurance payments. For the unemployed and the poor the welfare state at best pays little to keep people in poverty.

Blair promised to 'think the unthinkable' on welfare reform. The main policies developed by the Labour government since 1997 are the New Deal welfare to work scheme and social inclusion. Welfare to work is generally greeted with considerable hostility. Although, it is hard to argue that paying somebody to stay unemployed and living in poverty is somehow better than developing the skills to gain employment. Social inclusion is now the benchmark for the welfare sate, replacing the 'old' objective of income equality. Inclusion is about assisting the poor, lone parents, unemployed and disabled to gain skills and employment to become full stakeholders in a modernised Britain. Those who genuinely cannot work will receive adequate benefits. In part this is a return to the Victorian idea of the deserving and undeserving poor.

Gordon Brown, equally committed to this agenda, explained the new mission of the welfare state:

> *"We must look hard at our own welfare system to ensure that it provides pathways out of unemployment and poverty rather than trapping people in persistent dependency. For the risks and insecurities that the welfare state was set up to combat have changed dramatically over fifty years and the welfare state has to keep up with the times. The welfare state must be about supporting people as they respond to these challenges – extending their choices and opportunities; acting as a trampoline rather than as a safety net"* (Gordon Brown, Fair is Efficient, quoted in Driver and Martell 1998)

We now turn to look at some New Labour policies on the economy, welfare state, social inclusion and lifelong learning in more detail.

Modernising the economy

Drucker (1994) commented on the role of the social sector in light of the development of the information society. He pointed out that the idealised communities of extended family, village life, close knit working class areas have all but disappeared. The knowledge society will increase social mobility – the time space compression talked about by postmodernists. With the breaking down of community who takes on the responsibility for social welfare?

Our conventional view is that the government should take care of social needs. That is why the welfare state of varying kinds, has been developed in industrialised western nations. Although we may have an ideological commitment to state welfare services, we have to admit they are usually inefficient, bureaucratised and certainly not consumer friendly. Drucker suggests that for reasons of cost and efficiency welfare functions will move to the non-state sector. We can see this process happening already. Community care functions are increasing delivered by voluntary agencies rather than local state social work departments. Public housing in the UK, the provision of which was a triumph for local state socialism, is in rapid decline. By 1999, 1.7 million ex council homes had been sold. However, this figure will be exceeded by the shift of properties to the private sector. Glasgow the largest local authority landlord in Europe has transferred its housing stock to Housing Associations. It is estimated that the majority of the 3 million council owned homes will be transferred to housing association with 10 years.

The role of the non profit sector is, according to Drucker, *"to create human health and well being"*. In doing so they could provide a focus for the development of local citizen action and a process to rebuild a sense of community and collective purpose. Perhaps an essential role for development workers is to promote social entrepreneurship, to help local organisations to acquire knowledge and enter into the non profit sector to provide services to their own communities. Many socialists argue that such developments undermine the role and responsibility of the state and place extra burdens on local communities especially women. The counter argument is that in the context of modern conditions both the economic and ideological arguments for state intervention at this level have been lost. The opportunity is there for communities to empower themselves, provide employment and to ensure quality of local services. Not to do so will not lead to an extension of government action. It will lead to a shift of these services to profit making companies.

Lifelong Learning

There is a radical tradition of lifelong learning (see Gelpi 1979) which ranges from education with a political intent for change to the holistic development of the individual. In contrast the current establishment view of lifelong learning is derived from the European perspective of education for economic development. This is a sub theme within the European view of learning as a support for social democracy. However, the main stress, as evidenced by the European White Paper (DG22 1995) is on vocational and skills development as a response to the globalisation of the market place.

In the same vein, the New Labour agenda makes only passing reference to the personal and community value of lifelong learning. Its thrust through the Learning Age, Learning to Succeed White Paper and the Opportunity Scotland paper is focussed on the needs to equip the workforce with skills and knowledge required by the economy. The Secretary of State, in the foreword to Learning to Succeed, wrote *"Lifelong learning can enable people to play a full part in developing their talent, the potential of their family and the capacity of the community in which they live and work"*. The White Paper goes onto stress the economic need for learning, commenting that:

- 'Jobs for life' are a thing of the past. People are likely to change jobs many times during their working lives. They will therefore continually need to learn new skills and new ways of working.
- Skills and qualifications are increasingly in demand. The proportion of unskilled and semi-skilled jobs is decreasing, a trend set to continue well into the new millennium. Those who have not kept their skills up-to-date will be disadvantaged.
- The ever-increasing pace of change in information and communications technology is having a huge impact on the way organisations operate, and on the skills that individual employees need.
- Employers will value employees with the right skills. Skilled employees help to improve productivity and profitability; crucial to the success of our economy.

The White Paper points out that *"Productivity in the UK is lower than in other major economies. The Gross Domestic Product per worker in the UK lags behind the US by almost 40% and behind France and Germany by around 20%"*. Low levels of education leads to unemployment and/or low income and with it the risk of social exclusion. Education for employment is essential not only to keep Britain competitive in the global economy but also to reduce social divisions at home. The White Paper comments "Our *vision of the Learning Age is to build a new culture of learning and aspiration which will underpin national competitiveness and personal prosperity, encourage creativity and innovation and help build a more cohesive society. We want everyone to benefit from the opportunities that learning brings both in personal growth and the enrichment of communities"*. From this position a number of principles inform the lifelong learning agenda, they are:

- investing in learning to benefit everyone;
- lifting barriers to learning;
- putting people first;
- sharing responsibility with employers, employees and the community;
- achieving world class standards and value for money; and
- working together as the key to success.

Under this policy education is clearly directed to the needs of the economy and to support the related strategy around social inclusion

Social Inclusion and Regeneration Strategies

New Labour sees social exclusion as the wider effect of poverty. That is the inability of individuals and families on low income to access the normal expectations of everyday life in social, economic or cultural terms. Furthermore, the idea of social exclusion is based on individuals falling out of employment through inadequate skills and training. It recognises barriers to accessing the required training and notes issues around motivation, the need for welfare payments to reward effort and the difficulties faced by being a lone parent or carer. However, the emphasis is placed on individuals ensuring, with support from government agencies, that they work themselves back into mainstream society. This is a normalisation process geared towards unemployed and young people who otherwise will not only be *excluded from* society but will also fail in their responsibility to *contribute to* society. This agenda is *"culturally defined, economically driven and politically motivated"* (Barry 1998).

In this definition there is no acknowledgement of social and economic structural problems or the need for radical change. The approach depoliticises poverty and makes the individual responsible supported by changes to service delivery. In doing so it avoids raising any questions regarding the need for fundamental economic and social change. Furthermore, New Labour reflecting communitarian ideals sees social exclusion as a moral issue as well as economic. Tony Blair said in his first speech as Prime Minister (1997).

> *" There will be no forgotten people in the Britain I want to build... We need to act in a new way because fatalism, and not just poverty, is the problem we face, the dead weight of low expectations, the crushing belief that things cannot get better. I want to give people back the will to win again..... But that cannot be done without a radical shift in our values and attitudes".*

Specifically Blair identified the following areas for action that continue to inform government policy:

- *Reforming welfare so that government helps people to help themselves and provides for those who can't, rather than trying to do it all through government*
- *Where opportunities are given, for example young people, for real jobs and skills, there should be a reciprocal duty to take them up*
- *We should encourage people like single mothers who are anxious to work but unable to, to get back into the labour market. This is empowerment not punishment.*
- *We should root out educational failure, because it is the greatest inhibition to correcting poverty*
- *We should enforce a new code of laws that crack down on crime and other antisocial behaviour*
- *We should attack discrimination in all its forms*
- *We should engage the interest and commitment of the whole community to tackle the desperate need for urban regeneration*
- *Government should commit itself to using whatever means is the best to play its part without outdated dogma of left or right to hold it back.*

This is very much in the Third Way / communitarian ethos we have discussed above. The government has a responsibility to help the individual and their family and they have a responsibility to respond. The way out of the problem is through work. Poverty is technical issue to be corrected not a manifestation of capitalism. Work is seen both as personal empowerment and a duty. The welfare state will be reconstructed to these ends free of left or right ideology. This is not a traditional socialist agenda. It is a modernisation agenda for the contemporary world.

But what is the reality of the socially excluded. The Department of Environment, Transport and the Regions identified trends in deprivations (DETR 1999). They conclude that at the national level some aspects of deprivation are improving. This includes the levels of unemployment, educational attainment, health, infant mortality, income levels, housing conditions and derelict land. Getting worse, however are levels of violent crime, drug misuse, long tem unemployment, benefit dependency, income inequality and the number of lone parents.

These statistics need some careful thought. Although, the national averages continue to improve we know that there is a wide variation between well off communities and poorer communities. This process of averaging out the figures can hide the reality in those communities where the situation is not getting better or may be getting worse. Similarly, although violent crime may be increasing overall, in some communities it is improving. It is also important to consider what is defined as deprivation. For example lone parenting may be an indicator of poverty. However, just because you are a lone parent does not automatically mean you are poor. It may also be a positive life style choice and to characterise it in negative terms is morally authoritarian.

The statistics continue to identify regional variations for England. Merseyside is the most deprived area with higher than average rates of unemployment (including youth unemployment), low educational attainment and high death rates but relatively good housing. London has high unemployment as well as higher than average levels of income and drug use. Although the main job losses of the 1980's and early 1990's have been reversed since the late 1990's, this has been achieved in part through increased casualisation of jobs (part time and / or short term). The most deprived local authority areas still have unemployment rates twice that of the national average. Ethnic minority groups also tend to live in disadvantaged areas. Unemployment rates amongst Afro-Caribbean's, Bangladeshis and Pakistanis are high. They also tend to live in poorer and overcrowded housing. As it would be expected, a significant number of people in the classified deprived areas are subject to one or more counts of deprivation. However, there are a greater number of deprived people living outside these areas. There are 1370 deprived social housing estates identified by the DETR. In these estates there are only about 14% of the total unemployed and 16.5% of lone parents. Policies that concentrate their attention solely on geographical areas will therefore miss the majority of the socially excluded population.

The Queens Speech outlining the policies of the third New Labour Government in June 2005 illustrates the continuation of the above policies. The speech stated that the Government will *"build on its programme of reform and accelerate modernisation of the public services to promote opportunity and fairness. Government will bring forward legislation in the key areas of public service delivery: education; health; welfare; and crime"*. Emphasis is placed on the extension of state power to regulate behaviour. Building on Anti Social Behaviour Orders and Curfew Zones the Government intends to confront binge drinking and disorder to promote what it calls a *'culture of respect'*. A Housing Benefit bill will reduce barriers to work, increase tenant choice along with more responsibility for paying their rent. There will be continuing reform of education and the National Health Service.

One the one hand New Labour policy developments must be welcomed as they focus on deprived individuals and communities that for so long have been the ignored casualties of the economy. There are however other approaches to defining and dealing with social exclusion. The table that we considered in appendix 4 that identifies four responses to poverty illustrates the options for a more fundamental critique and possible responses to inequality. Also there are also many cultures based around religious and ethnic groups, travellers and 'new age' communities that choose to exclude themselves from the mainstream of society. A choice has to be made whether we support people's right to be different and live their own lifestyle.

The worker needs to have his or her own ideas on these subjects. However, it is more important to facilitate local people to explore these issues for themselves. Whether local communities choose to involve themselves in, or oppose, these policies is a choice they should make for themselves on an informed and reflective basis

Summary

In this chapter we have covered the following points:

- The social, economic and political policies since 1979 have been based on the idea that Britain needs to change to meet the realities of the Global economy
- These changes requires some movement away from a society dependent upon the welfare state to a more enterprising culture
- This means controlling taxation and welfare expenditure whilst giving incentives for wealth creation
- Enterprise values should cover all aspects of society including the public sector
- The current New Labour administration seeks to build upon the best of the Conservative legacy
- New Labour is significantly influenced by the concepts of the Third Way
- Ideas of class have been rejected in favour of stakeholding and social inclusion
- Everyone should
- to be as economically productive as possible and sets out the agenda for welfare (people into work), education (lifelong learning primarily for economic ends) and social inclusion

Further Reading

For a discussion of the Thatcher years see Andrew Gmble's **The Politics of Thatcherism,** (Basingstoke, Macmillan, 1994)

Barry explores the ideas of Hayek which underpin the economic approach of the last Conservative administrations in **Hayek's Social and Economic Philosophy,** (Basingstoke, Macmillan 1979).

To explore the debate on welfare over this period see the articles in Loney et al. **The State of the Market; politics and welfare in contemporary Britain,** (Open University 1995)

The importance of Thatcherite ideas for New Labour are explored by Driver and Martell in **New Labour: Politics after Thatcherism,** (Polity Press 1998)

Especially recommended is Marilyn Taylor's discussion of social policy and the implication for community level work. **Public Policy in the Community,** Basingstoke: Palgrave

To understand the current policy framework a range of policy documents need to be read. This includes the various New Deals for work, communities and Schools, and Lifelong Learning and Social Inclusion. As well as the parallel documents for Scotland and Wales. These can be found on the Government's web site from: http://www.tagish.co.uk/links/centgov.htm

5

Underlying Perspectives: Theories

"Life is making us abandon established stereotypes and outdated views; it is making us discard illusions". Mikhail Gorbachev

Aims of this chapter

In this chapter we take at look at competing theoretical ideas that attempt to explain the world. We briefly introduce the concepts of socialism, Marxism and capitalism. The chapter then reviews some of the current debates around liberalism and libertarians, communitarianism and the new right and the modernist v postmodernist debate. The importance of the ideas of Gramsci and Freire are discussed alongside theories of the state

What is theory

Is community work just a simple activity of organising local groups for basic tasks? Or is it about promoting real change in society, albeit in small ways. If it is the latter then we have to have a set of theories that help us understand how society works, how it is changing and how it may be influenced. This is the role of theory; to give us the intellectual tools and knowledge to make our practice more effective.

The Collins dictionary defines theory as: *"a system of rules, procedures and assumptions used to produce results ... a set of hypotheses related .. to explain or predict a wide variety of connected phenomena"*. Theory is essential therefore, to enable us to understand how to approach working in the community, how to resolve practice difficulties and to predict what approach is most likely to succeed. Theory is underpinned not only by logical interpretation of events and data but also by ideological preference. In the community development context theory must also relate to the relationship between the state, communities and community workers.

A brief introduction to major theories

Socialism

Socialism as a term was first used around the early part of the 19th century; the ideals being based initially on creating a classless society. During the century it became the non revolutionary route for social change in contrast to the revolutionary ideals of Marxism.

There has often been a religious or ethical side to socialism. For example Robert Owen, a wealthy mill owner developed his model village at New Lanark to improve the welfare of his workers and their families. Socialism provides a critique of capitalism. It argues that capitalism directs production for profit rather than social needs and it creates cycles of underproduction and unemployment. Socialists also worked with liberals to campaign for welfare improvements for workers and trade union rights. By the early 20th there were socialist parliamentary parties in many western countries.

Between the 1914-18 and 1939-45 wars, socialists were able to form governments, usually in coalition with or supported by others parties. They were thus able to be in power, albeit intermittently, in the 1920s in Great Britain and Germany, and in the 1930s in Belgium, France, and Spain. In Sweden, where social democrats have been more successful than elsewhere, they governed without interruption from 1932 to 1976.

Socialist ideals influenced independence movements in India and Africa, especially in the ex-colonies of Britain, France and Portugal. However, the formation of specific socialist parties has remained limited to Western Europe. The USA rejected the notion of socialism as a mainstream political party. In Asia the political debate was more concerned with modernisation of the state with communism being the main radical alternative to old colonial administrations.

In the west from 1945 the democratic socialist parties, after an initial phase of nationalisation of basic industries, increasingly moved towards promoting welfare within a capitalist framework, rejecting what remained of any Marxist influence. Socialists assumed that continued economic growth would provide the resources for their social spending programmes thus allowing an accommodation with capitalism. The main contribution of these parties has been the development of various forms of increased state welfare provision and sustaining full employment through the application of Kenynsian economics. In Germany social democrats also experimented with forms of industrial democracy within a capitalist context.

The oil crisis in 1973 undermined the assumptions of socialist parties. Rising unemployment, inflation, social unrest and government debt produced unsustainable pressure on welfare state expenditures. Conservative parties argued for the need to reduce state spending, to free business from regulation, the control of trade unions and improve worker 'flexibility'. Popular discontent with the inefficient and bureaucratic experience of welfare organisations made their defence more difficult.

Parliamentary victories by European conservative parties in the 1980's and 90's led to the reduction of welfare spending, denationalisation and deregulation. The political consensus that had supported socialist programmes since 1945 eroded along with the significance of the working class vote. The collapse of the Soviet Union and Eastern Europe undermined the concept of socialism as an alternative to capitalism.

By the late 1990's socialist parties have reinvented themselves in a more conservative from to capture the middle class vote. This move also recognised that that the old economic growth and spending strategy would no longer work and that the realities of the global economy had to be taken on board. Socialist parties, although in many cases it is hard to correctly define them as such, have political programmes that are along way from their roots. Current European socialist policy concerns include;

- Limited economic regulation within the European Union
- Harmonising European welfare programmes
- Protecting consumer interests
- Promoting the interest of women
- Working towards full employment

- Support to the developing world

These policies are little more than tinkering with the effects of capitalism. In any case there is an inherent contradiction within socialism. As Cleaver (1997) points out socialists believe that individuals can and will work together for mutual benefit. It is this neo utopian ideal that appeals to community workers. Socialism also promotes the idea that the state can plan to meet economic and social needs more effectively than capitalism. In reality the drive to impose a planning regime has always resulted in the development of authoritarian structures which have been imposed upon working people. Rather than work for each other, working people have been organised to work for the benefit of the state, within which the benefits of production have been unequally distributed. The result of socialist experiments have been the rejection by the workers, most dramatically across Europe in 1989, as socialism proved to be more authoritarian and less productive than the capitalism it sought to replace.

It is correct to claim that at the end of the 20th century socialism appeared to have reached an ideological dead end. The values of socialism remain; that is a belief in equality, collective support and social justice. The problem is that socialism was about solving these problems through providing an economic solution. In the face of the rejection of socialist societies by their own people, the success of capitalism in generating wealth and the requirements of the global economy, socialist economic alternatives no longer appear to work.

Many community workers appear to continue in their support of socialist ideals and talk about promoting some kind of socialist practice. The problem is what does socialist practice actually mean? For many it was about holding the line until a radical Labour government came to power. The advent of New Labour has disillusioned many people as the social policy improvements of the new government are seen to be outweighed by its commitment to promoting market solutions and the profit motive. The challenge for these workers now is to devise a practice theory that can sustain and promote socialist ideals in a global capitalist environment.

Marxism

As a background theory Marxism is of paramount importance. It informed much of the analysis of the CDP's and provides the personal ideology of many, although probably a minority, of community workers. Its value lies more in providing a critique of society rather than directly guiding practice. Although, Popple (1995) and others suggest that writings of Gramsci can be developed to inform practice. The work of Freire has also been influenced by his interpretation of Marxism.

Marx's works are based on early 19th century thought around socialism and developing the ideas of Hegel. His writings can be broadly divided into his early philosophical writings, for example: The German Ideology (1845-1846), pamphlets such as The Communist Manifesto (1848), the analysis of contemporary events such as The Civil War in France (1871), and the fundamental works - Contribution to the Critique of Political Economy (1859), and his most famous work Das Kapital (vol. 1, 1867; vols. 2 and 3 published posthumously).

Marxism however, has developed into a wide body of thought with numerous, often competing, branches. Most importantly, Lenin added to Marxism a theory of imperialism, a theory of the state, and principles of revolutionary organisation based on the dictatorship of the proletariat, known as Marxism-Leninism. This with adaptations from Stalin and Mao-Tse-Tung became the models for the Soviet Union, Eastern Europe and China.

Underpinning Marxism is a belief that there is no such thing as a fixed human nature. Society is the product of the way in which people interact with each other (historical materialism). How society is organised is a product of the economic system (the mode of production). In capitalist societies workers do not receive the full value of their labour. The capitalist class (bourgeoisie) appropriating the surplus value as profit. The goods produced by capitalism must possess use-value, otherwise they would not find buyers. But for capitalists they must have exchange-value so that they can be sold. Thus capitalist production is essentially production for profit and not for needs. In pursuit of increasing profit capitalists will expand their operations geographically (leading to imperialism), reduce the costs of production through cheaper labour and technological change leading to unemployment. Competition drives inefficient capitalists into bankruptcy and leads to concentration of money and power through the creation of monopolies.

Workers (or the proletariat) are alienated from their work and treated as disposable factors of production rather than human beings. In addition, a reserve army of unemployed is used to keep wages low. In this context people are dehumanised; the One Dimension Man as described by Marcuse (1964) and are unable to realise their full potential. What Marx did not foresee here is that skilled workers need to be paid increased wages, otherwise why would they bother to learn the new skills required by an expanding economy? This is also a benefit for capitalism because the extra wages can be spent on extra goods leading to higher profit. The introduction of credit also expands the market and leads to increases in the workers standard of living, albeit at the cost of increasing debt.

The function of the state is to maintain stability so that capitalism can develop unhindered by social unrest. Some welfare activity may therefore be required to maintain stability. In contrast a communist society would fairly distribute the wealth of the country so that private property would become less important. Freed from the pressure to work constantly for low wages people would have the time to develop as full and creative individuals. The power of the state would fall away as increasingly democratic structures were introduced not only for political decisions but also in the workplace. As we know things did not turn out that way in the Soviet Union due to inefficient bureaucratisation and the desire of the Communist Party to retain its power.

There are many debates about how far the nature of the economy determines society, values, beliefs, social organisations and power. Some Marxists argue there is a direct determination, whilst others believe that much of society is relatively autonomous but set within economically determined boundaries. A Marxist variant known as Critical Theory argues that the working class is firmly integrated into the capitalist system through the working of the culture and ideological processes. For example the norms that people learn through schooling and the mass media (Horkheimer and Adorno 1972). Real change therefore, can only be achieved through changing the economic nature of society. Everything else is mere reformism that often only functions to sustain capitalism through making revolution less likely.

What does this mean for community work? Marxists contend that community work is both a dangerous activity and a delusion. Welfare reforms, they say, have not empowered the working class. Community work seeks to create a consensus that class, gender and race issues can be overcome through notions of partnership with the state. However, what really happens is that community work operates as part of the superstructure, co-opting potential working class leadership into conforming to the needs of capitalism. If community activity ever becomes a real threat the state will quickly close it down. The end of the CDP's and the police operations against peace and environmental protestors are evidence of this.

The counter argument is that it is fantasy to talk about revolutionary struggle in Britain at the current time. In reality power in society is diffused and it is possible to both make real material gains and change people's perception of the world. Change will only come if people organise around their own oppressions, for example as a woman or a Black person, rather than for an abstract ideal society. Cockburn (1978) points out that welfare struggles over housing, education and health are both economic and ideological in content. Furthermore, there is doubt over the value of the notion of the working class being the sole agent of change. The analysis of class by Marx and Engles in the mid 19th century bears little relevance to the social and economic structure of Britain at the end of the 20th century (Gorz 1982).

In 1883, the year of Marx's death the industrial class in Britain was still a minority of the population. They received low wages, no pensions, no paid holidays, no heath insurance and little job security. During the 1914-18 war there were real fears of a proletarian revolution and in post war Europe unsuccessful communist revolutions were attempted. The successful revolution in Russia was not a mass uprising of the working class. Russia was essentially a rural country at the time. The successful coup was led by one of several small revolutionary groups.

By 1950 industrial workers were the largest single group in every developed country. They were generally well organised through trade unions and exerted political power through elected representatives. They had chosen the reformist rather than the revolutionary route. In return real wages had risen and extensive welfare systems were being put into place. The industrialised worker might, in Marx's terms, be alienated from the fruits of their labour but revolution was not on the agenda.

In most developed countries during the 1990's industrialised workers accounted for around 20% of the population. With the growth of service and knowledge industries Drucker (1994) estimates that by 2010 this percentage will decrease to around little more than 10% Capitalism may still produce profits by exploiting surplus value but the industrial proletarian revolution of suggested by Marx cannot now happen.

A further criticism of Marxism is that is reduces everything to the relationship of economic classes and the means of production. In doing so key areas of conflict over race, religion, culture and gender are reduced to manifestations of the class struggle, rather than areas that deserve attention in their own right.

Capitalism

The term capitalism comes originally from Marx to describe the economic system dominated by those who accumulate and control capital in society. Capitalists themselves prefer the term free market and the ideological position of personal freedom that underpins it.

Adam Smith in the Wealth of Nations (1776) argues that it is possible to seek private gain in ways that also furthers the interests of society as whole. Freedom to make money, acquire private property in an environment of competition will lead to the maximisation of production to the benefit of society by, in Smiths words *"an invisible hand"*. Only minimum government involvement is required, otherwise the working of the market will become distorted. Fundamental to this process is the division of labour into the most productive units. This view reflected the growing mechanisation of production and the movement from independent skilled artisans to the domination of factory work. The loss of personal independence is replaced by rises in the standard of living through the reduction in the real price of goods. Therefore, the Marxist argument that capitalism leads to increasing impoverishment of the working class is false. This argument overlooks the appalling working conditions in 19th century factories and extensive use of child labour that led to the creation of trade unions; as well as the export of low wages and poor conditions to the developing world.

Free market theory at this time also failed to explain the boom and bust cycles of the economy that led to periods of intense unemployment. Ironically, it was Marx who pointed out that these crises were an inherent cyclical part of capitalism. During the great economic slump on the 1930's British economist John Maynard Keynes wrote his General Theory of Employment, Interest and Money (1936). Keynes correctly argues that by varying its level of spending and taxation governments could regulate the economy to prevent the boom and bust cycles. This policy for government intervention clearly challenged the laissez-faire world view of Adam Smith. Nevertheless, in 1946 the USA Congress enacted the Employment Act that committed the American government to maintain high levels of employment. Other western governments up to the 1980's have followed similar policies.

The result of this change alongside continued welfare spending was the shift from the ideology of free enterprise to welfare capitalism in which government had a clear role to sustain the output of the economy, both in the general level of economic activity and as a social regulator. In the UK parliamentary elections from the 1950's onward have been contested on which party could best manage welfare capitalism. Today Marxists argue that the welfare reforms introduced through campaigning by trade unions and the labour movements (pensions, national insurance) have reformed capitalism sufficiently to ensure its survival for some time. However, capitalism will eventually fail because managing the contradictions between the expectations for rising standards of living and continued profits will eventually become unsustainable

From the 1980's the argument has shifted away from Keynsianism towards monetarism as proposed by Milton Friedman of the University of Chicago. Monetarist, and later neo liberal critiques of the post war economy argue that welfare state spending is too high, diverting capital way from economic production. State spending and regulation also leads to an inflexible labour force. In the climate of globalisation national economies can only survive if they are adaptable and free to respond to new technology and opportunity. This view leads to the privatisation of state enterprises and the reduction of regulatory controls leaving international monopolies greater freedom to manoeuvre. The main differences between the Keynsian and Monetarist approach are summarised below.

Keynsian Position	Neo Liberal / Monetarist Position
The free market without government intervention cannot sustain full employment	The free market will create more wealth in the long run despite periods of unemployment
Unemployment is a waste of economic and social resources and needs to be solved	Inflation is the main problem and unemployment can help reduce prices
Government intervention can smooth out the booms and bust of the economy and ensure steady economic growth	Government intervention distorts the market and reduces wealth creation
Government spending can help promote wealth creation	Government spending diverts money away from the private sector and reduces the opportunity for enterprise

By the 1980's there were three variants of capitalism. The Japanese (or East Asian / Chinese) model is based on direct government support to establish and sustain large conglomerations operating in many markets. The emphasis here is on developing and retaining a loyal and trained workforce and building co-operating between the company, banks and government. The German model based on a long term partnership between capital and labour so that workers see their economic interests being linked to the company. The USA/UK model in contrast is driven by a financial system that demands high short term profits. This works against long term strategic developments. It also means that labour is seen more as a disposable factor of production than an essential resource. This contrasts to the high value placed on retaining and training staff in the Japanese and German models.

Since the 1990's we have entered an era of post modern capitalism. In this stage of capitalism the generation of profits is still the central purpose. What has changed is how this may be achieved. Modernist capitalism was about expanding production, building ever larger factories to gain from the economies of scale and employing an increasing number of people. Ultimately this strategy starts to reduce profits, as organisational inefficiency, due to the size of the operation, becomes apparent. Shifting the responsibility for production and employment to third parties, usually in the developing world where labour costs and employment rights are minimal, has become the main route to regenerating profit levels. As a result management responsibility is devolved to the lowest possible level to reduce bureaucracy and costs as well as promoting innovation.

These changes have also been spurred by the change in capitalism itself. The product is no longer important. The object of capitalist companies is to develop a global brand that will be recognised everywhere on the planet; Pepsi, Burger King, Mars, Virgin, etc. The brand can be added to anything. Virgin is a prime example. What links a record store, vodka, cola, an airline, trains, insurance and mobile phones: simply the Virgin brand.

The objective is to outsource production, so the management of this becomes another company's problem, whilst the energy of the main company is put into marketing the brand. The value of a company is tied to its share price, and today share prices are linked to the global strength of the brand not the actual capital owned by the company. As companies become transnational, and increasingly wealthy, the size of their labour force declines. Success therefore is tied to branding and marketing. To illustrate this point Klein (2000) quotes the president of Levi Strauss:

> *"Our strategic plan ... is to focus on brand management, marketing and product design ... shifting a significant portion of our manufacturing to contractors throughout the world will give the company greater flexibility to allocate resources and capital to its brands"*

This contracting out of production is increasingly concentrated in free trade zones in the developing world. For example in the Philippines there are 52 such zones employing just under half a million people. In China it is estimated that there are 124 zones employing around 18 million people. These zones are characterised by long working hours, often 12 to 16 hours per day, no sickness, pension or other employment rights. Most of the workers are young women under 25 years. Pregnant women are often sacked. Low wages are the norm. Producers of Nike products in

China, for example, are paid 16 cents (11p) per hour for a 12 hour, 7 day per week employment.

Back in the developed work it is almost impossible to drive down wages of permanent staff. Instead companies are moving towards cutting costs through the casualisation of the workforce via the growth in temporary contracts. It is estimated that in the USA and Europe 36 million people are currently employed on temporary contracts with the number rising. After radical restructuring and casualisation of its workforce during the late 1990's, Microsoft's direct employment of staff fell by 19% whilst income increased by 91% (quoted in Klein 2000).

These trends are being accelerated through the development of e-commerce based on the Internet. In turn this has led to the highly optimistic and speculative suggestion of a new form of capitalism based around the idea of new economics (Kelly 1996). This rewriting of classical economics, argues that in future the world economy will be based on the marketing of knowledge and knowledge products. As knowledge does not depend upon raw material for production there is no limit to growth, economic expansion and profit. This economic growth is driven by technological monopolies, which need to be enabled to expand into poorer countries through a globalised free market. The 'trickle down' effect will lead eventually to the eradication of poverty even in the depressed economies of Africa, which many traditional economists have written of as a hopeless case.

It is an uncomfortable fact for many workers that community work has a defined role to play in capitalist society. Community work in this context should be concerned with enabling unemployed and unproductive members of society return to employment and promoting community based welfare programmes to underpin the reproductive needs of capital. Although out of favour under the Thatcher administration many Conservative controlled local authorities continued to fund community work. Under John Major community development was actively promoted. The New Labour commitment to social inclusion and the new deal can also be seen in this context.

With the end of the Cold War and the collapse of the Soviet Union, capitalist theorists appear to celebrating ideological victory. Francis Fukuyama in The End of History and The Last Man (1992) sees the triumph of capitalism and multi party democracy as the dominant ideology and world power. As he put it:

> *"We have become so accustomed by now to expect that the future will contain bad news with respect to the health and security of decent, democratic political practices that we have problems recognising good news when it comes. And yet the good news has come .... In essence it's incredibly simple .. a capitalist paradise at the end of history".*

Although, we can dispute the notion of paradise, Fukuyama is correct that with the collapse of Marxism and current intellectual dead end of socialism, there is no effective challenger to capitalism currently in sight.

Feminism

The women's movement and the development of feminist thought has had such a profound effect on community work practice, that it is important to explore the basic concepts in some detail at this point.

It is usual to identify the emergence of feminism as an ideology during the late 18th century. Concern with the rights of women and the demand for equal social standing with men arose during the French Revolution and the American War of Independence. In England Mary Wollstonecraft published *A Vindication of the Rights of Woman* in 1792. This book criticised the prevailing social system and demanded social reform. She wrote that wives were *"confined in cages, like the feathered race .. it is true they are provided with food and raiment, for which they neither toil nor spin; but health, liberty and virtue are given in exchange"*.

From 1850 onwards the campaign for women's rights focussed increasingly on winning the vote. Suffrage movements developed in a number of countries including Germany, Austria, Sweden and Poland. These campaigns expanded and by the 1920's welfare issues for mothers and children had been adopted.

The so called 'second wave' of feminism developed in the 1960's, from the American Civil Rights movements and socialist parties in Europe and Australasia. In the USA the women's liberation movement linked equality issues with a woman's right to control her own identity, sexuality and reproduction. Linked to this was the key concept that the 'personal is political'. This means that the oppression of women may be experienced on an individual basis but is a product of social economic and political systems. Amongst considerable debate two key texts influenced feminist thinking at this time. Simone de Beauvoir's The Second Sex originally written in 1949 developed arguments from history, biology, psychoanalysis, literature and Marxism to argue that men saw themselves as normal whist women were 'the Other': some kind of aberration. Kate Millet's Sexual Politics (1970) explored how patriarchy reproduces itself through the working of society and the family. As Millet put it *"The great mass of women throughout history have been confined to the cultural level of animal life in providing the male with sexual outlet and exercising the animal functions of reproduction and care of the young".*

From the 1960's the movement diversified with distinct positions being developed for Black Women's Liberation, and Lesbian Liberation. By the end of the 1970's the movements in North America and Europe could be divided into three camps; radical, socialist and liberal.

Radical feminists defined the problem as patriarchy.

"Men have defined the parameters of every subject. All feminist arguments, however radical in intent or consequence, are with or against assertions or premises implicit in the male system, which is made credible or authentic by the power of men to name" (Dworkin 1981).

The radical feminists argued for women only campaigns and organisations in an attempt to build a women's culture. They mainly focussed on issues around men's violence towards women, rape and pornography. Writers such as Mary Daly (1991) and Angela Dworkin believe that men use violence to control women and to force them into heterosexual relationships. Some Radical feminists believe that men cannot overcome their role as oppressors. Therefore, women have to work to overthrow patriarchy. This involves demolishing existing social structures including religious, educational and political organisations as well as the family. The new non-patriarchal society would be based on power sharing and collective organisations. The feminisation of society would enable the creation of a more sustainable and peaceful world.

Socialist feminists defined the issues as a combination of class and gender struggles. The liberation of women, they argue, is inextricably linked to the overthrow of capitalism. The role of women has historically been tied to the interests of reproducing capital. The social function of women is to produce and socialise children in conformity with social norms, meet the welfare requirements of male workers and the elderly, and provide low paid dispensable labour as required. This unpaid labour provides surplus value to employers who otherwise would have to pay increased wages and taxes. Working class men also benefit from this system as they are absolved of the responsibility for caring roles and it reinforces the superiority of men over women. In response to this analysis much of the socialist feminist energy has been spent trying to build strong feminist positions and platforms within existing socialist political structures and campaigns.

Liberal feminists hold a more reformist position. They seek legislative changes to promote equality, improvements to child care and maternity provision and to develop positive role models for women. Institutions that work to socialise child to social norms, especially schools and the family, need to change to reflect gender equality. Progress has clearly been made in this area even if the fundamental problems of patriarchy have not been confronted.

From the late1980's feminism has become increasing influenced by postmodernism. It is argued that the grand theories that attempt to explain everything fundamentally reflect a male view of the world. Essentially this has to be an authoritarian position. Postmodern feminism holds that all social norms are social constructs and that each woman should be free to develop her life, her sexuality and her body according to her own choice. This position challenges the notion that all women, by the fact of being a woman, share a common interest that can be the basis of campaigning. Smithies and Webster (1987) warn against naïve concepts of sisterhood as a substitute for analysis and planning for action.

Many feminists in the developing world contend that the way feminism is promoted in the west is essentially Eurocentric and imposes western views on other cultures. Black workers in the UK, for example Ng (1988) and Yurval (1992), have also criticised feminism for being white dominated and failing to understand the effect of racism on women. In Asia feminists have campaigned for liberal reforms against purdah (seclusion in the home) and the dowry system. However, the debate on the position of women within Islam is subject to much controversy. Black feminist continue to explore the response to the double disadvantage of race and gender. Although, some Black writers define ethnicity as strength.

Writers such as Maria Mies and Vandana Shiva (1993) have developed the concept of Ecofeminism, based in part on the Chipko experience in India. The Chipko movement led mainly by village women, works to protect both local communities and their means of subsistence from commercial exploitation. Ecofeminism sees a link between patriarchy, the destruction of nature in the name of profit and the process of globalisation. In the developing world the majority are still dependent for survival on subsistence activity. Shiva (1989) comments:

> *"the western male has produced only one culture, and there are other ways of structuring the world. Women's struggles for survival through the protection of nature are redefining the meaning of basic categories. They are challenging the central belief of the dominant world view that nature and women are worthless and waste, that they are obstacles to progress and must be sacrificed".*

Feminism has undoubtedly changed the nature of modern society. It has also changed the practice of community work. David Thomas (1993) hardly the most radical of commentators wrote: *"the feminist analysis is a restatement of community work's process goals and takes us further by identifying personal change as the beginning of the process of political development, both of the individual and of existing structures".* In doing so it has much in common with the work of Freire. It is no coincidence that both feminist and Freirians seek consciousness raising as a key objective. The feminist principles of power sharing, collectivity and creativity also have much to offer community based practice. Feminists rightly argue that much of community activity is based on male hierarchical models, reflecting the structures of local government and trade unionism. Committee systems and fixed office bearers in community groups are a replication of elitist male ways of working and are not necessary.

Whatever feminist analysis may be adopted, Kenny (1994) outlines a number of basic responses that must be integral to community work practice.

- Make conscious their own views of patriarchy and class, and relate them to their own life experiences
- Draw attention to the lack of resources for women, and how this restricts women's lives
- Work to expand real options and choices for women
- Treat women's own lived experiences with respect
- Encourage women to articulate and define issues in their own terms
- Be conscious of everyday language which perpetuates women's oppression and feelings of inferiority felt by women. For example, the comment "I'm only a housewife" should not be accepted by community development workers, for it belittles housework and women.

Current debates

Liberalism, Libertarianism and the New Right

Liberalism is based on the writing of Thomas Hobbes and John Locke in the 17th century who argued for just government and the protection of property. This was essentially the new rising middle and entrepreneurial class campaigning for their rights against the interests of a fading feudal state. In the late 18th century Thomas Paine in the Rights of Man set out a revolutionary claim for individual freedom and the pamphlet Common Sense which provided an ideological basis for the American Declaration of Independence.

In the early 19th century liberalism was a radical doctrine. Its basic concern was personal freedom and the freedom of the market. Freedom they believed was the route to creating the greatest happiness for the greatest number of people. However, this did not necessarily mean democracy as those with education and property had a greater stake in society and were therefore better equipped to make responsible decisions. This latter position changed during the century as liberalism become closely associated with social reform. It was the Liberal governments of the early 20th that laid the basis for the welfare state, constitutional and trade union reform. Despite the social reforms liberalism is intrinsically tied to a capitalist economy. From the late 19th onwards the working class increasingly looked to own its own (Labour) party to press for wider socialist reform.

Within modern liberalism there is a split between two factions. The 'positive liberals' continue to believe in action by the state to promote the interests of individuals. Poverty, and vested interests limit the freedom of the poor and government has a duty to intervene on their behalf. In contrast 'negative liberals' see any action by government as authoritarian. This latter view underpins the libertarian groups prevalent in the USA today as proposed by Hayek and the new right economics.

Hayek believed that government had no role in managing the economy and everything should be left to the working of the market. In arguing this position Hayek was not naive enough to suggest that such systems would be painless for the poor. He acknowledged that the reality of the market system is uncertainty and the need for constant adjustments. Overall there would be better use of resources and the meeting of individual needs. The suffering that might accrue to individuals through this process was unfortunate and could best be mitigated by the unfettering of the market to allow it to respond to changes in demand as quickly as possible.

A significant feature of this ideology is belief that there is no moral argument for the redistribution of wealth. Indeed, the pursuit of equality was a fantasy that could not be achieved and which did untold damage to the working of the market. According to Hayek morality had no place in real world affairs. There is no link between rewards for work and income. Wealth was the outcome of effort and skill as well as luck, accident and inheritance. The market is in reality a lottery. What is important is not the justice of the market outcome but the choice that is offered. To be born in a deprived community is therefore bad luck. It is no ones fault and nobodies responsibility to change it. The market will offer you as an individual various choices to work your way out of poverty. Whether you do so is entirely your responsibility.

The Libertarians and the New Right have a defined political agenda based upon free market ideals. The Libertarian Party in the USA have the following statement of principles. This is worth quoting extensively as libertarian views are gaining increasing acceptance in the context of globalisation and the possible decline of the nation state.

> *"We hold that all individuals have the right to exercise sole dominion over their own lives, and have the right to live in whatever manner they choose, so long as they do not forcibly interfere with the equal right of others to live in whatever manner they choose. Governments throughout history have regularly operated on the opposite principle that the State has the right to dispose of the lives of individuals and the fruits of their labour. Even within the United States, all political parties other than our own grant to government the right to regulate the lives of individuals and seize the fruits of their labour without their consent.*
>
> *We, on the contrary, deny the right of any government to do these things, and hold that where governments exist, they must not violate the rights of any individual: namely, (1) the right to life... (2) the right to liberty of speech and action ... (3) the right to property -- accordingly we oppose all government interference with private property, such as confiscation, nationalisation, and eminent domain, and support the prohibition of robbery, trespass, fraud, and misrepresentation.*
>
> *Since governments, when instituted, must not violate individual rights, we oppose all interference by government in the areas of voluntary and contractual relations among individuals. People should not be forced to sacrifice their lives and property for the benefit of others. They should be left free by government to deal with one another as free traders; and the resultant economic system, the only one*

compatible with the protection of individual rights, is the free market.

The New Right is a broader political movement that accepts much of the above position and is fully committed to laissez faire competition in the economy. It is also a development of conservative ideology and Social Darwinism. This doctrine believes that society will develop best through the survival of the fittest. The welfare state should be abolished: firstly, because public servants, not having to produce profit, are lax concerning efficiency and the costs of the service; secondly, the provision of a free service only creates increasing demand that cannot be sustained; thirdly, it promotes the idea that the state owes its citizens a living and this undermines individual responsibility and effort. Poverty can be reduced through tax cuts to the rich, leading to a growth in wealth which through increased employment will 'trickle down' to the poor. Equality is neither possible nor desirable as society should reflect the difference in individual ability.

The New Right often departs from the libertarian ideas through a preference for active government intervention on social policy issues. In both Britain and Australia this has lead to morally driven policy intervention to promote the family, impose discipline in schools and law and order measures. The promotion of the sense of duty to work and duty to the family is at odds with the belief in individual freedom. In the USA the New Right is often linked to the fundamentalist Christian groups who promote even more repressive social causes including anti abortion and restrictions on women's rights.

The New Right agenda can find considerable support amongst all classes of society through its portrayal of 'common sense' solutions to everyday discontents. The idea of paying less taxes, avoiding subsidising 'scroungers' on the state, opposing housing for young single parents and refugees can appeal to alienated workers trying to make a living. Users of services are redefined as consumers with consumer, but not necessarily any other, rights. The Conservative Party in the UK has adopted this approach with its so called 'Common Sense Revolution' which is really new right dogma dressed up sheep's clothing.

Community work values fundamentally support the ideas of liberty, self determination and personal rights which are inherent to liberalism. However, community work involves positive action to improve the quality of people's lives and sees this as a collective responsibility. The links therefore, between community work and the positive liberals are clear. The placing of the freedom of the individual above everything else that is part of the libertarian and new right agenda cannot be equated with the underpinning values of community work as it rejects the notion of social justice and positive action for the oppressed.

In considering these arguments the water becomes muddy. As Blagg and Derricourt (1982) point out the New Right's stress on self help and people taking responsibility for themselves comes close to the radical community work of the 1970's. A range of issues are raised here. Is self help an abdication by the government of its duty to help its citizens or is it empowering for local communities? Are volunteers responding to civic duty, an essential ingredient for a more powerful and organised community or exploited unpaid labour? Community workers need to more closely define their answers to these questions.

In the USA the Cato Institute is developing a social agenda that confronts the old certainties of the welfare state and which challenge many of the assumptions held by community workers. In testimony to the US Congress in 1995, Michael Tanner a Director of the Cato Institute argues that welfare services contribute to the growth of crime. Citing research (Wright, Green, Warren 1994 and Hill and O'Neil 1990) he claimed that increased welfare payments led directly to increases in single parent families, and statistically these families are more likely to contain children who will drift into crime. Welfare payments also reduce the incentive for single parents gaining education and employment or marrying. An effect of this is that young men do not develop responsibility for a family and single young men are also more likely to engage in drugs and crime.

In his book, The End of Welfare: Fighting Poverty in the Civil Society (1996) Tanner goes onto criticise liberals for their unfounded belief that job training schemes lead to increases in employment. He also attacks traditional conservatives for their belief in 'workfare' which he also claims does nothing to promote independence and social responsibility. Tanner argues that welfare cannot be reformed and all state driven attempts to end poverty will fail. Tacking a libertarian route Tanner suggests the way to solve poverty is through deregulation of economy to create more jobs and increasing private charitable support for those between work. What he does not say is that faced with the loss of welfare payments, people will be forced to take any employment or starve. This was the model of Victorian Britain which clearly failed to alleviate poverty and led to the growth of the welfare state in the first place. It could be argued that what drives this perspective has little to do with concern for the poor and more about the well to do looking for tax cuts. These radical arguments against the welfare state are also being developed in Britain. Community workers need to confront them with detailed arguments rather than simple slogans that the welfare state is a good thing.

A more compelling position from the Cato Institute is the argument concerning school failure. The failure and often repressive nature of public schools has long been a subject of debate. The classic argument against state schools being put by Ivan Illich in Deschooling Society (1971). In the 1970's the anti school argument was based on progressive libertarian ideals coupled with concern for children's rights and child centred education. An outcome of this debate in the UK was the development of 'free schools' that worked with often disturbed children to provide education in a supportive social environment. The Cato argument takes the same basic criticism of schooling but turns it towards a market, rather than social solution. Bruce Golberg in Why Schools Fail (1996) reviews educational theories over the past 150 years. He argues that the common flaw in these theories are that they see children as essentially interchangeable and there to receive education (the banking approach in Freire's terms). According to Golberg this is *"the denial of individuality, the idea that everyone must follow some general plan that is the core failure of the schools"*. He argues for the introduction of school vouchers. Such a scheme would allow the market to develop a range of provision allowing parents and children to follow an individual, rather than a standardised educational pathway.

In contrast the Illich argument (1971, 1973, 1976) is to question *"why so many people - even ardent critics of schooling - become addicted to education, as to a drug"?* Education according to Illich has become a growth industry driven by the professional teacher. The idea of Lifelong Learning promotes education at work, for leisure and personal advancement. Education ritualises, and reinforces the belief that learning as presently constituted is a valuable commodity. People are led to believe that they are personal failures because they have failed at educational institutions. Instead, Illich proposes that individuals engage in creative exchanges with each other based on personally defined needs. This process will lead to the creation of learning webs within which free interaction and genuine useful education can take place. This concept prefigures the development of the Internet which makes the idea of learning webs more possible. For community workers Illich's ideas raise questions about how we facilitate community groups and activists to learn. Can we promote and facilitate learning webs in communities and between organisations?

This contrast between the Illich and Cato positions illustrates the complexity in the area of personal freedom and libertarian theory. In some forms it can be progressive in creating choice and improving social provision, although always opposed to mass collectivisation and state control of services. In other forms it is market driven and thus only available to those with sufficient income to choose. Community workers need to carefully and thoughtfully work their way through this territory making sure their positions are in accordance with the value base.

Communitarianism and Normalisation

Communitarianism has a superficial populist appeal. It has a growing base of active support in North America and proponents at high levels of all the main UK political parties. The Institute for Communitarian Policy at George Washington University describes communitarianism as:

> *"recognising that a healthy society must have a correct balance between individual autonomy and social cohesion ... when you put 'community' back into the equation you find that the apparent conflict between the individual and government can be resolved by public policies that are consistent with core American values and work to the benefit of all members of our society"*

In contrast to the libertarian position above, the communitarian seeks active government intervention in society with possible constraints imposed on the market for the social good, although, this is definitely not an anti capitalist movement. The basic framework of its policies were laid down by Amitai Etzioni (1995) and have been developed to cover a wide range of social policy areas encompassing the family, child care, schooling, criminal justice, the political process and civil society in general. Communitarians argue that one of the main problems with society is that people claim too many rights while at the same time fail to live up to their responsibilities. People should *"provide for themselves and their families ... beyond self support, individuals have a responsibility for the material and moral well being of others"*.

Civil society is the basis of the communitarian argument and this in turn is based on morality. The core to rebuilding communities, it is argued, lies within the family. It is for both parents (as single parents are described as problematic) to honour child rearing, instil moral values and for one parent to stay at home whilst the child is young. Schools are seen as the 'second line of defence' who should take more seriously their responsibility for moral education. Morality here is defined as *"those values Americans share, for example ... a days work for a days pay ...saving for ones own and one's country future, dignity and tolerance"* (The Communitarian Network: Rights and Responsibilities). Specific policy initiatives should include replacing sex education in schools with classes on interpersonal relations and family life. The government should use the tax system to support family life as well as introducing mandatory premarital and pre divorce counselling.

Writing in the Times (21 June 1997) Etzioni suggested that Tony Blair may be communitarian. He cited the revised clause four of the Labour Party constitution which recognises the importance of community and of *"rights (that) we enjoy reflect the duties we owe"*. Etzioni commented that the election motto *of "responsibility for all, responsibility from all"* was as communitarian a notion as they come. Certainly social policy in the UK tends to follow North American initiatives and the communitarian agenda continues to inform the development of the Labour governments social policy.

The criticism of communitarianism is that it is based on questionable assumptions. Although it is concerned about social justice and improving the welfare of citizens, the moral position of communitarianism is culturally determined and essentially white middle class and conservative. It is based on a belief that everyone else should conform to its 'natural' position and government needs to intervene to make it so. This is potentially authoritarian and discriminatory as other value and moral positions are not easily tolerated. In adopting this approach communitarianism promotes the idea of normalisation.

The theory around normalisation developed originally in Scandinavia during the 1950's in relation to those with learning difficulties and as part of Social Comparison Theories. Wolfensberger (1972) later developed these ideas. He defined normalisation as *"the utilisation of means which are as culturally normative as possible, in order to establish and / or maintain personal behaviours and characteristics which are as culturally normative as possible"*. These ideas were developed to help people with disabilities. Stigma and social rejection could be overcome if the marginal groups acted as 'normal' as possible. There is no intention here to directly challenge the oppressive and discriminatory actions of others; it is for the victims and the oppressed to change themselves. The communitarian position builds on this view by blaming those that do not conform to the norms of society as the cause of social ills. It is the single parent, the divorced couple, the unemployed who far from being the casualties of a capitalist society are the cause of its problems.

This line of argument is inherently conservative as it ignores that society, especially a multi cultural society like the UK is made up of a variety of social groups with diverse cultures, ideologies and life styles. Normalisation implies that the dominant culture of the dominant social group is the norm and everything else is of less value or potentially destructive. Once we have rejected diversity and accepted mainstream norms as the correct norms for society it is just a short step to prescriptive or repressive social policies to impose acceptable behaviour.

Although Wolfensberger and many communitarians are concerned about social justice, their argument that promotes mainstream norms and morals as the ideal for a society is dangerous. Community workers concerned with empowerment should be promoting the celebration of diversity and the acceptance of other cultures and life styles, challenging oppression and working with the dispossessed. Community workers therefore have a duty to engage with the communitarian debate to defend the rights of minority groups.

Cultural analysis and social movements

Firstly we need to know what we mean by culture. The traditional definition of culture is based around bourgeois artefacts in museums and art galleries, as well as classical concerts and opera. In this view the middle class have culture and the working class do not. Raymond Williams, amongst others, debunked this view with his classic phrase and book title that *'Culture is Ordinary'* (1989). Influenced by Marxism, Williams linked culture with the economy and redefined it to include the organisation of production, the structure of the family, institutions, social relationships and the various forms through which people communicate. Culture therefore is relative to both a society and sub groups within a society. An understanding of local culture is essential for a community worker, because her view and understanding of the world may not be the same as that of the community in which she works.

Anthropologists Kroeber and Kluckhohn have identified 160 different definitions of culture. These definitions can be summarised as covering what people think, what they do and the material products they produce:

Topical	Culture is everything on a list of topics covering religion, social groupings, national identity, etc
Historical	Culture is the traditions and beliefs that are passed down through generations
Behavioural	Culture is the behaviour that is learnt through parents, school and society about how to live you life
Normative	Culture is a set of rules that guide what we should and should not do
Functional	Culture is the ways that people solve problems and adapt to new circumstances
Mental	Culture is the ideas that we have about ourselves and the world we live in
Structural	Culture is our understanding or, and response to, symbols and ideas that govern our everyday life.
Symbolic	Culture is the meanings that are collectively shared by a society.

Cultural analysis today explores a number of themes including the nature of identity, power, the individual in society and public policy (Gray and McGuigan 1997). It has been used to explore the effects of colonialism (Tomlinson 1991, Sardar 1997 and Ibrahim 1996), and developing insights into feminism and sexual orientation (bell hooks 1990). Cultural study ranges from the messages contained within soap operas, the power of advertising, cultural myths, culture of ethnic groups to the effects of technology and globalisation. Much of the current writing is based on postmodernist methods such as semiotics (the decoding of signs, texts and codes). It is useful for community workers to have a working knowledge of culture to inform their understanding of the communities in which they work.

For example, E. P Thompson (1978) argues that class is more than the Marxist view of simply the relationship to the means of production. It is the product of the interplay of a number of cultural trends over time. Popular mass culture evolves through changes in income, leisure time and opportunity. This interacts with received cultural messages through the media (radio, TV, movies, magazines) and cultural messages from the power elite through institutions such as schooling, work and the police. For a working class community there is dialectic between culture made *by* the working class and made *for* the working class by external institutions. As modern communities become more mobile and increasingly influenced by external factors the local culture becomes more fluid.

Community workers need both to understand the nature of the local culture and to be able to help people understand where their influences and world view comes from. The work of Freire is very useful here as it offers us a process to help people decode their culture as part of developing a critical consciousness. There are also clear linkages here to writings of Gramsci who can also help us see how hegemony of the ruling elite is internalised by working class people through the working of the media.

Related to understanding culture is the idea of semiotics that has been developed from the work of de Saussure (1974). We know that objects have meaning as signs. Every sign is composed of a *signifier*, that is a coded object (for example the picture of a child) and the *signified,* the decoding of the mental concepts relating to the object. The signifier can be read as text through discussion or discourse. As Peirce (Hoopes 1991) pointed out it is helpful to think of three types of signification. He called these types; firstness, that is the *feeling* generated by the picture, secondness, the *facts* depicted in the picture, and thirdness, the *mental* element; love, hate, adoration, etc derived from the picture. Peirce argued that some signs are 'open' that is they can have infinite number of meanings. Others are closed as they have a culturally agreed meaning.

Multiple discourses are possible depending on how we approach the subject. For example the child's parent will view and interpret the picture differently from a teacher, a doctor or a social worker. Most discourses, in turn, form part of larger discourses. In this case we are exploring the wider meaning of a political and cultural discourse derived from the signification of the mural. Derrida (1976) argues that the text of each sign has within it traces of all other texts. In theory this could be a continuous process of 'unlimited semiosis'. In practice this is limited by a shared understanding of what is meaningful.

Also of particular value to community workers is social movement theory. As we would expect there are competing views on social movements. Firstly, the *'collective behaviour theory'* developed by the Chicago School of sociologists argues that a healthy society does not have social movements. Everyday social and political activity should absorb any kind of discontent that must exist to create a social movement. When the formal and informal institutions that hold society together (work, family, etc) start to fail people are open to charismatic leaders and the threat of authoritarian movements such as fascism and communism.

In direct contrast the *'resource mobilisation theory'* claims that social movements are rational responses to new situations in society. For example the protests around nuclear weapons and women's rights are social movements responding to legitimate concerns and which extend the nature of democratic participatory politics.

Thirdly, the *'new social movements theory'* sees social movements as resulting from the tensions and strains within a post industrial society that cannot be contained by outmoded institutions and processes. The old political parties neither understand nor are able to respond to new demands based around personal autonomy and reactions to globalisation. Essentially post-industrial in outlook these movements are more likely to reject class as an issue and focus more on universal human rights and needs.

Fourthly, the *'action identity paradigm'* suggests that social movements are essential to move society forward and promote social emancipation. Traditionally the established ruling elite use cultural processes to control society through social norms and socio-economic relationships. In post-industrial society the dominant class according to Touraine (1981) is technocratic and the working class no longer exists as a mechanism for change. The key nature of conflict is therefore now socio-cultural rather than the socio-economic. Conflict revolves around the control of knowledge and capital investment. Examples of such movements include urban protests, student protests and mass environmental actions.

For community workers it is important to understand that significant social interests that are not incorporated into the existing political system will lead to a social movement of some kind. Usually this is a diffuse and indirect process rather than a direct outbreak of discontent. How far such discontents develop depends upon the ability of the state to either concede to demands or crush (using the media as well as force) the movement. The greater the degree of discrepancy between the state and the social movement the greater the degree of change demanded by the movement. This again raises issues for community workers on whether or not to support social movements. How many workers were involved in supporting the minors strike, the poll tax campaign, and environmental campaigns? The In and Against the State dilemma appears once again.

Modernism and post modernism

So far we have considered a wide range of theoretical perspectives. The modernist v post modernist debate moves this discussion onto a more fundamental analysis of modern society. First of all let's consider modernism.

During the 1700's philosophers started to believe in the idea of human progress. It was they believed, possible for society to develop through the application of reason, logic and science to create freedom and happiness. This time is known as the Age of

Enlightenment. Its best known proponents are Descartes, Locke, Newton, Voltaire and Kant. During the 1800's the belief in progress began to decline. This was due to many causes, for example the horror of the thinking classes at the violent excesses of the French Revolution, the poverty and pollution caused by industrialisation, wars from the Napoleonic to the mass slaughter of the 1914-18 war.

By the late 1800's many philosophers had rejected the possibility of progress and reason. Freidrich Nietzsche went further proclaiming the 'Death of God' and of morality in general. In his writings, including Thus Spoke Zarathustra (1883-1885), Beyond Good and Evil (1886), and The Will to Power (1901) he commented on the herd instinct of the masses lost forever in a slave culture, social chaos and the meaningless of life. Only a 'Superman' affirming all aspects of life including pain and suffering can develop true independence from the mob. There is considerable debate whether the superman thesis encouraged both the development of fascism and the cult of the leader dictatorships of Stalin and Mao. Either way the belief in enlightenment had gone.

Out of the intellectual ruins of the enlightenment comes modernism. In an attempt to transcend the meaninglessness of everyday life painters, writers and thinkers began to explore how to make the world new and for the artist to find meaning in chaos. This process was driven by the progress being made in science and technology. If a better life cannot be achieved through reason then it may be achievable through technological change. An example is the Bauhaus movement led by architect Walter Gropius. The Bauhaus was based on the principle that modern art and architecture should reflect the influences of the modern industrial world and that good design must be both aesthetically pleasing and technically sound. Mass production of consumer goods, and the employment that this created would also lead to improvements in the quality of life. The benchmark in the belief of social benefit from technological progress is the introduction by Henry Ford in 1914 of the five dollar eight hour day for the mass assembly of cars. This mass production and mass consumption process has become known as Fordism and is an integral part of modernism.

In contrast to the Fordist claimed benefits of consumption and production, technology has also created Nazi death camps, nuclear weapons and has clearly failed to deal with global poverty. Modernist optimism by the late 20th century has, many would argue, proved to be unfounded. Modernism also has an inherent oppressive nature. Max Weber identified four types of social action which he termed:

- Traditional action based on custom and habits
- Affective action based on emotion
- Wertrational action based on values
- Zweckrational action based on pre defined goals

Modernist culture and economy, driven by technological imperatives has embraced the Zweckrational mode. This has led to the creation the bureaucratisation of work and much of social life. As a result the individual has few spaces in a modernist environment to find themselves. Their needs and identity are submerged for the greater good of the company, institution or political party. Habermas (1971) has explored how citizens have been depoliticised as decisions, economic and political, are supposedly taken on rational and technical grounds rather than on ideology. To oppose such decisions is to oppose efficiency and progress. In contemporary Britain, the Labour Party no longer talks about socialism but of modernisation.

These processes create difficulties for community workers who believe in Wertrational value based activity. Instead community workers often have to follow goal driven social planning activities, explain to service users why budget cuts are being made or how a service is being reduced or changed to rationalise resources. To be employed by a bureaucracy as a community worker, whilst trying to promote an empowering agenda requires the ability to 'look both ways at the same time'- a reprise of the In and Against the State dilemma of the 1980's. It is no wonder than many workers consider their work is neutralised by their employer.

Postmodernism is a contested term with debates on whether it is part of the modernist tradition, a separate entity or does not exist at all. However we may choose to define it, postmodernism attempts to understand contemporary society. David Harvey (1990) argues compellingly that:

> *"there has been a sea change in cultural as well as in political – economic practices since around 1972. This sea*

change is bound up with the emergence of new dominant ways in which we experience space and time".

Frederic Jameson (1984) argues that postmodernism is simply the latest phase of capitalism. In the last thirty years the growth of transnational corporations has dominated all parts of the world. Even Russia and China, once bastions of state socialism, have now taken the capitalist road. At the personal level even our inner thoughts have been tainted by capitalism through the mass media and advertising. The individual in a postmodern world lives a fragmented and alienated life. Confused by endless fleeting images we become passive TV watching consumers. What we need, according to Jameson, is 'aesthetic cognitive mapping' or a scientific approach to tell what is real about the world and what is illusory. For Jameson we need to revive Marxism as a workable meta-narrative.

There is no doubt that Jameson is correct in pointing out the economic, social, political and cultural changes that that globalisation has produced. However, many would argue that the extent of changes in society is more than simply products of an economic system. It is also argued that Marxism is essentially, despite recent updating, still a 19th century world view that fails to give us the tools to understand 21st century society.

Postmodernists claim that the modernist belief in meaning, morality and truth is false as they do not exist objectively. They are simply cultural constructions of society, formed and shaped through language. Andre Gorz (1982) comments that:

> *"Just as the belief in progress through scientific, technological and industrial development has died away, so too has the positive outlook which equates the state with supreme good and politics with religion or even morality. We know now that there is no 'good' government, 'good' state or good form of power, and that society can never be 'good' in its own organisation but only by virtue of the space for self organisation, autonomy, co-operation and voluntary exchange which that organisation offers to individuals".*

Gorz goes further and questions the entire modernist product of capitalism and Marxism. He wrote *"There is no point wondering where we are going or in seeking to identify laws immanent in historical development. We are not going anywhere. History has no meaning"*. This loss of belief in progress is based on the failure of the modernist projects to deliver the promised better life. It also relates to the movement away from Fordist mode of production to smaller more flexible patterns of production, globalisation, the development of the Internet and the resulting social and cultural changes.

The French intellectual Jean-Francois Lyotard sees the grand theories of the enlightenment and modernism as stories (meta-narratives) that attempt to provide a universal explanation for society and the individuals role within it. Marxism, Christianity and Fascism are all meta-narratives. Lyotard (1984) argues that since the 1939 – 45 war nobody really believes that any meta-narrative really explains all we need to know about the world. Instead there are an almost infinite number of contradictory micro narratives; small stories that explain a particular part of life in a way that works for some people. The micro narratives may be a sub part of a meta-narrative or just small individual ideas. Rather than listen to an official storyteller of a meta-narrative who will give us guidance (e.g. priest, party leader) we become our own storytellers. We individually explain our lives through a unique set of micro narratives. We may share some of our micro narratives with others at our workplace, a different set with social contacts and friends and yet another set with those of the same political persuasion.

The argument of meta v micro narratives is of profound importance. As community workers do we believe, for example, that socialism provides all we need to know about the world in order to both understand it and to work for change. If we do then socialism is our meta-narrative. Do the people we work with in communities have to believe this to? If we reject the totality of the socialist, or any other, meta-narrative we need to explore what our set of micro narratives may be. We should then expect a diverse set of micro narratives in the community from which we have to try and build some commonality.

Jean Baudrillard, like Jameson comes from a background of Marxism. He is also concerned with alienating effect of the mass media and modern life in capitalist society. Unlike Jameson, Baudrillard believes that the Marxist meta-narrative is now inadequate as an explanation for society and we need to look deeper into society and ourselves for meaning and understanding.

Baudrillard has explored semiotics, and the structure of various systems of meaning such as myths, language and fashion, to understand modern culture. He argues that in a mass consumer society the Marxist analysis fails. Marx defines class as the relationship of people to the means of production. In the modern economy, according to Baudrillard, the level and nature of consumption define class. Elite's are defined as such because they consume goods that the masses cannot have (large country houses, penthouse flats, luxury yachts) whilst the socially excluded are defined as such by their inability to consume according to the norms of society. For the majority the nature of consumption (shopping) and work is the critical purpose of life.

In The System of Objects (1968) Baudrillard argues that we grow up in a society dominated by objects (i.e. consumer goods). In effect we become an object ourselves. Instead of being defined by what we do and what we believe, we define ourselves and are defined by others by what we own: by our clothes, car and where we live. Fashion and style replaces thought and values. Life therefore, only has meaning through consumption and to consume we must work and through this become locked into the capitalist framework. The Descartes dictum of *"I think therefore I am"* becomes changed to *"I consume therefore I am"*. Those who cannot consume are outsiders to society and present a reminder to us all what might become of us if we fail to conform.

Modern life is also changing in response to the 'communication revolution'. Baudrillard comments on this in his writings on the Simulacra. He defines the simulacra as copies of the real thing. Originally, there were only real objects: for example the paining of the Mona Lisa. As technology developed it became possible to make limited copies of objects through craft activities, in this example the basic printing press. Baudrillard calls this The First Order of the Simulacra. The Second Order arrived with the industrial revolution and the possibility of mass production and infinite copies. The Mona Lisa then ceases to be a unique work of art. Instead it is decoration on tea towels, used to advertise consumer products, etc. The Mona Lisa therefore no longer has any real meaning. It becomes a sign that we respond to but loses any intrinsic value. Market forces, rather than the intrinsic worth of an object become the main determinant of society. Contemporary society is entering the Third Order where life is dominated by models that we either select or reject, mirroring the binary system of computers. We either select Labour or Conservative, Republican or Democrat, Pespi or Coke, or any other of the predetermined choices we have to consume. Although, it appears that life offers us an immense variety of choices, there is in fact no choice at all other than the consumption of meaningless objects. The process is becoming absurd, or hyper-real in postmodern speak. A Rolex watch has considerable but inherently meaningless status attached to it. Yet many people buy 'genuine imitation' Rolex watches to gain some of the supposed status of the real good. In some cases the imitation object has a higher status than the real one.

The implication of all this for those concerned with social change is outlined in Baudrillard's book In the Shadow of the Silent Majorities (1983). He contends that society has become hyper-conformist in which we would rather watch spectacular, if staged, events on TV than take political action. The media, the source of our information about the world, is itself locked into the reflection of models. The messages we receive through TV and the press has little to do with facts. Rather it is the repetition of pre-programmed responses and interpretations reflecting the status quo. People are suspicious and sceptical of change because they realise that any serious threat to the status quo will be co-opted or crushed. This signals the death of the possibility of social action.

In a more hopeful vein, Michel Foucault takes a more positive view of the possibility of change. Concerned with the relationship between power and knowledge, Foucault argues against both monolithic power structures (the state, transnational corporations) and meta-narratives. For Foucault power only resides at the micro level. Power and knowledge are inherently linked. To gain knowledge is to gain more power, to restrict knowledge to others is to reduce their potential for power. Everywhere there is power there is various degrees of resistance to that power. Change can be achieved through localised struggles and linking interested parties to a common agenda and the development of knowledge. For community action this suggests the focussing of campaigns on local, rather than national issues and the building of coalitions for specific actions.

Foucault also argues against meta-narratives because he sees them as attempting to impose an order on the inherently chaotic nature of life. Meta-narratives according to Foucault are based around a 'central core' that involves the words and deeds of great heroes (Marx, Engles, Lenin, Christ, Mohammed) mainstream cultures and conventional histories. In doing so they tend to ignore and compress the diverse reality of people's experience in order for it to fit the pre conceived model.

For much of the 1970's and 80's a major development within communities was concerned with the idea of identity. This involves individuals defining themselves, for example as a black woman, a gay man or a Muslim male. However labelled, identity is supposed to set out a fixed notion of what a person is, their cultural location, historical background and their self definition. As such it is a modernist statement. Bauman (1998) argues that this is no longer the case as *"the world of durable objects has been replaced with disposable products designed for immediate obsolescence. In such a world identities can be adopted and discarded like a change of costume".*

Identity has given way to superficial and changing lifestyles. Unlike an identity, a person can have several conflicting lifestyles at once and certainly many different lifestyles over the course of their life. For example, at work I assume the lifestyle of a University lecturer and this contrasts greatly to my previous lifestyle as a neighbourhood community worker. At home my lifestyle is built around being a parent and this contrast both with my work lifestyles and my previous life as a single person. The nearest I come to a fixed identity is being a white English male but this, in the changing context of postmodern culture also has little meaning.

Bauman argues that lifestyles are superficial and changing, individualised, transient and often lonely. For the community worker the task is no longer about helping people determine a fixed identity that will give them meaning for the rest of their life. Rather it is concerned with assisting people to move between lifestyles and to deal the resulting personal conflicts. This is similar to the life politics of postmodern feminism. An understanding of changing lifestyles is essential for working with community groups. For example the persona adopted and developed by a woman in a group may conflict with her other lifestyles, such as a mother and wife.

The idea of chaos is important to understanding postmodern culture. Take for example trying to understand life in a community. There are many variables to be considered. The variables may include the daily actions of individual citizens, the networks between organisations and the effects of outside agents. Each day the pattern of activities will be different. However, what has happened one day will affect some of the actions the following day. The size of these effects cannot practically be predicted. Like the example of a butterfly flapping its wings over China leading to a thunderstorm in New York. Two people having an argument one day may lead to the collapse of a community organisation several months later. The community therefore is what is called a non-linear system (in that it constantly changes) and it is subject to feedback (what happens one day effects what happens the next).

Non-linear feedback systems are subject to the theory of chaos; a mathematical concept that can be applied to the social context. Within the modernist view of the world, communities, indeed cities can be understood and successfully planned to ensure social problems are solved. Under chaos theory attempts at large scale planning becomes problematic because of the complexity of the undertaking. This has serious implications for social planning, which we have seen, is the dominant model of work in the UK. Social planning cannot be very successful because communities are complex chaotic entities. There is an increasing amount of research that reflects this view. For example Mary Murphy (2002) in a discussion on social partnerships in Ireland concluded: *"social partnerships have borne very limited fruit and there has been considerable opportunity cost in terms of loss of time dedicated to other actions for social change. Public awareness raising, legal challenges, social analysis, networking, and straightforward campaigning are necessary"*.

What can be applied to cities is the notion of fractals. A fractal is ways of measuring chaotic qualities that otherwise have no clear definition. Geographers can map activities in cities as fractals. This shows that patterns of activities at a micro level are broadly repeated at the macro level. In doing so the city creates its own form of self-organisation. That is cities work without the intervention of planners or controls. The extension of this understanding is that rather than try and control a city (through social planning) the only viable option is to encourage participation in the city to allow self organisation to function more effectively. The implication for community work here is to enable as many people as possible to participate in community and city affairs.

In the late 1960's Jacques Derrida developed the concept of deconstruction. Difficult to define, deconstruction is based on the idea of Centres in Derrida's term, although essentially they are meta-narratives. Like Foucault he believes the ruling elite will define a world view or meta-narrative which reflects their own interests. Alternative views and opposition groups will be marginalised and when necessary actively repressed. All meta-narratives therefore, are inherently oppressive. Again this is a reflection of the binary system. For example western society has the following binary systems:

Power Elite	**Marginalised Group**
Men	Women
Family	Gay , Lesbian
Caucasian	Black
Judeo Christian	Pagan
Wealthy	Poor
Industry	Nature
Socially Included	Socially Excluded
New Labour	Old Labour

The system of deconstruction focuses on the binary opposites. It illustrates the relationship to identify how one side is seen as natural and the other abnormal. The deconstruction process then makes the oppressed side dominant and explores meaning from that perspective. Although deconstruction is essentially a literacy technique it has usefulness for community activities. For example, a government policy will promote a firm line and set out specific proposed actions. Deconstruction techniques applied to policy will seek to identify what has been marginalised and excluded from that policy. And what alternative actions could considered if the marginalised elements were made the centre of the policy framework. It would then go onto explore the relationships between the powerful and the marginalised. If we applied this method to the UK Government policy on social exclusion we would gain more insight on exclusion from the perspective of marginal groups. We would realise that the proposed policy framework seeks to maintain the power of the mainstream institutions and develop a clearer understanding of the power relationships between government, institutions and the excluded groups.

Marxists and many feminists criticise deconstruction because it fails to provide a firm base from which to develop political action. Derrida and his supporters would say that this may be uncomfortable but in reality society has no absolute meaning and political action can only come from a narrative and all narratives are inherently subjective.

The final postmodernism concept we need to consider is space-time compression. David Harvey (1990) argues that the effect of capitalism is to increase the pace of life. Together with modern communication this reduces the effective size of the world. Before the Enlightenment the world was seen as full of mystery, known only to God. During the Enlightenment the world became viewed as knowable by man and subject to exploration for commerce and colonialisation. Modernism saw the world as interconnected through trade and communications and subject to change through further technological advances. From the Marxist perspectives the world was capable of being transformed through revolutionary action. In the postmodern era space and time have collapsed. We can share events happening almost anywhere in the world through TV, the telephone and the Internet. Global travel is an everyday event for millions of people. Daily we consume goods from across the world. In effect life has become a global supermarket where we consume objects of our desire, from almost anywhere whenever we wish. It is as if we are living in an MTV video; multiple images, instant consumption but no real meaning.

Robert Kaplan (1998) travelled through North America exploring these effects in what Baudrillard (1989) saw as the worlds first post modern culture. Commenting on urban development projects in the USA he notes that the best developments were organic ones: places where local people opened shops and took the initiative themselves to improve their community. The big expensive top down government led projects do not appear really to contribute much to the quality of life for the average person in terms of reducing unemployment, income and crime. The wealthy communities grow richer. The poorer communities are left to their own devices. For some urban areas in Southern California technology and communications means community is seen in terms of other similar areas on a global basis, rather than the communities down the road.

American cites are, of course, also organic at the macro level. Trade and employment patterns are fragmenting the concept of the nation state. Vancouver in South Western Canada and Seattle in North Western USA have more in common with each other than with the rest of their own countries. Their trade and focus is between themselves and westward across the Pacific rather than eastward. This process is accelerated as the power and influence of central governments declines in contrast to the increasing influence of transnational corporations. It is not hard to see, suggests Kaplan, both Canada and the USA fragmenting effectively into smaller nation states. These smaller groupings would be economically viable and successful. The GNP of Southern California would place it 20th in the world ranking if it was a separate country.

Many people in Northern Italy want to sever ties with the south of their country. In Spain, Catalonia wants to break away from the rest of the country. As the world becomes more integrated we need to find new a new sense of identity and this makes us look for smaller grouping to which to relate. There are hard questions to be asked. Is devolution in the UK part of this fragmentation process? What does South Wales, economically dependent upon European trade and transnational corporations have in common with agricultural rural Wales? In Scotland the central belt is also linked into the international economy. What then is the real, as opposed to romantic, relationship to the Highlands? In the new millennium what does it really mean to be Welsh, Scottish or English other than a romanticised notion of the past. These questions are increasingly important and community workers need to help people explore these issues. It may be that our current view of culture, community and nationhood will not survive as people look for more meaningful groupings in response to social and economic change.

Many radicals, especially in the developing world see the concept of postmodernism as another Eurocentric form of oppression. Islam is viewed across many parts of Africa, the Middle East and Asia as the meta-narrative that will confront capitalism. Yet most western postmodernist thinkers ignore the importance and effects of Islam. Secondly, postmodernism denies the possibility of an all embracing political agenda. However, in Central America coalitions of organisations come together to fight on a collective agenda. Stuart Hall (1991) rightly points out that once people engage in conscious reflection and dialogue there is *"a proliferation of new points of antagonism, new social movements of resistance organised around them, and, consequently, a generation of politics ... a politics of health, of food, of sexuality, of the body"*. Perhaps the road to change in the postmodern context is through the celebration of diversity and bringing together micro narratives in coalitions of action. Current activities on sexuality, gender, race, and the environment may set the organisational model for the future.

For community development to be effective under postmodern conditions where globalisation and information drive the process of change, we need to develop knowledge driven practice. The OECD (1996) argues that *"education will be the centre of the knowledge-based economy, and learning the tool of individual and organisational advancement"*. Education is becoming so important to globalisation that the World Bank, amongst other institutions talks about *knowledge capitalism* as the next stage of the globalisation process. Michael Peters (2002) suggests that this will entail *"knowledge wars, a struggle not only over the meaning and value of knowledge both internationally and locally, but also over the public means of knowledge production"*. At the micro level Burton-Jones (1999) argues that the distinction between managers and workers, learning and working are becoming blurred. In effect we are all becoming *knowledge capitalists*. Peters prefers the term *knowledge cultures*, and it is this context that includes consumers and community groups. If we live within a knowledge culture where power is based upon the control and application of knowledge, then it is reasonable to conceptualise community based work fundamentally as knowledge driven practice.

The table on the following page suggests some of the difference in conceptualising traditional community development as it has evolved under modernist conditions, and how it is may develop in postmodernity.

Aspect	Modernist CD	Postmodernist CD
CD role	Intermediary	Animateur
Purpose	Improved welfare	Personal liberation
Focus	Uniform community	Diverse consumers and groupings
Mode	Social control	Empowerment
Means	*Task driven* through planning activities and capacity building	*Knowledge driven* for self exploration and determination
Organisation	Formal groups, long term stability, partnerships	Informality, short term, loose alliances, possible conflicts
Communities	Subjects for welfare	An arena for self determination
Group experience	Hard work, devotion	Fun, Innovation
Leadership	Traditional political structures	Autonomous and community based
Human beings	Determined	Moveable lifestyles
Belief in change	Reform through political process	Possible only at individual and micro level
Needs	Rational, known by experts	Driven by consumption
Meaning	Through structures	Consumption and lifestyle
Knowledge	Absolute truth: to inform decision making	Relativist: for personal transformation
Culture	Mediated by bourgeois standards	Simulations tied to consumption
Power	Distant, exerts control over resources and people	Contested at local levels

(Purcell 2003)

Community work and theories of the state

Community work in the UK suffers from a general lack of theory of its own and largely failed attempts to relate it to other more general theoretical models. For the majority of workers in the UK the base theory of community work is usually some variation on the theme of pluralism. This is defined a seeing society as based on competing groups each with some, though different, degree of power and influence. The competition between groups is an essential component of a vibrant democracy. The role of the state is to mediate between these competing interests. Social planning being one method of mediation. This is a reformist analysis where the workers role is to enable groups to compete (against each other) more effectively, to improve the quality of services and to make the status quo function more effectively. Community work theory in the pluralist tradition is more concerned with the techniques of the work than wider social and economic analysis. Community capacity in this context concerns training people for tasks within the community rather than any liberatory purpose. Henderson and Thomas Skills in Neighbourhood Work is the classic pluralistic text which builds on this tradition from Batten onwards.

Society is of course more complex than the pluralists would have us believe. To develop an effective theory for community work we must first understand the nature of the state.

The state can be seen in a number of ways. Firstly, there is the concept of the *independent state*. This view argues that the state should only adopt a minimal role, in its extremist role limited to foreign affairs, defence and policing. State institutions are inherently neutral and act to promote the widest public interest. Citizens should be free to succeed or fail depending on their own ability and effort. Concepts such as equality and redistribution of wealth only interfere with the natural working of the market and should be avoided. Hayeck is generally seen as the main proponent of these theories. If we accept this view then the role of community work is the equip communities to compete on a self help basis independent of significant direct help from the state.

Secondly, is the *instrumental view* of the state. In this view the state functions, either totally or partially, to further the interests of the ruling class. This is fundamentally a Marxist analysis. One view argues that the state is subject to the will of the leaders of capitalist enterprises. And that it uses the organs of the state, the police, and army and to a lesser degree education, to control the population for the interests of capital. A more sophisticated variant of this approach argues that state institutions have various degrees of autonomy and some independence from the ruling class. Althusser (1977) splits the state in two. The *Repressive State Apparatus* represents the direct use of force through the army and police. However, the state usually acts more subtly through the *Ideological State Apparatus* that includes the institutions of society, education, culture, religion and family life. The state's role is to maintain the conditions in which capitalism can operate. This may involve giving concessions to the working class. The welfare state both provides benefit to workers but also maintains social stability. In this situation community work can choose to either organise direct opposition to the state, or forge a compromise by extending concessions for working class communities.

Thirdly, there is the concept of the *Interlocking State*. In this case the state and the economy have become inextricably linked (Habermas 1974). The growth in power and influence of transnational corporations is such that the nation state is powerless in comparison. The role of the state is therefore to train and control a workforce as well as manage the economy effectively to provide a stable environment for consumption. The practice of community work in this setting is possible as long as the goals are limited and do not fundamentally conflict with the interests of capital.

The notion of the *Contested State* argues that the state has many facets and roles that are not necessarily consistent. One state body may act in contradiction to another. This provides space within which to exploit opportunities to make progress for social change. In the UK the London Edinburgh Weekend Return Group (1980) explored the dichotomy of the state. Some aspects of social policy and the welfare state can be defended, other aspects attacked. Gradually this will lead to a shift towards welfare socialism. This argument can be developed in the context of a postmodernist analysis that the state is in effect irrelevant. What is key for community work is to analyse the sources of power in any given situation and in many cases the state may only be a minor or non-existent player.

O'Donovan (2000) argues that recent development in critical state theory have led to the development of the concept of an *interactive state*. She argues that traditional theories of the state see community work as either reinforcing the needs of capitalism through providing cheap welfare services or legitimising the state and the status quo by creating the impression that change is possible through working within existing frameworks and institutions. The concept of the interactive state suggests a number of ideas. Firstly, that local people can become critically aware and develop their own agenda for change which may conflict with that of the state and its support for capitalism. Secondly, that organised and powerful communities and pressure groups can redirect social policies. This is of great significance for those of us working in various forms of regeneration and social inclusion partnerships.

Furthermore, some commentators, for example Mann (1987) argue that state regulation and resistance are interconnected. The more the state attempts to control through authoritarian action the more likely there is to be a radicalisation of opinion and militant action. However, we need to be careful here. In the 1980's part of the far left was supporting the election of a right wing conservative government in the belief that the resulting worsening of working class conditions would lead to revolutionary action. Regulation and resistance may indeed be linked but the connection can often be weak and we should avoid a strategy that promotes a worsening of social conditions.

Finally, interactive state theory recognises that the state is not a unified monolith. Different parts of the state, for example different national government departments, local v national government, managers v political representatives, may all have competing views. It is possible to work with various state agencies to make gains if a thoughtful and organised approach is undertaken. Underpinning such an approach is the prerequisite of an organised and knowledgeable community.

As we have said, community work theory is underpinned by ideological preference. This means an individual's theoretical analysis of how to work in the community will be informed, consciously or not, by their wider understanding of how society operates. Regardless of where an individual worker stands in relation to personal ideology, the critical factor is to be aware of personal beliefs, understand how they influence your analysis of community work and be open and honest about it.

Gramsci and community work

Antonio Gramsci is currently seen as the Marxist theorist most likely to hold the way forward for community work. Born in Cagliary in Italy in 1891 he became involved in socialist activity in Turin from 1913. He visited Moscow in 1922/3 and returned to Italy as leader of the Communist Party. Mussolini imprisoned him in 1926. From 1929 he starts to write his prison notebooks. He died in 1937.

Gramsci's most important contribution to Marxist theory is that of 'hegemony'. The concept appears to have originated in Russia as part of the Social Democratic movement around 1900. Gramsci developed the idea to explain why the working class was not just anti revolutionary but in places prone to fascism. Gramsci believed that:

- Class struggles must always involve ideas and ideologies and these can be both revolutionary and counter revolutionary.
- Change comes about through human activity; simply expecting economic crisis to cause change does not work.
- Belief that everything is driven by the economic mode of production is false. The state has significant autonomy, as does culture and ideology.
- Workers accept the domination of the ruling class because they believe it is in their own interest to do so and that they defer leadership to powerful people and institutions.

Hegemony can therefore be defined as the:

"dominant groups in society, including fundamentally but not exclusively the ruling class, maintain their dominance by securing the spontaneous consent of subordinate groups, including the working class, through negotiated construction of a political and ideological consensus which incorporates both dominant and dominated groups" (Strinati 1995).

Applying this concept of hegemony to the present day UK it could be argued that the dominant class has succeeded in persuading the majority of the population to accept its political, economic and social leadership. This assumes that the majority of the population consents and conforms to the prescribed norms and actions of the ruling class. In effect the majority of the population accept the status quo as being common sense responses to everyday issues. For those who do not accept such norms coercion through moral pressure, sanctions and ultimately violence will be applied.

Gramsci's insight was that the working class could also exert hegemony. This can be achieved through developing networks, alliances and coalitions amongst minority groups. Partners in this arrangement could come together to create a popular front for major struggles (for example the Poll Tax), but be autonomous for their own sectional interests. This is a rejection of the Leninist approach to organising that subjugates all struggles to the centralised authority of the revolutionary leadership. Williams (1992) sums this up as:

> *"the key to revolutionary social change in modern societies does not therefore depend, as Marx had predicted on the spontaneous awakening of the critical class consciousness but upon the prior formation of a new alliance of interests, an alternative hegemony or historical bloc, which has already developed a cohesive world view of its own".*

In current western societies such a strategy would take a long time. It is necessary to engage in hegemonic struggles with a wide range of social institutions including trade unions, churches, community groups, education and the media. The struggle has to be fought as both battles of ideologies and through culture; that is the way people define and live their lives. This idea links directly to the feminist position that the 'personal is political'. To lead such a battle a new generation of intellectuals is required. Ideally, the intellectuals should come from within the working class, although this contradicts the experience of most revolutions where the leadership is usually middle or upper class in the initial phase.

However, the intellectuals do not have a monopoly of knowledge. Gramsci is very clear that workers also have essential knowledge. What is required is the integration of theory and practice (praxis) through rigorous analysis. As we shall see this position prefigures the work of Freire. It is for the intellectuals to enable praxis to happen. Only in this way can short term campaigns and isolated groups develop a wider ideological perspective that will lead to long term collaborative struggles.

Within this analysis community work has potentially a crucial role. Gramsci identifies a 'middle stratum' of professional groups between the working and capitalist classes. These groups usually act to sustain the status quo and reinforce the dominant ideology by defining the boundaries of action and thought. If we are honest this is the role played by the majority of community workers. It need not be this way. Community workers can promote discussion to explore the contradictions that people experience between the status quo 'common sense' view of the world and aspects of their own lives. Freire is very important here as he gives us a method for creating such a dialogue that will lead to the development of a critical consciousness and a revised world view. Community workers also have the task of making links between groups and building campaigns for the longer term. For community workers this is a clear choice. As Freire said *"not to side with the poor and oppressed is to side with the rich and the powerful"*. There is no neutral position.

Freire and community work

Paulo Freire is perhaps the most important Marxist theorist who has contributed to practice in community settings, as opposed to political or economic struggles. His seminal text Pedagogy of the Oppressed (1972) developed a radical approach to promote literacy through the creation of critical consciousness. A process termed by Freire as 'conscientisation'. His ideas are based upon the fusion of Marxism, academic studies in education and his practical experience of developing literacy programmes in Brazil. Exiled by the Brazilian military regime in 1964, Freire has worked in Chile, Africa and Europe. His techniques are practised extensively in the developing world. They can be applied to almost any group setting in the UK. For example see the work of the Adult Learning Project in Edinburgh (Kirkwood and Kirkwood 1990).

Freire argues against the tradition roles of teachers and experts who claim to hold useful knowledge. This he calls the *'banking'* approach where experts lead and others passively receive knowledge that it has been decided is useful and acceptable for them.

The role of the worker in the group setting is to act as a facilitator. The workers task is to pose problems that enable the group to reflect on their personal circumstances, to gain a greater understanding of their personal, family and community situation. Open questions are 'posed' against a 'code' that illustrates some aspect of the personal or community life. The code can be a drawing, photograph, poem, mural, play or any other device that when discussed will help people critically reflect upon their experience.

For liberation to be achieved group members have to develop a more critical level of consciousness. For Freire *"conscientisation is about intention. It is a quality of critical awareness which enables people to consider a range of options in the ways they act, and enables them to choose a course of action deliberately and with the intention to change some aspect of their reality"* (Freire 1972). He identifies three main levels of consciousness. Firstly, there is *'Magical Consciousness'* where people accept the oppressions of external powerful forces; they do not fully comprehend the socio-economic or other social contradictions that exist in our world or believe in the possibility of change because they are caught in the *'Culture of Silence'*. This can operate at a community level, for example in a community living in substandard housing, where there are few job opportunities and where schooling and health services are inadequate. Magical consciousness also operates at the personal level, for example among women subject to domestic violence who feel trapped and where their suffering is unheard and unacknowledged.

The next level is defined by Freire as *'Naïve Consciousness'*. This is where people can reflect on their situation and begin to make connections with social, economic and political issues. However, the worldview at this level is very much one of individualised experience. For example, the non-availability of good housing may be blamed on single parents or the shortage of jobs on immigrants. At this level issues are subject to simplistic analysis and emotional responses often with other social groups being classified as deserving or undeserving.

The major step of viewing life through a *'Critical Consciousness'* does not come until the context of the outside world is engaged on an analytical basis. The impact of structural and cultural discrimination is understood, and problems move from being private troubles to public issues (C. Wright Mills 1959). It is essential to the development process that the object of the work and activities are generated by the group themselves as a result of this process of consciousness development.

Related to these levels of consciousness is Freire's concept of *'Boundary Situations'*. He believes that we all repress ourselves through imposing a boundary on our own actions as a result of internalising the cultural norms of oppressive institutions and belief systems. The community worker should, through using a problem posing technique, facilitate the group to question these assumptions, to develop a more critical view of themselves and their community and shift their self defined boundaries. If this is achieved belief in the possibility of change becomes conceivable. The group are then able to move from the *Reflective* phase to developing a *Vision* of a better personal and collective future, and go forward to *Plan* and undertake *Action* to these ends.

This consciousness development integrated with the **reflection - vision - planning - action cycle** can have profound effects on both individuals and communities. Fritz (1982) reflecting on a group work process with young women commented on the importance of the Freirian process for individuals:

> *"In a process from naive consciousness to critical consciousness a lot can happen. I had to get myself out of the culture of silence, asserting myself, building up self confidence and stating my own opinions, in order to act. The experience of being a single parent on social security made me look at life in a different way. I can distance myself and look back at my own process, which is a never ending process, breaking through boundaries and meeting new ones all the time".*

The process enables individuals to make connections with the wider world. Again Fritz comments: *"a lot of patience was needed with this kind of work. Big things and small things happened during the course. For most women it was the first time they had looked from a distance at their own lives in a more structured way. Now and again they started linking up their lives with the world outside".*

Freire's methods have been criticised as either non-revolutionary because they do not necessarily link people's conditions with the wider social structure and an analysis of capitalism. Alternatively, they are said to be totalitarian in that they indoctrinate vulnerable groups to a radical programme. Both criticisms reflect either bad practice or more likely the ideological bias of the commentator. If you want people to accept you own meta-narrative (Marxism or Libertarianism for example) then the Freirian methodology will not do that. What it will do is facilitate people to develop a critical understanding or themselves and their situation. The analysis and links they make will be theirs. In this respect Freire's methodology is inherently post modern. This is ironic given Freire's Marxist background and perhaps explains the criticisms from the traditional political left. Its ability to radicalise people explains the opposition from the political right.

An overview of theoretical perspectives

Theory is a complex area. Yet it is our road map to help us find our way in confusing and uncertain times. As we have seen there are many and contradictory views of how the world operates. Even within a body of thought, say Marxism or Feminism, there are diverse and often contradictory views. Nevertheless, we cannot afford to avoid developing a theoretical view. If do not have a theory then our work in communities will be unfocussed and directionless.

Firstly, we need to come down on one side or the other in the modernist / postmodernist debate. Is postmodernism simply a diversion from understanding capitalism and gender oppression as many Marxists and Feminists claim. Do we believe in a meta-narrative that informs us how the world works at the individual, family, community and global level. If so, what is it and how do we take this theory and use it to inform both the purpose and the nature of our practice in the community.

Alternatively, if we reject meta-narratives as oppressive and unworkable in the modern world then we are free to select any combination of ideas to construct our own personal world view. The challenge then is does our selection make sense, is it inherently contradictory and again how does it inform our practice.

The table below outlines the contrasting perspectives on development work depending on which side of the debate is taken.

Modernism		Post Modernism
Uniform model of development		Diverse models of development
Power seen to act through nations / international institutions and transnational corporations		Power seen to operate at the micro level
Development driven by economic activities		Development driven by a diverse range of activities – economic, social cultural
	Global Issues Urbanisation Poverty Unemployment Rights Environment	
Response to global issues based on western capitalist ideal, free trade and supported via the IMF and World Bank		Response to global issues based on local and sustainable projects
UK policy through social inclusion approaches and the new deal and new welfare initiatives		UK policy based on sharing lessons from the developing world and building floating coalitions on specific issues

Secondly, we need to take a position on the personal freedom – state regulation and state economy – market economy continuums. Our position here will be guided by our ideological preferences for particular theories and by how we link this to our values base and interpretation of the importance and application of human rights. The following diagram illustrates where particular ideologies fit against these continuums.

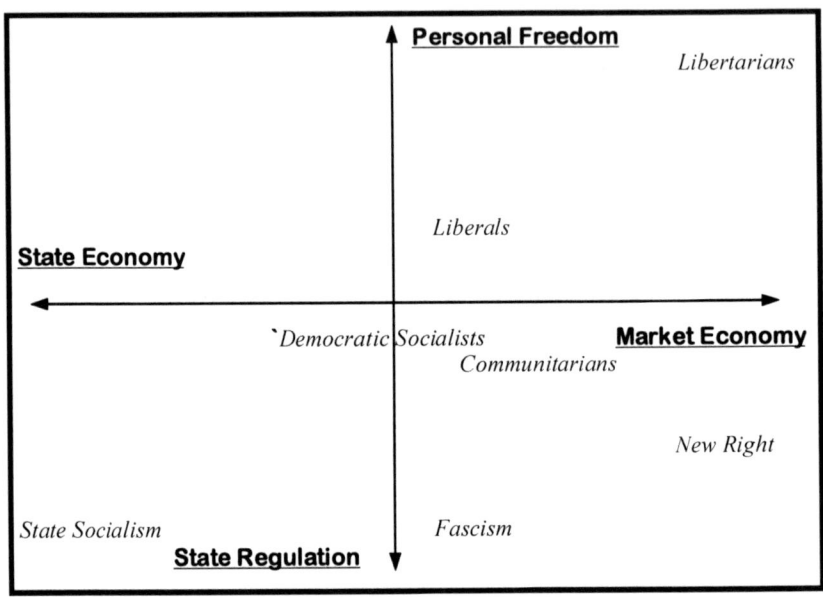

Theory is never static. Whatever we decide today will be based on our interpretation of life experiences. It is important to be flexible in this and develop our theoretical understanding as we read more and continue to reflect upon our lives. What we should not do is adopt a meta-narrative and make our life experiences conform to its dictates. Neither should we impose our theoretical views on others. The task of the community worker is to facilitate others to undertake the same reflective process.

Summary

In this chapter we have covered many theoretical positions that are often contradictory. The challenge of theory is to find a way through that informs rather than confuses our understanding of the world.

Introductory Ideas

- The varied ideas around socialism have been influential in providing a reformist and humanitarian perspective to the world.
- Marxism in its various forms gives a revolutionary critique of capitalist society. Essentially, Marxism demonstrates how the mode of economic production has a fundamental effect on shaping society and power relationships within it.
- Socialism and Marxism also suggest possible alternative social and economic structures
- Capitalism is the main economic system in the world today. However, capitalism can take a number of forms and is currently changing in response to globalisation and the impact of new technology
- Feminism provides a critique of patriarchal society and an analysis of the position and needs of women. It also has a lot to say about the process of community work, the importance of gender relations and the idea that the 'personal is political'.
- In the USA there are a number of debates around libertarianism, communitarianism and the New Right. These debates provide often contrasting views on modern society. This is important because of the influence they have on shaping both North American and UK social policy.
- Culture shapes our understanding of the world. It is subjective and varies both between and within societies. Community works must understand and work with the culture of communities.
- Social movement theory is useful in helping us to understand how change takes place

Modernism v Post Modernism

- The technology and ideas of the late 19th and 20th centuries have shaped modern society - this is termed

modernism. Socialism, Marxism and capitalism are all products of modernist thinking and rooted in the ideas of the 19th century.
- Lyotard suggests that all embracing theories and idea (meta-narratives) do not work
- Baudrillard tells us that we have lost the power to promote change and that we have become passive consumers
- Foucault is more positive and suggests that power exists only at a local level and that the key to power is knowledge
- Modern life is immensely complex and chaotic. Our ability to understand and shape events is in reality severely limited.
- Derrida's ides of deconstruction helps us understand that what is presented as normal is really the view of the powerful. Using semiotics and deconstruction techniques we can begin to explore the ideas of the less powerful and excluded.
- Many Islamic theorists suggest that post modernism is a western construct. Islam they say is the worlds response to the negative effects of capitalism

Community Work and the State

- Community work is often concerned with assisting local communities to negotiate with either the local or national state.
- Theories of the state necessary to help understand the nature of these relationships.

Gramsci

- Gramsci suggests that society is controlled through 'hegemony'.
- The working class is also able to achieve hegemony if it can develop sufficiently wide ranging alliances with other groups
- Promoting change is a battle of ideologies and cultures

Freire

- Education is necessary as a prerequisite for change
- In taking action to change their lives and their community, people have to confront boundaries that have been imposed on them through cultural conditioning
- The effect of these boundaries is for people to be trapped in a culture of silence in which their needs and aspirations are never expressed
- Knowledge is never neutral it is always politically and culturally biased
- Education is either dominating through imposing the 'banked' knowledge of the powerful on communities, or it can be transformatory through assisting people to explore their reality
- For change to occur, therefore, people need to reflect on their lives and develop a critical consciousness

Further Reading

The writing on socialism, Marxism and capitalism are virtually endless. Starting points could be:

Basic Writings on Politics and Philosophy - Marx and Engles, London, Fontana and McLellan D, **Karl Marx: His Life and Thought,** Basingstoke, Macmillan

A contemporary discussion socialism is given by Cleaver in **Socialism** in Sachs W, **The Development Dictionary,** London, Zed Books. Another view is Andre **Gorz Farewell to the Working Class: An Essay in Post Industrial Socialism,** London, Pluto Press

For capitalism see Shutt **The Trouble with Capitalism** , London, Zed Books and Jameson's essay **Postmodernism: or the cultural logic of late capitalism,** New Left Review 146. For the theory of perfect competition see Adam Smith **The Wealth of Nations,** Oxford, Clarendon Press. And to understand the views of Hayek, try his book **The Constitution of Liberty**, London, Routledge and Keagan Paul

A start to exploring feminism can be found in **What is Feminism?** Oxford: Blackwell by Juliet Mitchell and Ann Oakley. The links between feminism and social change are explored by Sheila Rowbotham in **Women and Movement : Feminism and Social Action**. London. Routledge. Also see Bryson V, Feminist **Political Theory**, Basingstoke, Macmillan

The calssic text on the ideas behind communitarianism is Amitai Etzioni **The Spirit of Community**, London, Fontana

For an introduction to culture see Gray A, McGuigan J, **Studying Culture: an introductory reader**, London, Arnold and Storey J **Introduction to Cultural Theory and Popular Culture,** Prentice Hall,

Readings on modernism and post modernism are generally for the committed. However Daivd Harvey is one of the more accessible writers with **The Condition of Post Modernity**, Blackwell. The ideas of post modernism and specifically those of Baudriallard, Derrida and Focault can be found in the **'for Beginners'** series published by Writers and Readers

An interesting discussion on theory of the state can be found in O'Donovan, **Theorising the Interactive State; reflections on a popular participatory initiative in Ireland,** Community Development Journal, Vol 35, No 3. Also see Mann in **Ruling Class Strategies and Citizenship,** Sociology 21,

To understand Gramsci there is no real alternative to reading the original. The most accessible version is **Selections from the Prison Notebook,** edited by Hoare Q and Smith G, London, Lawrence and Wishart .

A lot has been written both by and on Freire. His basic ideas are outlined in **Pedagogy of the Oppressed** published by Penguin. More accessible is Freire in conversation with Ira Shor in **A Pedagogy for Liberation; dialogues on transforming education,** London Bergin and Garvey. An exploration of Freirian practice in Scotland is given in **Living Adult Education; Freire in Scotland, by** Kirkwood and Kirkwood, Buckingham, Open University Press. The four volume **Training for Transformation** series by Ann Hope and Sally Timmel published by Intermediate Technology Publications, provide a workbook approach to Freire.

For a very detailed analysis of both Gramsci and Freire see Peter Mayo **Gramsci, Freire and Adult Education,** London, Zed Books,

6

Underlying Perspectives: Understanding the Urban

"It is the city of mirrors, the city of mirages, at once solid and liquid, at once air and stone" Erica Jong

Aims of this chapter

In the world today the majority of the population live an urban lifestyle. For community based practice to be effective we need to understand the nature of urban life in the 21st century. This chapter challenges the existing view of city as a spatially defined entity. It suggests that the city is essentially a collection of socio-economic processes that flow beyond its notional border. Two case studies are used to illustrate how these themes operate in particular communities. But first we need to consider the nature of urban communities.

The traditional view of community is based on Tonnies and the Chicago School of urban sociology. Tonnies (1957) saw community as being either *'gemeinschaft'* that is a close intimate society (traditional rural village) or *'gesselschaft'* individually focused and based on multiple relationships (city life and modernity). The Chicago School (for example Park 1925) saw community as a social process operating within a geographically defined area. They argued that city has social characteristics of its own that divided it, both geographically and socially, from the rural. It is this structural view that underpins the 'area' approach of UK social policy where lines are drawn on maps to delineate the 'excluded" from the "included", and the 'disadvantaged' from the 'normal'. This approach, although administratively convenient, is flawed as there are more excluded or disadvantaged people living outside the designated areas as within them.

Cohen (2000) argues that Tonnies was wrong, and that his rural and urban stereotypes miss the variety and complexity of communities that can be found in either setting. The Chicago School was also incorrect in seeing community in terms of structure. Instead Cohen suggests that communities are based on culture rather than structure, quoting Geertz (1975) *"man is an animal suspended in webs of significance he himself has spun"*. Community therefore exists within the minds of its members and are conceptualised through a boundary that defines who we are and who we are not. This binary process helps to give meaning to our localised understanding of class, gender and ethnicity depending on the nature of the community involved.

A community boundary can be hard or flexible. Boundaries are defined in symbolic fashion: for example, graffiti or neighbourhood watch posters for geographic communities, initiation processes (membership forms, attending meetings, paying subscriptions, dress codes, and use of language) for communities of interest. The meaning of these symbols depends upon the cultural position of the viewer. The more a community is under threat (from geographic or socio-economic change) the more symbolic action may be taken to reinforce the boundary. Often this is achieved through reasserting tradition or community myths, not as nostalgia but as a resource for the present. For community workers such an analysis of community is very useful in helping to understand the social processes at play.

Castells in his book The Urban Question (1977) also rejected the existing views of the city. Instead he sees the city, like Cohen, as a more dynamic entity based on social relationships as well as a process of collective consumption as part of the overall capitalistic structure of the state. Castells sees society as *"fundamentally made of flows exchanged through networks or organisations and institutions. By flows I mean purposeful, repetitive, programmable sequences of exchange and interaction between physically disjointed positions held by social actors in organisations and institutions of society"* (1999: 57). Castells is specifically writing about the flow of information and its interrelationships with economic power in a globalised world, but the analysis also applies includes flows of ideas and culture. These flows, according to Castells, operate at four levels:

- Networks that organise the position in society of people, organisations and institutions. These networks create structural hierarchies form both within and between societies. Bourdieu might add that relative position here depends upon the control of cultural capital
- The more dominant the position in the hierarchy, the more powerful is the opportunity to influence society (hegemonic power). These hierarchies may be unstable as the relative flows of power change.
- Within networks there are asymmetries between positions. Key people in mid level posts may wield significant power. An example here is the editors who control and define media news broadcasts. Castells comments that *"who sends the message and who shapes the channel of transmission of the flow largely condition the social effects"* (1999: 58). Some networks operate largely autonomously (for example financial markets)
- The logic of flows is uneven across and within societies. Where the effects of globalisation are strongest there is a tendency for these flows to break down existing social and political structures. This process leads both to new social and cultural forms as well as a community based assertion of old identities based on territory, ethnicity, religion and history; such as the rise of religious fundamentalism or the growth of nationalism

The effects of these flows therefore, affect not only society at the macro level but also the individual at the interior level. Castells writes:

"the constant changes in roles and situations in a society defined by innovation, flexibility, and unpredictability in all spheres require people to constantly redefine themselves in their roles at work, in the family, and with their friends. Therefore, the restructuring of the personality to adequately fulfil the new functions demanded by society requires a bringing together of all the new codes and messages from

> *the different networks relating to the various dimensions of people's lives. The construction and reconstruction of the self is tantamount to manage the changing set of flows and codes that people are confronted with in their daily experience" (1999: 63)*

Castells also promoted the analysis of state intervention into the domestic area through public services to extend social control. Collins (2002) also explored the relationship between community and the state in Ireland and concluded: *"that the emergence of community based, participatory democratic processes in Ireland and elsewhere was ... an induced - if not driven - State innovation to expand its frontiers in constituencies where its presence was weak or predominantly repressive - as in policing, housing or social welfare"*. These processes play out through a series of areas of conflict:

- between the public and private areas of city life
- personal liberty or social control
- cultural diversity or the imposition of 'normality'
- the extension of state power over domestic life
- through the control of space through street architecture

It is therefore only possible to understand what is happening in a city, if the analysis is placed in a social, economic and historical context. However one chooses to frame this debate, it is no longer acceptable to simply talk about public services as through they were politically neutral. Neither is it effective to practice to limit our understanding of urban cultures to the specific groups with which we work. Effective community work comes from locating practice within an understanding of urban process and broader cultural groupings. The two case studies below on 'street life' and urban festivals illustrate the level of analysis we need to make.

Case Study 1- The Street

In one sense the street is simply a conduit for moving people through the city. On the other hand as Jane Jacobs said *"a city sidewalk by itself is nothing. It is an abstraction. It means something only in conjunction with the buildings and uses that border it"* (1972: 39). It could be argued that the street and street corners are public spaces that *"become a kind of neutral grid on which cultural difference, historical memory, and social organization are inscribed"* (Gupta and Ferguson 1992: 7); that is they become a place where the diverse forms of city life unfold offering a full range of economic and social opportunity. Philip Kasinitz (1995) wrote that public spaces *"in which strangers can come together to meet, communicate, transact business or just enjoy the sight and sound of each other are at the very core of the urban experience"* (1995: 273). Street corners, as public space, can therefore act as a metaphor for the city itself.

Low (1996) suggests that the density of urban life and economic and social interaction leads to the transmission of local knowledge. Low references Rotenberg (1993) who speaks of the 'salubrity of sites' as a way of understanding the interrelationship between knowledge and the urban landscape. Rotenberg (1995) elaborates this idea through studying the history of open spaces and gardens in Vienna and exploring how these spaces have become a 'spatial template of urban symbolic communication'. The street corner is also one of the locations where this transmission of knowledge takes place; where diverse communities interact both with each other and with passing strangers.

The themes reflected on street corners include the acting out of a city divided by class, culture, gender and ethnicity and the different codes and patterns of behaviour. The street corner can also be a site of conflict between tradition and development and the related processes of deindustrialisation, gentrification, and immigration. The street corner is a contested space also in terms of the tension between private and public use, domestication and social control and the battle for reclaiming the street through graffiti and festivals. These themes are explored by reference to the ethnographic studies of Duneier (2001) of the New York Sidewalk, Liebow (1967) on Negro street corner men in Washington and Whyte's (1993) study of Italian men in Boston

Liebow in his account of Negro street corner men makes the point that although the study relates to the specific individuals under observation, their particular experiences on the street are replicated across the city and in similar cities. Liebow comments of the street corner that *"this inside world does not appear as a self-contained, self generating, self sustaining system or even subsystem with clear boundaries marking it off from the larger world around it. It is in continuous, intimate contact with the larger society - indeed it is an integral part of it"* (1967: 209). Liebow also makes the point that in the socially deprived community street corner activity reflected a *"way of trying to achieve many of the goals and values of the larger society"* (1967: 222). Whyte argues in his study of Boston, that although the social structure of these street corner groups does reflect wider patterns of urban belief and behaviour, the overall social organisation of the corner is detached from the mainstream of urban life. To move into the mainstream and adopt a more middle class lifestyle involves leaving behind, and being rejected by, your original street corner social group and all this implies.

Whilst many broader urban themes are replicated on the street, specific locations can only reflect a sub set of themes. Each street corner has to be analysed and understood in its own socio-economic context. For example Whyte in his account of Italian migrants in Cornerville showed that the corner is the location for young men to develop friendships, grow up and learn about society and their role within it. The corner group has a defined hierarchical structure with set roles, responsibilities and patterns of behaviour. Whyte comments that *"the corner gang, the racket and police organzations, the political organization, and now the social structure have been described .. in terms of a hierarchy of personal relations based upon a system of reciprocal obligations"* (1993: 272). This reflects an extremely high level of bonded social capital and as a socialisation process it may be more important that family. In the case of Cornerville some of these patterns of behaviour can be traced back to the rural origins of the people who migrated to the city. Whyte gives the example of the annual Festa of the patron saint. This event includes a Mass but is mainly comprised of band concerts and processions that follow a ritualised route and set activities, which reinforce hierarchies and gendered relationships.

Duneier suggests that analysis of life on the street can tell us about the informal life of people, the multiple uses of street, the limits of social control and the regulation of people, and the construction of decency. An important point made by Liebow is that what *appears* to be happening on the street is not necessarily the same as what is *actually* happening. We all read street situations through a semiotic process. Differences in interpretation will be affected by gender, age and other cultural positions. These conflicting interpretations also reflect our perception and understanding of the city and responses to street life. For example Liebow gives the example of a young male standing on a street corner that may to some people signify unemployment / criminal / drug dealer / underclass / personal threat. To others it might signify a man escaping poor housing, or meeting friends, or simply at leisure on a non working day.

Anderson (1995) argues in his study of Greenwich Village that for the majority of the population *"the public awareness is color-coded: white skin denotes civility, law abidingness, and trustworthiness, while black skin is strongly associated with poverty, crime, incivility and distrust"* (1995:332). These ideas are embedded in the local culture and affect how people behave on the street to reduce potential conflict. One aspect of this is based on time; when to go out on the street and when not to because other communities or strangers are at large. However, Anderson thinks this view, what he calls 'street etiquette' is really based on class and a reflection of the dominant power relations within the city. It could equally well be argued that it is also based on gender relations. Anderson also suggests there is a more sophisticated approach, 'street wisdom' based on a more insightful decoding of street life that incorporates a range of coping strategies to deal with unexpected encounters on the street. Goffman (1973) points out that these rules and procedures are largely internalised and unconscious until street conventions are violated

A further point relates to the social and economic level of the street corner. A corner in an economically disadvantages ethnic minority area will exhibit differences to that of wealthy shopping neighbourhood. The higher the economic status of the neighbourhood, the more likely women will be equal participants of street life. The parts of the city we know and understand are felt to be more comfortable and safer than the parts we don't. It is often claimed by the ruling elite that so called 'marginal' areas like Cornerville are chaotic and unorganised. However, the street does regulate itself through well developed norms of behaviour and informal patterns of community control. Whyte's study demonstrates that Cornerville has a well defined social structure within which everyone knows their place and the roles expected of them. Duneier comments on the number of people working as street vendors who had taught others how to set up their own street businesses and provide personal and social support for incomers to establish themselves locally. Duneier suggests that *"order must not be prized as an end in itself; rather, order is a by-product of a system of social regulation that is grounded in an understanding of city life in its uneasy complexity"* (2001: 316).

Jane Jacobs thought that the presence of people on the street made it feel safer and more vital. In Jacobs's phrase, there are many 'eyes upon the street'. She commented that *"a well used city street is apt to be a safe street ... the trust of a city street is formed over time from many, many little sidewalk contacts"* and that the public peace is kept not the police but by *"an intricate, almost unconscious, network of voluntary control and standards....enforced by the people themselves"* (1972). Duneier suggests this may not always be true, citing evidence that passers by watch crime take place but do not get involved. Perhaps a busy street is no ones particular responsibility. Again the answer may depend on the social mix of who is on the street. This can change during the course of a day. For example, in Greenwich Village during the day the streets are dominated by professional white residents. During the night and weekends it becomes, according to Duneier, a playground of Latino and Black hip-hop subculture.

The street corner also reflects the broader theme of social control and the domestication / privatisation of public space through architecture. That is changing the design of buildings and gating off otherwise public spaces so that there is nowhere to sit, sell goods or to sleep. Linked to this approach is surveillance. In the UK there are now more than 4 million CCTV cameras observing daily life along with private security guards who patrol shops and their immediate surroundings.

Duneier argues that the street and other public spaces in the USA are an increasingly regulated space and that this process can be seen as part of the so called 'broken windows' strategy (Wilson and Kelling 1982). The proponents of this strategy claim that crime increases in response to signs of neglect: such as a broken window in a street. This approaches leads to driving informal businesses, the homeless and potential criminal activity off the street through aggressive policing. For example *"in New York it is now illegal to wash a car's windshield without the drivers permission or panhadle by the doors of ATM's....in Santa Barbera and Seattle it is against the law to sit on the sidewalk"* (2001: 312). Davis (1998) has explored a similar process underway in Los Angeles where public space and residential streets are reconstituted as defendable private enclaves. Jacobs (1972) has commented extensively on the use of urban development to move so called 'marginal' people out of the city centre and control pedestrian movement. Jacobs writes that *"the forms in which money is used for city building – or withheld from use – are powerful instruments of city decline today"* (1972: 331)

The street corner can also reflect the different use of time and the attempt by city authorities to control time as a manifestation of competing power discourses. Low quotes Rutz (1992) who argues that *"a politics of time is concerned with the appropriation of the time of others, the institutionalization of a dominant time, and the legitimation of power by means of the control of time"* (1992:7). Low notes that this process is also commented upon by Rotenberg (1992) in his analysis of Viennese urban schedules, Lovell's (1992) New York study of street time and Gounis's (1992) documentation of the daily homeless shelter routine. Low makes the point that the control of time and space are critical, not only to people going about their daily routine, but also specifically to the survival of homeless people who live in the street (Hopper 1991). This debate about what is acceptable behaviour on the street can therefore be seen in terms of Foucaldian discourse: a conflict between the social views of those who attempt to plan and control the city and those who try to make their life on the street.

The street and the street corner can therefore offer some a full social life, for others it is perceived as a place to avoid. The street can also be seen as a secure conduit between gated residential communities and places of work or the place where residence and informal work are played out together. It is also about whether the city openly reflects the diverse culture of its population, or about normative concepts of public order being imposed from above. These contested positions will be worked out in each locality. Every street corner therefore, has its own character that will reflect to varying degrees some of the overall themes of urban life.

Case Study 2- Festivals

This case study explores how the analysis of urban festivals may contribute to an understanding of class, ethnic and gender relations. Initially, it explores some of the writing around the function of urban festivals. In particular it considers two ethnographic studies: Wazaki (1993) on the Daiminji festival in Kyoto, Japan and Cohen's (1993) study of the Notting Hill carnival in London.

Sadi (1980) traces the origin of contemporary festivals to smaller social gatherings built around music (and often dance), linked to ritual and mythological traditions. In a similar vein Martin (2001: 7) suggests festivals originated around themes of fertility, life and death and representations of power. Contemporary festivals may take many forms: some linked to tradition and / or religion, whilst other festivals are modern creations for cultural or commercial purposes. However, even the modern commercial festival may also function at a social and personal level, to reinforce a sense of place and feelings of belonging

Waterman (1998) writing about the cultural function of modern arts festivals suggests they are:

> *"a ubiquitous phenomenon in western culture... festivals transform landscape and place from being everyday settings into temporary environments, albeit with permanent identities, created by and for specific groups of people.*
>
> *.. as well as contributing to the cultural landscape, festivals provide a means whereby groups may attempt to maintain themselves culturally, while presenting opportunities to others to join that group. Festival is also an occasion for outsiders (sponsors, subsidizers) to endeavour to force or lead the group towards an acceptable course for the continuity of its culture". (1998: 55)*

Festivals can be perceived as reflecting high culture or popular culture. Either way they have wider cultural meaning. Festivals can be constructed by the ruling order as hegemonic devices to promote the dominant social discourse and instil feeling of nationalism or ethnic identity as a way of limiting social change.

Several writers (for example Cohen, 1982; Jackson, 1988; Western, 1992) argue that festivals allow marginalised groups to release their discontent through ritual. Often an inversion or ambivalence of social roles are acted out in the festival, but this is often promoted through fantasy (e.g. dressing up, imaginary characters, use of masks, humour) and is therefore removed from a direct link to social reality. The M11 link road protest in London (Butler 1996) was frequently conducted through street festivals and 'art events'. Superficially the festivals were a device to challenge the power of the government to push through the road, although this was really more symbolic activity than direct political confrontation. It is probable that the main function of the street festivals was to develop a sense of group cohesion amongst the protestors and their immediate supporters.

Martin (2001) provides the example of the Paris festival in 1848 that lead to confrontation and the overthrow of King Louis Philippe and the creation of the Second Republic. However, Martin argues this is a rare case of major social change being produced from a festival event. Although festival activity may promote a class or counter cultural political analysis, appear to challenge the social order and open up the prospect of social change, it is tolerated (possibly even supported) because of its short termed nature. Disorder is therefore allowed because order will reassert itself at the conclusion of the festival.

The idea of time and space is important for understanding the power of festivals. Giddens (1990, in Teather 2001) argues that the mobility of modern society stretches traditional communities and the sense of place. Traditional time linked to seasonal change has been replaced by 'clock time'. Festivals allow the stepping out of clock time and the recapturing of a sense of place and meaning. Writing of the Qingming and Chongyang (grave sweeping) festivals in Hong Kong, Teather notes that although 200 years old, these festivals remain relevant in times of rapid social change as a link to the past, ancestors, family and a sense of continuity and belonging. In addition they provide a base model for the formation and operation of new social relationships. In this sense festivals can be seen as a conservative force that links to tradition and as a form of resistance to, or co-existence with social change.

Many festivals, galas, fetes, etc operate on a small local scale. However, these events may be of major significance for the local community in which they take place. They can provide a 'charter' (Malinowski) that legitimises current actions. Festivals often function to reinforce the symbolic boundary of the community through who is included or excluded. As Waterman notes "*many arts festivals can and do exclude or include on the basis of ethnicity or class, and perhaps gender or race, in ways that range from the sophisticated to the crude, the transparent to the tacit*". (1998: 67)

As an ethnographic example of these processes, Wazaki (1993) writes about the Daiminji festival in Kyoto. Taking place annually in August, the festival is a mixture of Bon ceremony, ancestor worship and fete. Participation in the festival activities can be at various levels depending on the activity. For example, the dedication of woodsticks is an open event that symbolises a universal following based on the idea of peace. Wazaki notes that not only does the festival have a collective function, but also provides a mechanism for individuals to make sense of their individuality and self identity in an otherwise alienating urban environment. In an expanding urban setting, traditional ties through kinship are weakened and people fall back on ideas of ethnicity to sustain social relationships. This is true for the traditional 22 'ritual' families that are charged with conducting the festival, as well as incomers to the area.

Wazaki identifies how the festival has responded to the growth of the city by developing four categories of participants: households still residing in the original community, households that have moved out but still have links back to the festival, newcomers accepted by the 'old timers' and incomers who chose to participate. As membership has broadened other folklore and social groupings have been incorporated. This broadening out of membership serves to maintain the festival and to provide a social mechanism for developing new relationships. In doing so the community is shown to be able to sustain its relevance by evolving over time and in response to changing social conditions.

As Cohen argues above symbolism and ritual are required to give meaning to community. The ritual of the festival also creates an overlay of meaning on the physical place of the city. Wazaki comments that: "*by creating the story of 'a city as a whole' which the inhabitants can share with each other, they cement their mutual belonging*" (1993: 138). According to Wazaki there are three levels of activity within the festival. Firstly, a religious function related to

Bon, undertaken in each local community according to heir specific tradition. Secondly, shared activities between communities (and therefore across boundaries). Tensions between communities are eased by the ritual process of coming together. Thirdly, there is a series of wider commercial and tourist events linked by various degrees of legitimacy to the festival.

Linking these three events is the need of individuals to give meaning to their lives. This is achieved by finding individual satisfaction through shared ritual activity. Wazaki comments *"almost all Kyoto households extinguish their house lights in response to the endeavour of the Daimonji community. It is an act which unites the ritual's performers and spectators of the festival as an urban community ... at this level the distinction between self and others is dissolved... self is projected onto a common horizon, transcending individual subjectivity and indicating coexistence"* (1993: 145). By drawing on tradition the Daiminji festival, like the grave sweeping festival, reinforces self identity and what this means in terms of traditional culture and belief, gender and social roles.

Cohen (1993) in writing about the Notting Hill Carnival identifies its origin as an attempt to create a multi racial event based on a traditional English rural working class fair. The model for such fairs dates back at least to Catholic pre-Lenten festivals, if not to the pre Christian era. Cohen describes such carnivals being *"characterised by revelry, playfulness and overindulgence in eating, drinking and sex, culminating in ... massive street processions by masqued individuals.. playing music or ecstatically dancing"* (1993:3).

Since the Carnival started in 1966, there has been the creation of a contested mythical history. Some people claiming the Carnival is African in origin, others that its dates from the ending of British slavery in 1834, and therefore a symbol of Black liberation. At various times, it has been, or claimed to be a non political multicultural event, a front for Black politics, a front for militant campaigning against corrupt landlords, a front for criminality, an anti racist event or a mainly white tourist event. In some ways the Carnival can be used by individuals and communities for it to be whatever they need it to be.

According to Cohen local Afro-Caribbean residents also see the festival as representing 'liberated space' from an otherwise implicitly racist society. He argues that for Afro-Caribbean's music is the dominant form of cultural expression. As the carnival is predominately a musical event (dance and the procession being essentially supporting activities), it is felt to be an expression of the essence of Afro-Caribbean life in the UK, linking back to its cultural origins in the Caribbean. In doing so it enables the sub cultures from the various Caribbean islands (that have diverse colonial and ethnic histories) to be experienced as a single entity. This creates a stronger and more integrated community.

Notting Hill has a history of overt racism. In this context it is necessary for the Afro-Caribbean population to form associations and to develop social processes that resist racism, empowers local community and help sustain and define the position of the self with regard to ethnicity and gender. Cohen points out that the tradition in the Caribbean is for looser communalist organisations linked to religion rather than tighter and more formal organisations. The loose pattern of conjugal relationships within the Afro-Caribbean community and the extensive social networks this creates also promotes communal organisation. But communal organisations tend to focus more on the social and the informal than organisation and getting things done. In this context the Carnival became the main form for bringing people together and building cultural identity.

The meaning of the Carnival though, is transmitted back to the wider community through communal organisations and other groupings, in a variety of ways depending on its meaning for them. Cohen refers to Abercrombie (1980) in seeing this process as the 'apparatus of transmission'. He gives the example of transmission through *"sound system sessions, poetry reading sessions, calypso performances, etc"* (1993:152). This process allows exploration of meaning through the continual reinterpretation of local events. In turn this helps build identity around race, ethnicity, gender, class or however the group or community concerned defines itself.

Cohen sees the Carnival as both a political and a cultural movement. In one sense it is political because it involves the local state and the police in making decisions about supporting or opposing an event that at times has involved criminality, local political action, expression of Black militancy and in 1976 mass violence. In another sense it is political because art and culture are a contested area of hegemony. In a Foucauldian sense it is about whose discourse will dominate. The attempt to make the carnival a depoliticised tourist event is a reflection of the dominant capitalist hegemony attempting to both neutralise the Carnival and exploit it for commercial ends. The local community's resistance to such a change could be seen as a counter hegemonic activity (a similar process has been working out with the Daiminji festival).

In conclusion, festivals contribute to help individuals and communities define themselves and the world. Depending on the nature of the festival it may promote a conservative world view resisting social change, a safety valve for discontent or a mechanism for the promotion of change. Festivals also function symbolically to reinforce notions of community. In doing so, they build upon existing socially constructed identities, sustain and promote community myths and reinforce local conceptions of gender and ethnicity.

Summary

In this chapter we have suggested:

- that community is a symbolic entity that resides in the minds of its members
- that communities have boundaries which are reinforced by ritual activities
- that urban areas are artificially divided up in geographical units for administrative purposes, and that these units may bear little relationship to real communities
- that to understand urban communities we need a sophisticated understanding of the economic and social processes at play
- these process operate as flows of information between networks, organisations and institutions
- the working of these processes can lead to a range of conflicts
- effective community work process is based on understanding how these processes and power relationships work

Further Reading

The seminal work on urban life is Jane Jacobs **The Death and Life of Great American Cities**, Harmondsworth: Penguin. This should be followed by the Mike Davis's **The Ecology of Fear: Los Angeles and the Imagination of Disaster,** New York: Henry Holt and his recent book, **Dead Cities and Other Tales,** New York: The New Press.

7

Underlying Perspectives: Organising for Change

"Not to be on the side of the poor and oppressed, is not to be neutral, but to be on the side of the rich and powerful" Paulo Freire

"I know of no safer depository of the ultimate powers of society but the people themselves". Thomas Jefferson

Aims of this chapter

The chapter starts with a discussion towards developing a revised model of community work practice that encompasses ideas from the forgoing chapters. We then consider the use of participatory methods, organisational strategies and power, to build powerful community organisations. And in the light of this reflect on capacity building, social capital and leadership

Towards a new community work model

We need to do better in the communities in which we work. We need to improve our understanding of the diverse threads of globalisation and capitalism and think through what this means for practice. It is time for a revised flexible community work model. Such a model can only be produced by analysis and discussion amongst workers themselves. All I attempt here is to make some tentative drawing together of ideas and suggest some possible ways forward.

During 1996 Sheela Patel Director of SPARC a NGO in Mumbai, India made a study tour of the UK. Her report (Patel 1997) is a synthesis of Indian and UK experience. In particular she identifies a number of problematic practice areas. In her view the bid culture has come to dominate. Community projects are driven by short term funding regimes at the expense of developing a long term strategy. More importantly, the objectives of community organisations are shaped by where funding is available rather than local needs. I am sure most community workers will, if they are honest, agree with this analysis. Patel made a number of specific points:

- Funding goes to the worst areas. There is therefore a disincentive for communities to break out of the worst levels of deprivation. Success leads to the loss of funding; a reworking of the classic poverty trap.
- Community development needs to move beyond service delivery. Real changes only come through changing the ways things are and not simply plugging the gaps.
- The emphasis on delivering service ratter than enabling individuals and communities lead to increasing dependency.
- Community representation and leadership is often limited, under resourced, untrained and marginalised.
- Value for money could be improved from the more direct involvement and employment of local people rather than increased employment of professionals.
- The issues around volunteerism need to be explored. How can exploitation of volunteers be prevented? How can more men and young people be encouraged to participate?
- The safety net of the welfare state has created a dependency mind set; the feeling that the solution to problems will come from elsewhere rather than from personal responsibility and action.

Patel goes on to suggest a new model for sustaining community development. This suggested revision of practice she calls 'A New Focus' and contrasts it with the 'traditional approach'.

	Traditional Approach	A New Focus
1. Mode	Service delivery	Solution oriented
2. Time Scale	Short term (3 to 5 years)	Long term (10 years +)
3. Style	Pragmatic and opportunistic	Strategic
4. Characteristics	Relief via projects	Regeneration via processes
5. Key Partners	Government and NGO's	NGO's and the local community
6. Project Design	Vertical	Horizontal
7. Project Bias	Pro-professional	Pro-poor

(from Patel 1997 p8)

As a model of a possible way forward this has a lot to commend it. The SRB's and Social Inclusion Partnerships have, for example, taken in the longer time scale required for fundamental change to take place in communities. However, the thrust of regeneration work in the UK is still towards improved service delivery with local groups responding pragmatically according to funding criteria. The process of rebuilding and genuinely empowering the community is largely ignored. Local and national government agencies are still dominant, power resides at the top and the whole process is effective run by professionals.

For community work practice to more effective it needs to adopt the 'New Focus' and become more centred on strategic work with communities. It has to help identify and respond to needs and rights driven agendas developed at the local level. In doing so it has to shift the balance of concern from the social planning agenda to that of the poor. More importance must be placed on the process of the work without losing site of the product. The difficulties of doing this should not be underestimated while community work continues to be under the hegemony of the state. The old community work debates on how to work against the state whilst being funded by it are still pertinent. However, the shift of community work towards better responding to local needs has to be accomplished. This does not necessarily mean continued opposition to government funded agencies or the rejection of partnership. Rather, it is about community workers developing some freedom of manoeuvre in order to be able to respond to local needs and issues.

We may also add to the 'New Focus' the insight from Routledge (1997) about the levels in which campaigning and development activity takes place. Traditionally community development work has had a local focus between community based groups and usually the local state. Even large scale national campaigning, for example against the Poll Tax used traditional forms of protest developed from trade union activity to oppose national government policy.

The new developments concern campaigning that exists primarily in 'media space'. Routledge is correct to see this as an aspect of postmodern politics. It is an activity that Naomi Klein discusses in a global context in her books No Logo and Fences and Windows where campaigns are run through the Internet, using web sites to promote and discuss the issue. Email, telephone, video and use of the news media are the main vehicle for promoting the campaign. The traditional tactics of putting people on the street to protest becomes an adjunct to using the media, rather than as the prime form of activity in itself. Routledge quotes the following to illustrate the point:

> "The more we get on TV the better. Were trying to use TV as a media to get people off their arses, to get them angry, and get them involved" Jake, Pollok Free State

> "A two minute take is what the public perceives the struggle to be about, so for those two minutes it is important to manipulate reality as you wish to see it represented" Lindsay, Earth First

These techniques have been pioneered by many in the environmental movement and have now taken on global significance: for example the recent Live 8 campaign against international debt. Used properly, campaigning in media space can have an impact far beyond that possible by traditional means.

Community work is essentially about promoting a process committed to community empowerment. It is true that empowerment is a much contested concept and that its vagueness has led to many practitioners abandoning it all together. This is a mistake. Forrest (1999) provides a useful discussion on empowerment and argues for:

> *"an understanding of the contest taking place over empowerment and how the consciousness of control, participation, a shared vision, self organised leadership and ownership can become elements of a liberatory empowerment process will underpin praxis. This is conscientised empowerment"*

In Monitoring and Evaluation of Community Development in Northern Ireland (Barr, Hashagen, Purcell 1996) we defined the promotion of community empowerment as the core process of community development. Empowerment, in our view, comprises four *key dimensions*. To these a fifth dimension has been added (Purcell 2004)

1. Personal empowerment
2. Positive action
3. Development of community organisations
4. Power relationships and participation.
5. Leadership

These five dimensions can be sub divided to give a clearer identity to the purpose of the community development process. Whilst wishing to avoid crude reductionism, it is possible to use the criteria in appendix 5 as a checklist for practice. This checklist provides a mechanism for ensuring that the core perspectives are included in our work. Furthermore, this close definition of what our work is trying to achieve enables us to ensure that we have clarity of purpose and direction and that we are committed to specific outcomes.

Implemented properly this empowerment process also leads to real outcomes in terms of more confident, knowledgeable and skilled individuals, raised awareness of critical issues, the development of powerful community organisations with some political clout.

But this is not the sole purpose of development. The fundamental aim is to improve the quality of life within the community on a sustainable basis. Far too many community projects are dependent upon the continued presence of paid workers and external funding. Sustainability of the work has to be an integral in most situations.

The NGO Habitat II conference further defined quality of life in terms of sustainability:

- Social sustainability
- Sustainable economics
- Sustainable livelihood
- Physical sustainability
- Sustainable culture

Such improvements therefore can take many forms depending upon local circumstances but are likely to include:

- Economic gains – around employment, extra resources spent in the community and anti poverty strategies
- Social gains – improved quality and access to education, health care, housing and welfare services
- Environmental improvements
- Safer community

The diagram in appendix 1 provides an overview of the community development process. Inputs to the process of empowerment may come from agencies outside the community and / or from agencies and local organisations which are part of the community themselves. It is important to remember that inputs include the activities of local people, paid and unpaid, as well as the use of physical resources and money.

The *underpinning perspectives* informs *how* the work is to be done (e.g.: with respect to a feminist analysis, identification of local needs, social and economic context, rights and values, etc).

The *process* of community development is the key part of promoting empowerment. The *5 key dimensions* providing the check list of activities which helps identify *what* is to be done (e.g.: activities to promote personal empowerment, positive action etc.). Essential to the successful development of the empowerment process is basing the work on the Freirian reflection – vision – planning – action cycle and understanding that community development work is fundamentally and educational activity both for the individuals concerned and the community organisation as a whole.

The outputs and outcomes help us to decide what we are trying to produce as a result of our work. Outputs are things over which we have direct control and may be split into two categories: *specific outputs* such as new buildings and activities, and *capital outputs* such as human, economic and social capital.

Outcomes are larger scale results over which we, as community workers may have some influence but not control; for example women gaining qualifications and employment as a result of an information service. By constantly checking the results of our work against our planned outputs and outcomes we know how well the working is going and whether we need to change our approach.

Making participation work

Participation is another of the key words of community development that is seldom defined and often misused. The concept of participation is ideologically based and related to the use and/or distribution of power.

All mainstream political parties the libertarian and new right factions favour participation. Indeed the whole partnership approach is based on a stated commitment to community participation. Arguments in favour of participation include the belief that free individuals have the 'right' to be actively involved in decisions and processes that affect their lives. This is the key point. Participation is a right it is not a favour to be granted by council or government officials. Furthermore, decisions made by the people concerned are often more realistic and effective than those made by bureaucrats. And that personal growth takes place from the experience of being involved in participative processes.

The alternative, hard left view (see for example, Coit 1978) is that participation creates a myth that we live in a classless society. In doing so it diverts potential militant action into negotiation. This results in watering down of demands and possible gains for working class communities. In addition the community 'representatives' who sit on participative bodies either form another elite group above the local community, or leads to the siphoning off of working class leadership. Other left writers, for example Cockburn (1997) accept the dangers of co-option through participation strategies but point out real gains for working class communities that can be made this way.

Participation by members of the community is essential to community development. The common view is that the degree of active participation is in decline. This is often attributed to people being apathetic. However, blaming people for being apathetic by failing to do what the community worker wants them to do is at best naïve, at worst arrogant. We need a more analytical understanding of why people do or do not participate in community affairs.

Ohio State University have identified reason why citizens may become involved in community activity. This is when people:

- See positive benefits to be gained from the activity
- Have an appropriate organisational structure available to them for expressing their interests
- See some aspect of their way of life threatened
- Feel committed to be supportive of the activity
- Have better knowledge of an issue or situation
- Feel comfortable in the group

People will become involved if the community work job is being done properly. Often people do not participate, not due to apathy, but due to the workers misidentifying the issues or even trying to tie local people into the worker or agency's own agenda. Knowledge is also important and this is best developed through reflective discussion. People need to make the link between the issue and their own situation. Freire gives us ways of enabling these connections to be made. Simply distributing leaflets and expecting people to respond is nothing more than lazy practice. If you want people involved you have to talk with them.

The Ohio documents also suggest ways in which participation can be increased:

- Stressing the benefits of participation
- Organising or identifying appropriate groups receptive to citizen input
- Helping citizens find positive ways to respond to threatening situations

- Stressing obligations each of us have towards community improvement
- Providing citizens with better knowledge on issues and opportunities
- Helping participants feel comfortable within the development group.

Some of this simply comes down to good groupwork practice which will be discussed below.

There is no doubt that participative bodies themselves have often failed to contribute much more than a public relations gloss. However, properly understood and used, participation is the cornerstone of development activities. The Community Workers Cooperative (1997) has outlined what participation is and is not:

Participation is	Participation is not
• A process which empowers people	• Giving information and assuming it is enough
• Active involvement of people	• Asking people what they think and then disregarding it
• Process which enables people to develop skills, confidence and knowledge	• Deciding what is 'good' for people
• Process which is deliberately chosen and resources	• A cheaper and quicker alternative to centralised planning
• Process which requires effort and time	• Involving people in planning but excluding then from implementation and monitoring
• Process which targets those who are marginalised and excluded	• Involving people in activities without prior involvement in planning
• Promotes active involvement of end beneficiaries and users	• Just contact the visible mainstream groups without targeting the marginalised and excluded
• Power sharing and negotiation between stakeholders	
• Based on the articulation of interests	
• Underpinned by a commitment to eliminating exclusion and inequality	

The classic text on participation comes from Arnstein (1969). She saw a wide range of activities being carried out under the name of participation. In Arnstein's views the goal was for citizen participation. She defined this as:

> *"the redistribution of power that enables the have-not citizens, presently excluded from the political and economic processes, to be deliberately included in the future. It is the strategy by which the have-nots join in determining how information is shared, goals and policies are set, tax resources are allocated, programmes are operated, and benefits like contracts and patronage are parcelled out. In short it is the means by which they can induce significant reform which enables them to share in the benefits of an affluent society"*

Arnstein identified 8 hierarchical steps on a ladder of participation.

Level	Type of Participation	Nature of the Experience
8	**Citizen Control**	Degrees of Citizen Power
7	**Delegated Power**	"
6	**Partnership**	"
5	**Placation**	Degrees of Tokenism
4	**Consultation**	"
3	**Informing**	"
2	**Therapy**	Non Participation
1	**Manipulation**	"

Whatever it may be called activities at levels 1 and 2 are clearly not participation. These levels are characterised by attempts at public relations to gain support, through leaflets and the media, for decisions that already have been made. Levels 3, 4 and 5 involve a greater degree of citizen involvement but the purpose of the exercise is mostly to inform citizens through leaflets and public meetings, rather than effectively engage then in a real debate about decision making. At levels 6, 7 and 8 citizens have either equal power with government bodies (level 6) or have decisions delegated to then (level 7). At the top level citizens have taken absolute control over the service or resources in question.

Petty (1994) quoted in Blackburn and Holland has developed a useful typology of participation from perspective of local people. He sees participation as operating at 7 levels:

Level	Attributes
7. Self mobilisation	People take the initiative themselves – this may or may not challenge existing distributions of power
6. Interactive participation	People participate in the formation of joint plans which lead to action. Some control involved over local services and resources
5. Functional participation	People form groups to meet objectives predetermined by others e.g. forming a steering group for a project planned and funded by an outside agency
4. Participation by material incentive	People participate by contributing resources e.g. undertaking a local survey, expecting in return material improvements. Usually, results do not meet local expectations.
3. Participation by consultation	External people discuss proposals with the community, but the decision on how to proceed is taken externally
2. Participation in information giving	Participation is based on answering questions but do not have an opportunity to discuss or check the findings
1. Passive participation	People being told what is going to happen, or has happened. Information being shared is owned by officials

(adapted from Petty 1994)

Levels 1 to 3 are clearly just tokenism and should be avoided by all development workers. Sadly, levels 4 and 5 are reflected in much current community work practice where the agenda for development lies with external agencies. Level 6 reflects the current model for much regeneration and social inclusion work. The critical question here is how far local people are equals in the process. Level 7 is the goal which is often shied away from by community workers.

Wilcox (1995) takes the opposite perspective and writes from the viewpoint of social planners. He identifies five levels or participation. This is based on Arnstein but is more concerned with current modes of working in the UK. His five levels include the tokenistic levels of *Information* and *Consultation*. He then identifies levels of partnership as - *Deciding Together – Acting Together – Supporting Independent Community Initiatives.* This is a useful subdivision of Arnstein's partnership level. There are crucial differences between partners who are only involved in deciding on a course of action, to those involved in implementing action. The failure to be clear about this difference can lead to confusion and mistrust in partnerships. However, it requires an understanding of the balance of power within the partnership to be an effective model. For example, do we all decide together equally or do some have more influence in decision making than others?

These typologies raise a number of crucial points. There is a difference between having a formal place on a board or organisation and having the skills, knowledge and resources to be able to effectively use the place. If we are serious about making participation work then it is essential to give the time, resources and support to community representatives so they are equipped to do the job. A further dimension is the importance of ensuring that marginalised groups are included in participatory processes. It is easy to 'give' places to established representatives from well known community groups. It is less easy, but essential, to ensure that women, Black and ethnic minorities, young people, etc are effectively involved. The location and timing of meetings, provision of crèche facilities and travelling expenses are all basic factors that have to be taken into account to support meaningful participation.

Even if full participation cannot be achieved there may be merit in supporting limited participation – as long as this is the basis of further developmental work and not simply justifying tokenism. Smith (1998) argues that in developing countries limited participation does assist communities. He identifies five forms of benefit, which he terms utilisation, contributions, enlistment, co-operation and consultation.

Utilisation concerns the improved take up of services. This argues Smith, contributes to empowerment as people may become materially better off or start using resources that can be the basis for future development. Contribution is the other side of utilisation where local resources (often mostly labour power) are used to run or create a new service. Such a development can lead to the provision of a resource that otherwise would not be available to the community and perhaps the community management of services.

Enlistment is the training of volunteers to work in the community as lay professionals. Community health services are the usual example for the developing world. Although in the west credit and money advice may be a better example. The mobilisation of local unpaid workers can have a 'knock on' effect through shaping services to local needs and providing role models for others to become active in their community.

Co-operation is the acknowledgement that for many projects success is unlikely without at least the passive support of the local community. Gaining such support can be the first step to greater involvement and influence by the community. The next step is consultation. Although low on Arnstein's ladder, consultation provides an opening for the community to make an impact of services to their community.

For community workers the basic questions to be considered for promoting participation are:

- Who participates – from which constituencies
- How do we ensure marginalised groups are included
- In what processes
- How de we ensure all stakeholders support the agreed process
- What are the support requirements – time, resources, access to information, crèche etc.
- Through which organisational forms
- With what degree of power (where on Arnsteins ladder is this, where does the community want it to be?)

Organising for community work

Every worker and community leader prides themselves on their ability to make things happen and to organise activity. However, this is often a one dimensional activity. Case studies show workers repeating methods of organising regardless of the situation. Just because an approach has worked before does not mean that it will work in every situation. To be effective workers need to have an adaptable theory of organisation, a tool kit of methods and a professional approach to supporting community organisations and promoting change. As Alinsky points out a social problem becomes an issue to be won *only* when there is an organisation capable of fighting it. A community that is not organised is simply a community suffering. Building an organisation is more than printing leaflets, calling meetings and creating steering committees. It is hard work and depends upon the application of theory according to the local situation.

Gramsci argues through his writing on hegemony *that all aspects of social reality are dominated by or supportive of a single class* (quoted in Mayo 1999). He goes on to argue that people working for social transformation have to engage in what he calls a 'war of position' relating to social organisations and cultural influence. Unless community organisations are prepared, when required, to resort to campaigning and conflict there is little chance for effective shifts of power at the local level and sustainable increases in the level of community empowerment.

The realpolitik of community work means that the 'war of position' has to be developed thoughtfully and creatively. In many instances communities have to promote constructive engagement with other power holders. As Saul Alinsky said *"compromise always puts you ahead of where you started"*. Deprived communities are usually in a very weak position and direct confrontation with government agencies is often unlikely to be successful. Working from a position of continuing opposition therefore will only alienate possible allies and lead to a culture of continual defeat for the community. To quote from Sun Tzu's Art of War, *"to win without fighting is best"* and the resort to confrontational strategies should be a considered last resort.

Some Marxists oppose the idea of constructive engagement on the basis that it diverts attention and energy away from the real structural issues affecting society. However, the idea of constructive engagement is based on the idea of the community identifying its own needs and building its organisational strength. It accepts the need for joint working with government and compromise and that proposed change has to be realistic, but allows for range of tactics including confrontation when required. Other Marxists and postmodernist radicals tend to support constructive engagement as its helps to build a 'culture of opposition' from which further gains and social change can be built.

In the context of constructive engagement, Barry Checkoway (1995) identifies six strategies of community change. He defines them as:

- Mass Mobilisation around key emotive issues. This was the strategy employed by Ghandi and Martin Luther King
- Social Action through building powerful organisations at the community level as described by Saul Alinsky
- Citizen Participation through involving local communities with social planning and service delivery organisations
- Public Advocacy through using the systems of representative democracy
- Popular Education, based on the work of Paulo Freire which seeks to help people to develop a critical consciousness by reflecting on their current situation
- Local Service Development where communities take control of and provide their own local services.

The implementation of any of these strategies requires the building of an organisation. One way to assist us with developing an effective organisation is to adapt from management theory a 'natural organisation' approach. Generally, natural organisations have three components:

1. they serve a clearly defined purpose
2. they are based on the collection and interpretation of information which provides the basis for action and
3. they are totally flexible and adaptable to changing circumstances

The purpose of community work has been outlined above. The community worker and community organisation should be able to clearly express what they are trying to specifically achieve. This needs to be in terms of specific outputs and outcomes and not vague generalisations like 'more facilities for children' or 'a better environment'.

The struggle for success is largely based upon changing the perception, opinions and actions by politicians, local government and other agency officials of; the local community, its needs, the power and validity of its organisations, an often vague sense of social justice as well as personal self interest. Community work wins or loses on its ability to change the perceptions of these people to coincide with the interests of the local community. Foucault's adage that *'knowledge is power'* could be developed to *'those who have knowledge of their opponents and who control the nature and flow of information have power'*.

At this point many readers may object to the idea of controlling information. Is this manipulation if not censorship? The answer to this is that information is not neutral and you need to promote information that supports your position and be less open with information that undermines it.

For example, a residents group may be campaigning for local environmental improvements. In doing so the group will deploy arguments about why the environment needs to be improved, why money should be spent on this area, claim that needs are greater in this community than elsewhere, that the residents group have the support of the local community in arguing this position and that in general the group know what they are talking about.

The residents group are not going to point out that their AGM was yet again poorly attended, that the management committee has vacancies, that the office bearers have been unchanged for years, that their playscheme grant has not yet been accounted for and that Christmas social programme for the elderly was a catalogue of organisational errors.

As Alinsky reminds us most situations are in reality 52:48 for and against and nobody is going to commit themselves to a position for the sake of 4%. If you want to win you have to make your position 100:0.

Success is based upon gathering, interpreting and using information to identify and exploit the weaknesses of the opposition whilst manoeuvring away from their strengths. We should consider everything before taking action. There is no substitute for effective analysis and planning. Case studies show that this is also true of effective community work practice. Although, many case studies also show communities based campaigns marching into action with plans based on little information, or in some cases in direct contradiction to the information at hand.

Case studies on community activity also suggest that much of the high failure rate in community work is due to inflexible approaches. This rigidity is partly due to insufficient information and understanding of what the alternative options might be as well as insecurity of trying new approaches.

Modern management theory sees an effective organisation as a fluid entity committed to a process of continuous change to continually improve its performance. Organisations must be able to adapt according to changes in circumstances. Potentially, community based organisations are ideally suited to respond in this way. However, the traditional approach to community work in Britain is based upon a committee system with regular meetings very much like that of a local government body. For small community based organisations to work this way is not only unnecessary but also counterproductive. The advantages of being is small is the ability to be flexible. Yet the majority of community organisations, in Britain at least, throw away this advantage.

Success depends upon the application of a number of factors:

You are in competition. This is not about competition for the sake of it. It means that community workers and leaders need to recognise they are in competition for scarce resources. The reality is that for your community to win some other community will miss out. You should not embark on campaigns for poorly thought out projects or for resources you do not really need. Neither should you act out of emotion – the estate down the road has a new community centre so we want one too, or we don't like the nearby traveller's camp so we want it out – these are not reason for taking action.

Leadership determines success. What is leadership in the context of community organisations? Many community workers and community organisations reject the notion of leadership. To them it implies being dictatorial and hierarchical. Indeed we all have the memories of organisations who have been 'led' ineffectively and aggressively by a single individual for many years. It is weakness in leadership that leads to failure. This is defined as; recklessness, timidity, emotionalism, egoism and courting popularity.

The dictionary definition of leadership is *the position or office of a leader*, but more meaningfully it is also talks about the *capacity or ability to lead*, that leadership can be based on a *group of leaders,* and that it involves both *guidance and direction of activities.* Community leadership therefore is not about individual power; rather it is an (often small) group of people with the knowledge and skills to take an organisation forward. Without effective leadership an organisation has no future. Like most skills, leadership has to be learnt through reflection on experience. It is one of the roles of a community worker to develop effective leadership within community organisations.

What then are the characteristics of good leadership? It can include; self discipline, a sense of purpose, commitment to meeting the needs of the community, owning personal actions and decisions, constantly improving knowledge and learning from experience, working co-operatively with other and leading by example.

Be effective. The only point of being involved in the community is to promote personal and collective change. Achieving change is built upon effective planning. This in turn is based upon acquiring and assessing accurate information. Taking action follows the planning stage. We can contrast this with 'mindless activism' where people are very busy rushing from one meeting to the next, but without any sense of purpose or objectives. Effectiveness is based on the quality and purpose of your action not the quantity of activity.

Prepare for the worst. Murphy's Law says that if it can go wrong, it will! This is something to be always kept in mind. To avoid things going wrong it is best to keep plans and actions simple, do not be over ambitious and do not tackle projects where you do not have the capacity or resources to succeed.

There are many community work campaigns that have been run against impossible odds on matters of principle. Community based campaigns against new laws, or by small groups against large local authorities are examples. Sometimes these campaigns can be won, the Poll Tax in Scotland is an example, but usually this is due to mass political pressure rather than simply through local community action. With some of the community groups I have worked with, it appears that they go into battle expecting defeat as if to prove how unjust the world is and how strong their principles are. This is nothing more than empty posturing and does the local community a great disservice. If you are not confident of achieving your goals then do not start the campaign.

Take your opportunities. Speed and innovation are the keys to success. Most organisations the community tries to organise against are large, bureaucratic and slow. The community's advantage is smallness and the potential to respond quickly to opportunities. Do not throw this away by waiting for the next monthly meeting to make a decision.

Make people commit themselves. It is important to know who supports you and who does not. People and organisations are either committed to your side or not. There should be no grey areas here. People are motivated by a number of factors; the importance of the issue (this depends on how you present it), expectation that you will win, personal interest (or family, community, career), enjoyment and fun. This is legitimate; the idea that community activity must involve personal suffering, boredom and only be hard work is another practice myth. If we treat people with respect and train them well the success will come our way.

Be creative. When campaigning think and act creatively. Nothing fails more quickly than doing the same old things in predictable ways. Creativity does not require genius. It is based on learning from experience, doing simple things better trying new ideas and approaches and aiming to improve all the time.

Train for action. When reviewing case studies of community organisations, it is astounding to see how local people are expected to manage resources, develop services, undertake campaigns and constantly put themselves in challenging situations with little or no preparation. It is to the credit of community leaders that they constantly subject themselves to these pressures with little real support. However, without adequate preparation it is hardly surprising therefore that so much community activity is unproductive.

In my experience many local leaders place a low value on training. This is usually the result of their poor experience of schooling and previous courses. Training is often boring and irrelevant. How often is it said that the best part of the training course was the informal conversation in the coffee breaks! There is also often a difference between effective training and local capacity building programmes. Many of these programmes are driven by a top down analysis of what local people need to know in order to fit into the local partnership structure. Sometimes capacity programmes ask people what they want to learn, but unless this is linked to a reflective process of identifying community needs it is unlikely to be meaningful.

Effective training is about helping people acquire knowledge and skills to undertake tasks, which they have defined as important. To be successful training needs to be focused, well structured, participative and appropriate for the audience. Most of all it has to be an enjoyable experience.

Create surprise. Sun Tzu in the Art of War said *"what does it matter if the enemy has greater resources? If I control the situation, he cannot use them"*. In essence this sums up effective organisation; analyse the situation, see the opportunity, plan for action, respond with the unexpected, do it well.

Understanding and using power

It is impossible to effectively practice community work without understanding power. But what do we mean by power? In one sense it is simply the *motivation and capacity to act, to make changes and to influence the actions of others.* Foucault explains how power is related to knowledge and ideas. Power comes from knowing what you want and how to achieve it. Many community workers think that having power is a bad thing. However, power in itself is neither good nor bad, it is what people do with power that is the problem. Power can be indeed be destructive. However, used differently it can also be productive. It can also be integrative, that is used to create organisations, inspire loyalty and commitment to a cause. Community workers need to understand the nature of power, who has it, how it is used and how might it be used for the benefit of the community. This latter point takes us back to the principles of openness and accountability.

Foucault argues that power is not, as many people think, just the use of physical force. Power is the dynamic that determines the relationship between people. This is an obvious point. How often are we physically made to do something? The majority of the time we do things because we accept the authority (power) of somebody else. Thus we voluntarily limit our actions because we either accept the power of another person or because we ascribe power to them. Freire describes these as boundary situations where we control ourselves because of our conditioning by outside forces.

Sometimes power is used directly say, between a policeman and a speeding motorist. Other times it operates through hegemony. As know from Gramsci the state and the dominant social groups in society maintain their power through the education system and the media who promote a message of what is to be seen as normal and acceptable. Hegemony also operates at a local level and within communities. Although hegemony works because people accept the status quo, coercive power (the use of force) is often applied when this acceptance by the populace starts to collapse. The miners strike is the classic example in the UK.

Power may be used formally via rank or title, such as policeman. Or it may be based upon informal relationships. In the community setting it is essential to know who the real power holders are. As Alinsky pointed out those with powerful titles might not really be the ones who operate power. For example, the leader of the local council is theoretically the most powerful person in the council structure. However, it may be senior managers who are seldom seen and who are unknown to the general public who hold and exert the real power in the council.

In the community many people have the potential for power, in that they can control resources (volunteers, community activists and their activities). The role of the community worker is to identify who are, and who may become, powerful leaders in the community and work with them to this end. In doing so it is necessary to take account of divisions within the community based on area of residence, age, gender, religion and ethnicity. Community leaders often have their power limited by setting. For example an individual may be leader in terms of housing issues but his views are not respected on other community matters. Community workers need to understand the reality of these situations and not simply ascribe power in the community beyond its real boundaries. Whilst it is preferable to unite a community this may only happen when each part of the community is united and can join together as equals. Sometimes the existing leadership in the community may be a barrier, perhaps due to inefficiency or deference to the local council.

There are a number of well tried methods for understanding power. Firstly, the *'positional method'* is based upon analysing who holds the key positions in formal situations. However, it is important to be clear which people actually use their power and those who are simply figureheads. Secondly, the *'reputational method'* identifies people who have power in a more informal sense. Usually, their power is based upon their knowledge and the acceptance of others rather than a formal position or title. Thirdly, the *'decisional method'* can be used to see who actually made the key decision on a key issue. Fourthly, the *'social participation method'* can be used to identify who is seen to hold power informally within the community.

Finally, the use of power seldom leads to a confrontation. Usually it is about convincing power holders to do something else in the interests of the community. This may be achieved through direct persuasion or through the use of the media and public events. Sometimes it comes from giving the illusion that the community is powerful and will take action if its demands are not met. Alinsky points out that the threat of taking action is often more powerful than the action itself. Ultimately, conflict may arise but the community needs to make a very careful judgment on the relative power relationships before this happens. There is no point engaging in a conflict that you are going to loose. There is no such thing as a glorious defeat.

If you find yourself in a confrontation then Alinsky is the prime source of inspiration on how to respond. Like the section above on organisation, the use of tactics is the key to success in dealing with power. Alinsky said *"tactics means doing what you can with what you have ... tactics is the art of how to take and how to give."* He developed and proved thirteen tactical rules for use against opponents vastly superior in power and wealth ...

1. "Power is not only what you have but what the enemy thinks you have.
2. Never go outside the experience of your people.
3. Wherever possible go outside of the experience of the enemy.
4. Make the enemy live up to their own book of rules.
5. Ridicule is man's most potent weapon.
6. A good tactic is one that your people enjoy.
7. A tactic that drags on too long becomes a drag.
8. Keep the pressure on.

9. The threat is usually more terrifying than the thing itself.
10. Major premise for tactics is development of operations that will maintain constant pressure upon the opposition.
11. If you push a negative hard and deep enough it will break through into its counterside.
12. The price of a successful attack is a constructive alternative.
13. Pick the target, freeze it, personalise it, and polarise it.

Alinsky was hated and defamed by powerful enemies, proof that his tactics worked. His simple formula for success ...

Agitate + Aggravate + Educate + Organize

Capacity building, social capital and community leadership

We have argued that successful community work requires an empowerment process that is built upon participatory approaches, an understanding of power and effective organising strategies. This leads to changes in the ability of the community, through the development of personal skills and knowledge and stronger local organisations. Such changes are defined in terms of capacity building, social capital and leadership.

Community Capacity Building

The UNDP (1997) commented that

> "*capacity development is becoming the central purpose of technical co-operation .. the past four decades practices of delivering foreign aid are being called into question for poor achievements in sustainable impact, national ownership and appropriate technologies ..new global factors such as globalisation, the information revolution, the growth in*

> *international markets .. and decentralisation of national authority are causing UNDP and other international development organisations reassess their roles and competencies... Capacity development with its emphasis on capacities to be developed in support of long term self management, shifts the focus."*

The term 'capacity building' like much of the UK's social policy comes from the USA. Originally, capacity building was linked to economic development as promoted by the USA Community Investment Act. Recently the idea has been broadened out to include the social dimension of development. Undertaken properly it is more than simply training and includes developing structures to better promote and manage change within a community. Sadly, what passes for capacity building in the UK is often limited in cope and concept. The UNDP notes that:

> *"The role of public institutions in development is now changing. Conventional ideas about organizational engineering are being supplemented by broader notions on promoting learning, empowerment, social capital and an enabling environment. Attention is being given to the culture, values and power relations that influence organizations and individuals. Donors are using different intervention points into capacity systems. The informal patterns of personal and societal behaviour-the rules of the game-are now better understood. And there is more appreciation of the need to complement, not replace, indigenous habits and practices. All of these are slowly forming into a body of concepts called capacity development".* (UNDP 1997)

In detail, capacity building means the promotion of a number of activities, for economic and social purposes, relating to building both individual capacity and the capacity of community organisations to meet local needs. In doing so it is about *building on existing activities* within the community in the following ways (Skinner 1997, UNDP 1997):

- Agreeing **objectives** between the community and local agencies that provide a common purpose for planned development activity.
- **Prioritisation of key themes**. In the UNDP case these are poverty eradication, position of women, sustainable livelihoods and management of the environment.
- Creating an **environment** in which partners can work together in an open and honest way to collectively defined objectives.
- Providing **educational opportunities**, ranging from individual training for work to skills development for community organisations
- Creating **structures** with clear systems to support individual and community organisations to achieve their goals
- Establishing **partnerships** between supporting agencies and community organisations to ensure needs are met and services and funding opportunities are co-ordinated
- Participatory **monitoring and evaluation** to ensure objectives are being achieved

There is a tension within capacity building programmes. On the one hand it seeks to better equip the community to identify and, in part, meet its own needs based upon the norms and values of that community. On the other hand, it assumes that this can always be undertaken in partnership with service and government organisations. Like most UK social policy and the New Labour vision of social inclusion it derives from the idea that everyone can reach a consensus on objectives and processes. Inequalities of power are either thought to be irrelevant or it is assumed that power holders will always act in the interest of communities.

The UNDP document recognises the need for an attitude and policy shift by agencies to give more primacy to community organisations. There is little evidence of this happening in the UK where the tradition of simply linking the community into local government agendas, albeit with increased token representation, appears to continue. The key questions of: *capacity building for whom, for what purpose, and how to do it,* need to be asked.

Social Capital

Tony Blair in his speech on the Active Community in 1999 said:

> *"Too often in the past government programmes damaged social capital – sending in the experts but ignoring community organisations, investing in bricks and mortar but not in people. In the future we need to invest in social capital as surely as we invest in skills and buildings"*

Superficially, social capital is similar to concept of capacity building, as both are concerned with processes within the community. Often the two terms are confused or integrated so that a capacity building programme becomes social capital building. However, social capital is actually a wider, more robust and controversial idea, which poses some fundamental questions about the nature of, and changes within, society. The current interest in social capital comes as part of the same trends that sees education and social policy as a servant of the economy, the marketisation of social welfare and the respectability and transference of economic ideas and concepts to the social sector. Social capital is therefore an attempt to apply the idea of 'capital' from the economic to the social sphere. In effect linking the disciplines of economics and sociology, to improve the potential for development.

There are various definitions of social capital. It can be summarised *as 'the institutions, relationships, knowledge, attitudes and values that affect interrelationships between people and their contribution to economic and social development'*. This definition is not just concerned with relationships, but also the quality of how they work and the degree of effective participation, networking, reciprocity and trust to create what is called 'civic society'. A limited view of social capital is concerned only with horizontal relationships. That is the nature and strength of relationships within a given community. This can be through the *bonding* of an existing social group or through the building of *bridging* relationships between local groups. A wider definition also includes *linking* social capital through vertical relationships to external agencies and thereby includes consideration of the distribution and use of power to social ends. This vertical relationship can be just between a community and the institutions that have a direct effect upon it or include a wider social analysis.

Tom Schuller (in Baron et al 2000) explores the nature of social capital compared to human capital and cultural capital. He defines human capital as a purely economic concept that sees individuals acquiring skills and knowledge, which in turn enables them to increase their income, and by aggregation community income. Bourdieu (1985) explores the relationship between social and cultural capital to explain how power structures are maintained.

An example of using social capital to analyse social problems is Putnam (1996), concerning the decline in the numbers of people engaged in community clubs and organisations (down 50% since 1965) and informal socialising (down 25% since 1965). As in many instances the UK exhibits similar trends to North America, Often this is simply put down to apathy, which just says people are not active without providing any explanation for why this may be so. Putnam set out to provide an explanation for this dramatic reduction of civic life in the USA. Putnam's view was the decline in social interaction was also a decline in social capital. As capital declines so does the resources and potential for a community to undertake activities for itself. As social networks decline the potential for dysfunctional behaviour (crime) increases as the glue that holds community together comes apart.

Having surveyed what he calls the 'usual suspects' of mobility, pressures on time, changing role of women and the family and the disempowering effects of welfare agencies, Putnam concludes the decline is social capital is due to television. If this is correct, then Putnam provides useful evidence that lone parents and working women are not in themselves negative developments. It also enables us to ask how we might make community activity more appealing if the alternative is primarily watching TV.

The argument here is that for development to take place a community needs to build its social capital. Building social capital means developing genuine participation and enabling as many people as possible to develop skills, knowledge and confidence to take action both for themselves and for their community. Community workers should therefore explore with local groups how social capital can be increased in the community and work towards that end. Dhesi (2000) notes that *"when formal and informal institutions are in conflict, social capital gets weakened and community action becomes difficult. Before development can be initiated, an attitude reorientation towards accepting change may be required"*. This attitude change is often required by power holders as much as local people. Institutions and agencies operating in local communities can be analysed in terms of how they contribute to, or negate, the development of local social capital.

Community Leadership

It not clear from the UK policy documents exactly what the government means by this. Is it another form of social entrepreneurship, the community representation on partnership boards, the leadership of autonomous community organisations or an amalgam of all three?

Traditionally, many community workers have been opposed to the concept of leadership. It is seen as representing individualism, opposed to the collectivisation of issues and anti democratic. This is naïve and is based on a vague notion of collective working and confuses the leadership role with decision making. Leadership can be authoritarian and unrepresentative, but it can also, and should, be transparent and democratic. Leadership can also be collective.

The African revolutionary leader Amical Cabral said *"to lead collectively is not and cannot be, as some suppose, to give all and everyone the right to uncontrolled views and initiatives, to create disorders, empty arguments, a passion for meetings without results"* (quoted in Hope and Timmel 1995). Many community workers and community groups could benefit from understanding the nature and importance of leadership. Too many groups meet for an undefined purpose, discuss randomly in an unstructured fashion and decide little. To paraphrase Alinsky, a community problem only becomes an issue you can tackle when you have an organisation to fight it. And an organisation without leadership is a rabble.

Cabral went on to say *"collective leadership must strengthen the leadership capability of all and create specific circumstances where full use is made of all members.... To lead collectively, in a group, is to:*

- Study questions jointly
- Find their best solutions
- Take decisions jointly
- Benefit from the experience and intelligence of each person

To lead collectively is to:

- Give the opportunity of thinking and acting
- Demand that people take responsibility within their competence
- Require that people take initiative
- Co-ordinate the thought and action of those who from the group

Hope and Timmel develop this theme and identify three types of leadership: authoritarian, consultative and enabling. *Authoritarian leadership* is where the leader makes the decision and presents it to the group. Discussion may be invited but only in the knowledge that the decision will stand regardless of what is said. *Consultative leadership* is based on the group discussing options and recommending courses of action. However, the leader(ship) have the final say on what is to be done. In community development only *enabling leadership* is acceptable where the group has the power to make the final decision. Here the role of the leadership is to facilitate the discussion and ensure that an informed decision is reached.

We can also learn from business models, in particular the VCM leadership model. This sees leadership as having three essential components: vision, commitment and management skills. Ideally, leaders or a collective leadership will have a balance of all three components. The benefits of collective leadership are that it is more likely to find these three skills within a group than in any single individual.

In North America where community leadership is highly valued, experience shows that quality leadership does improve the performance of community groups. The role of community leadership therefore, is to help drive the vision of change, support individuals, enable the development of skills and knowledge within an organisation and be at the front when the going is difficult. The role of community work, as Alinsky pointed out, is to identify existing and potential community leadership and nurture it so that the community can run itself without the need for external community workers.

Summary

In this chapter we have explored the following points

- We need to link or theory to practice and develop community work practice models that meets the needs of communities
- Traditional models of practice needs to be substantially revised in the age of globalisation
- New campaigning methods and strategies have to adopted to build on the potential of new technology and media interest
- The process of community work should be based on empowering individuals and communities
- The product of community work is to improve the quality of life in communities on a sustainable basis
- Participation is key to successful community work
- Participation needs to clearly defined and implemented at the highest possible level
- For change to happen the community needs to be well organised and appropriate strategies adopted and properly implemented
- The goal of organising is to obtain more power for the community
- Power is often based on acquiescence rather than the direct application of force – that is egemonic power
- It is necessary to understand where power lies and how it can be influenced
- Community work strategies need to help build community capacity and social capital
- Leadership within the community needs to be better supported and valued

- All the above factors need to held in mind by community workers if they are to effectively analyse the needs of communities and possible responses

Further Reading

Patel discusses her views on development in **From the slums of Bombay to the housing estates of Britain**, CIVA,

Classic texts on organisation and power are Sun Tzu **Art of War** online at www.sonshi.com and Green R_**The 48 Laws of Power**, London, Profile Books. Whilst the classic text on community organising is Saul Alinsky **Rules for Radicals,** New York, Random House

Community capacity is discussed in Steve Skinners **Building Community Strengths,** London, CDF. See also Debra Eade **Capacity Building: an approach to people centered development** Oxford, Oxfam.

Social capital is explored in **Social Capital: critical perspectives**, Oxford, Oxford University Press by Baron S, Field J, Schuller T. See also the article by Dhesi **Social Capital and Community Development,** Community Development Journal Vol 35 No 3. John Field's **Social Capital,** London, Routledge also provides a comprehensive overview of the subject

8

Practice Perspectives: Working with Groups

Aims of this chapter

An essential but often overlooked aspect of participative work is the nature of work with the community group itself. This chapter explores why people join community groups and their various styles. It goes on to consider the learning needs of groups and the value of the 'learning circle approach'. We then look at a simple groupwork model that can be applied to the community development setting. The chapter ends with a checklist for improving groupwork practice.

Why Community Groups

In general people will become engaged with community development groups for a number of reasons. Henderson and Thomas (2002) suggest the following reasons, which may alter with time:

- to protect their personal and/or family interests
- for social and cultural activities and support
- to improve the quality of life within their community
- to preserve or create community assets
- to examine opportunities or repel threats whether real or perceived

Success in building a community group depends upon tapping into these felt needs. This might seem an obvious point. However, too much community work is practiced the wrong way round. Frequently, the worker or agency decides what needs people have and then go out to try and build a group around it. Sometimes this works, often it does not. If it fails then the community are often blamed for being apathetic. It is seldom the worker or agency's fault for being arrogant or out of touch. If we adopt a participatory approach that puts the exploration by people of their own needs as paramount, then these failures can be avoided.

Like the leadership styles discussed above, community based groups can generally be categorised as falling into one of the following three styles: authoritarian, consultative or enabling. Authoritarian groups tend to have a dominant leadership based around either a small clique or an individual. Very often these groups have been in existence for a long time and the current leadership may see themselves both as the embodiment of the groups history and the arbiter of what should happen. Group members are usually told what to do and little open discussion and sharing of ideas and feelings take place. Such groups may be efficient in carrying out basic tasks if the leadership is competent but offer little development potential.

Consultative groups appear more open and may have free flowing debates. However, the leadership in such groups tend to have their way. These groups may appear friendlier and can be effective in recruiting members. Again the success of the group largely depends upon the competence of its leadership. Enabling groups, in contrast, use their leadership to create an environment where open and supportive discussion can take place. Decisions are taken by the membership. For this to happen effectively and to avoid slipping into indecision and conflict, the leadership must be effective in managing the process openly, fairly and efficiently. Given the value base and the principles of community development enabling groups are preferred. They are certainly an essential part of a participative approach. Enabling groups are also more likely to facilitate the development the groups needs. These needs are the ability of the group to:

- Make all members feel they are accepted and valued by the rest of the group
- Create an environment where ideas, concerns and feelings (both positive and negative, happy and sad) can be openly shared

- Work productively to identify needs, plan action and learn the lessons from these actions without recrimination and egotism.

Groupwork can be very challenging. The worker needs to explore with group members how they may choose to work as outlined above. They also need to understand the position, role and feelings of individuals in the group. For example, many women through their community work experiences begin to challenge their roles within the family and at work. This develops to a new and more empowered view of themselves. Freire describes this process as people challenging their boundaries, and through developing an increasingly critical consciousness, moving their boundaries of belief and action. We may also choose to consider the organisation form of the group. Do we always need a formal constitution, a fixed chair and office bearers? Other forms of organisation that enhance the potential for development are possible. For example, the following discussion of Learning Circles the associated REFLECT approach.

The Learning Needs of Groups and Learning Circles

Community groups have an increasing need to acquire new knowledge and lean new skills. How this happens is important because, as Freire pointed out, education can be either a tool of domestication or liberation. It all depends on what is learnt and how it is learnt. The participatory approach to learning can take various forms. One common and successful method is the learning circle.

Learning Circles have a long history. They have grown out of the original idea of a study group and are based on the principles and practices of effective adult learning. Learning circles can be defined as:

> *"small, on-going gatherings of people who come together to share their ideals, goals, practices and honest experiences in service learning. In all cases, learning circles seek to be free spaces where open discussion of hard questions can take place in a collaborative and enriching environment that brings together people from different constituencies"*

The circles provide a welcome alternative to the traditional office bearer / committee structure which tends to both dominate and restrict community groups. For participative work, learning circles can encourage user involvement through creating a supportive enabling group environment.

Circles can serve to explore knowledge on particular issues, to build confidence and relationships, to plan and take action based on upon the learning and to review and evaluate the action taken. Circles can be a group in their own right or a smaller grouping within an organisation that explore issues and ideas on behalf of the main group. In many ways learning circles are like Freirian groups exploring codifications for the development critical consciousness. The process and environment are indeed similar. The difference being that learning circles are less dependant upon the generative theme which is central to the Freirian approach, and more focussed on immediate tasks and issues that need to be explored. The open, supportive and participatory nature of learning circles facilitates participants to:

- Become more aware of their own thinking and reasoning
- Make their thinking and reasoning more visible to others
- Inquire into others thinking and reasoning
- Inquire into what are the observable facts behind a statement
- Inquire whether everyone agrees on what the facts are

However, circles only work when everyone is committed to the basic rules:

- Participate fully in the circle
- Communicate your needs
- Tell circle members and the facilitator if your needs are being met or not.
- Help members clarify their needs
- Respect their needs
- Help members exchange feedback, inquiry, and resources to meet their needs.

The key to the success of a learning circle is the facilitator. And it is crucial to understand this role. Whilst experience of adult education can be important to facilitate group, it is essential to realise that the facilitation role is not training in the traditional sense. This is an important distinction, because the community work role is increasing about providing training for community groups. For example, where I work community workers are often employed to tell local groups what social planners have decided they need to know. Or to train group members to meet the roles planners have decided they should fulfil. Committee skills, business plans, completing funding applications, how to work acceptably as a partner, community group responsibilities are all part of the current community work training agenda for groups. This may be necessary in some cases but critical and liberatory education it is not.

The other side of this approach is that community groups are then diverted from identifying their own learning needs. Unless groups do this, empowerment and the building of autonomous and powerful community organisations is impossible. Based on the ideas of Freire, the role of the facilitator therefore, is to enable the group to explore their world in a critical way. This involves the group obtaining and decoding new information about their world. It is not about the facilitator providing pre-determined training (banking knowledge as Freire describes it) or leading the group down a pre-determined route, or achieving pre-determined learning outcomes. It is a shared open-ended journey of discovery. Paulo Freire describes the facilitators role as:

> *"Authentic help means that all who are involved help each other mutually, growing together in the common effort to understand the reality which they seek to transform. Only through such praxis -- in which those who help and those who are being helped help each other simultaneously -- can the act of helping become free from the distortion in which the helper dominates the helped".*

Learning circles are flexible, easy to set up, fun to be part of and inherently creative and liberating. For community activists whose main experience is that of the formal constituted group, circles can be a revitalising experience. They are also a challenge for the community worker as they mean letting go of the agenda and going wherever the group wishes to go.

The Life Cycle of Groups

It is important to see a community group as a living entity. They are born, grow, may encounter life threatening crises, have high points and low points. Eventually they die, hopefully after a successful life that can be acknowledged and celebrated. They may also be reborn as a new group.

Tuckman (1965) produced a model that explores the development process of a group, through the stages of 'Forming', 'Storming', 'Norming' and 'Performing'. The model was later elaborated to include 'Mourning and Reforming' stages. All groups go through a variation of this model. It is useful to know the stages to gain ideas about what is happening to the group and how to respond.

The **forming** stage is where people are coming together for the first time. They are getting to know each other, making decisions about whether they wish to be involved in this collective enterprise and exploring what the nature of the group might be and which objectives are most important. The key role for the worker here is to help the new group members set an open, inclusive and reflective tone to the group.

The **storming** stage unusually comes soon after the formation of a group. This is where initial tensions are acted out and decisions made. Who holds the power, how will the group be organised, what is the work program? Conflict may also arise over gender issues and roles, age differences, race, religion and individual prejudices around, for example, lone parents or people from a particular part of the community. It is important to acknowledge that storming happens and the role for the worker is to assist people through it with as little interpersonal damage as possible. However, it is a mistake to try and avoid storming. The tensions that come out at this stage are real. If they are not openly dealt with then they fester under the surface and break out later in more destructive forms.

Norming is where the group develops a sense of togetherness at a personal and organisation levels. It is important that the group achieves something at this stage otherwise the positive feelings can quickly turn to disappointment. It does not matter what is achieved – a small gain is often all that is required. It is the symbolic message that we can do things together that is important. Many workers make the mistake of going straight away for the big (and difficult) objective. However, the group needs a victory of some kind at the norming stage to give it the confidence to tackle the difficult tasks.

The next stage **performing** is where the real work of the group is done. To perform the group needs resilience, clarity of purpose and a clear sense of self-belief. They will only have this is the early stages of group development have been handled properly. All groups will encounter one or more crises during their life cycle. A strong well founded group will survive them. A group that never really resolved the storming issues can easily collapse under the pressure of a crisis.

Eventually all groups will come to the end of their natural life cycle, the **mourning** stage. Many groups and indeed community workers appear to believe that a community group can and should live forever. This is unrealistic and damaging. A group that has been set up to campaign for housing modernisation has come to the end of its life when the modernisation is complete. The majority of the existing membership will drift away because their reason for being there no longer exists. Usually, a small group of members carry on. Often this rump of members becomes angry at the apathy of local people and the apparent ungratefulness of the community for their hard work. What has been a success starts to feel like a failure. Community workers must avoid this situation occurring. Although they often collude with it as they feel that the ending of a group is also a failure on their part.

Success, as we have said before, needs to be celebrated. A thriving community group should be fun not hard work and misery. Workers need to know when a group is coming towards the end of its natural life and help group members consider if this is the time for a decent burial. A wake which celebrates the past history of the groups, its success and brings people back together is critical for sustaining community activity.

Out of the burial often comes the **reforming** of the group. However, this needs to be seen as the daughter of the old group. A new group, based on previous success, but with changes in membership and new objectives. A fresh enterprise, a new beginning with the life cycle starting again.

A Community Development Groupwork Model

As we have said community development is a change activity. It seeks to galvanise people who are disadvantaged or excluded to examine their experiences and commonalties and to determine and prioritise their needs. Through this process people are enabled to organise around their common needs. This animation of people can be in a geographical location or around issues or experiences that motivate people to take action.

In community development, perhaps more sharply than in some forms of groupwork, there should be clear outputs (products of the action; e.g. establishing drug advice services) and outcomes (effects of the action; e.g. change in drug use patterns). The process that facilitates this also receives significant attention. There are both individual and group components, but community development is founded on the principle that the medium of collective action is essential.

> "...that every human being,........is capable of looking critically at his world in a dialogical encounter with others. Provided with the proper tools for this encounter, he can gradually perceive his personal and social reality as well as the contradictions in it, become conscious of his own perception of that reality and deal critically with it." (Schull 1972 in Freire 1972 p 8)

Workers also face a number of personal and practice issues that need to be understood for effective groupwork. This can be explored through the COMPASS model developed by Kelly and Sewell (1989). The model raises questions along the two axis: whether we are inside or outside of the process and if we are acting on our own or the peoples agenda.

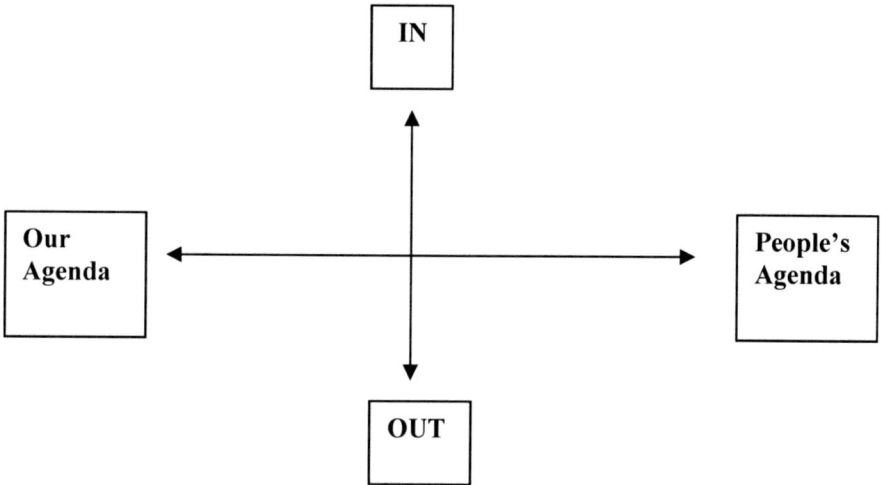

The COMPASS Model

Questions around the *In / Out* dimension explores the degree of trust granted to the community worker by the community group. By the nature of their education and training community workers are different in many social and cultural ways from the members of the communities within which they work. This is true even of those who were born and continue to live in those communities. Workers can become 'honorary' insiders through being open, honest, transparent, reliable and committed. It is a position that has to be earned through work on the ground. Workers need to accept that they need to achieve this position with local groups and should chart and reflect on their progress to this end.

The other axis, *Our agenda / People's agenda* confronts the issues we have explored above about the conflict of social planning agendas and the identified needs of local people. It can also concern debates over value positions between the worker and the group and questions over the formal and informal power of the community worker. Seldom does a worker completely locate themselves on the people's agenda side of the continuum. What is important is the transparency with which the worker conducts themselves and the way in which potential conflict of agendas are openly discussed and dealt with. It can be helpful for workers to regularly map themselves on the COMPASS chart for each of the groups they work with.

For community development to succeed we need to build upon the group dynamics and the stages 'forming – storming – norming – performing –mourning -reforming'. Workers need to understand what groups need to do to achieve their goals. Taking an overview of the tasks that confront community groups, Henderson and Thomas (2002) developed a process model that community development groups have to accomplish to effectively promote change. These tasks can be identified as:

- Making contacts and people coming together
- Forming and building an organisation
- Clarify goals and priorities
- Keeping the organisation going
- Dealing with friends and enemies
- Leavings and endings

The achievement of these processes that lead to accomplishing the above tasks are not necessarily linear, and they may take place or repeat themselves throughout the life cycle of a group. It is necessary, however, to link the group stages of development ('forming –storming – norming –performing – mourning/reforming') and group process tasks from Henderson and Thomas together. And to do so in a way that also unites the personal aspects of development with collective change.

The nature of personal change that occurs through community development groupwork is best explained through reference to Johari's Window. So called after its proponents Joe Luft and Harry Ingham. The window illustrates how we can improve both our knowledge of ourselves as well as understanding how others see us. Community based groups that are reflective and supportive should enable this process to take place.

	Known to self	Unknown to self
Known to others	**FREE**	**BLIND**
Unknown to others	**HIDDEN**	**MYSTERY**

Johari's Window

'The *Free* area represents knowledge that both you and others know openly. The *Hidden* area represents and area about yourself that that you choose to hide from others due to insecurity or other reasons. The *blind* are relates to aspects of your self that others know but which you do not. Finally, the *mystery* area contains aspects of your self that neither you nor others are conscious of. One of the purposes of groupwork is to extend the free area as far as possible into the hidden, blind and mystery areas, to give you a better understanding of yourself. This self development is integral to the growth of critical consciousness. It is also often essential for the group to have this kind of knowledge of group members to both develop trust and confidence in each other and to be able to offer support when required.

This discussion of personal development and critical consciousness brings us back to the work of Freire, with the following diagram illustrating the overlap of these diverse aspects of community development groupwork.

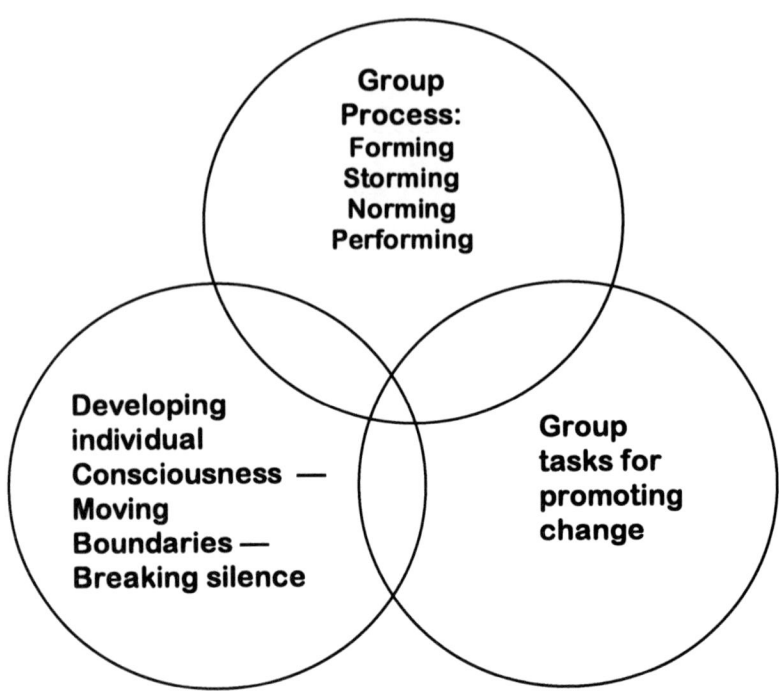

As we know from chapter 5, Paulo Freire has explored how his techniques can help people develop their critical understanding of themselves and their life. Freire's approach is used widely in the developing world and his approach also works well in the UK. It can be applied to any group setting.

Freire argues that the role of the worker in the group setting is to act as a facilitator. The worker in a community development context should not be leading the group to a predetermined end, but enable group members to gain a greater understanding of their personal, family and community situation. For this to happen group members have to develop a more critical level of consciousness. To recap the levels of consciousness are:

'*Magical Consciousness*' when people accept the oppressions inherent in society. This manifests itself through an often self imposed '*Culture of Silence*'. Such silence can operate at both a personal and community level as the product of hegemony or oppression. The next level is '*Naïve Consciousness*' where people think about their life and make some connections with social, economic and political issues. These connections though, are often at an emotional level and blame others for the current situation. *'Critical Consciousness'* is achieved when a critical and analytical understanding of the world structural and cultural discrimination is understood.

Related to these levels of consciousness is Freire's concept of *'Boundary Situations'*. He argues that we all repress ourselves through imposing a boundary on our own actions as a result of internalising the cultural norms of oppressive institutions and belief systems. By using a problem posing technique, the worker should facilitate the group to question their existing assumptions about themselves and their community, to develop a more critical view of society and their own possibilities and as a result shift their self defined boundaries. If this expansion of boundaries is achieved, belief in the possibility of change becomes possible. The group is then able to move through the *Reflective – Vision – Planning – Action* phases. In this way Freire links personal development with community orientated action.

Success in community development groupwork therefore involves working on multiple processes simultaneously. The process involved in the stages of forming, storming, norming and performing are common to many groups. In addition the development of group members' critical understanding of themselves and the wider group tasks is necessary. As these processes unfold, changes in the aims, purposes and activities of the group can be expected. (Mullender and Ward 1991; and Lee 1994; 1999). The challenge for the groupworker is to understand these multiple processes and to facilitate their progression. The reward is the empowerment of individuals with collective strength and cohesion to contribute to positive change in their communities; to break the 'culture of silence' and promote a more active exchange between policy and community.

Critical Questions for Community Workers

The pressure to achieve results and the balancing of competing demands by workers can easily lead to the neglect of the groupwork process. Sometimes the community group itself can be perceived to be a barrier to successful work, rather the means through which success can be achieved. It is essential that, like the rest of community work practice, groupwork is undertaken in a thoughtful and reflective manner. The following points (developed from Drysdale and Purcell 2001) are presented as a checklist to help keep the focus on the community group and our own practice.

Positive practice: *these are things we must do*

- Really listen to what is being said, instead of being preoccupied on what we are going to do next
- Staying and being seen to be impartial
- Drawing out the quieter group members
- Offering personal support when required – either in the group or outside it
- Being explicit about the values and principles of community development
- Challenging discrimination within the group
- Using open questions to encourage discussion
- Helping to keep the group focused on the key tasks and issues
- Helping the group to make, and follow through, democratic decisions

Negative practice: *these are things we must avoid*

- Letting the group treat you as the expert
- Letting the group 'dump' routine work on you, for example minute taking
- Backing out from asking the hard questions
- Ignoring conflict rather than exploring and trying to resolve issues
- Having a hidden agenda
- Not be open about your employers agenda
- Not being honest when you don't know, or can't do something

Critical Questions for Groups: It can be useful to reflect upon how community groups operate, and to consider how the working of the group and building membership can be improved. These are some of the questions that can usefully be discussed with a group.

Effectiveness of the group

- Does the group share common objectives
- How far is the group involved in, and committed to, achieving these objectives
- How well does the group work together
- How well does the group make decisions
- How well does the group support new members
- How well does the group care its members
- How does the group deal with internal conflict
- Does the group celebrate success
- Does the group analyse failure

Practical issues for groups

- Does the group meet at a convenient place and time for everyone
- Can transport to and from the meeting be improved
- Is the location and travel safe for everyone
- Are roles equally shared between men and women, young and old, etc.
- Are the meetings fun
- At the end of a meeting does the group feel it has made progress
- How does the group advertise its activities– does this work

Summary

In this chapter we have explored the following:

- That people join community groups to meet specific and identified personal, family and community needs
- Community groups take various forms, not all of which are enabling and empowering
- The learning needs of groups need to be recognised
- Community groups should identify their own learning needs
- Learning circles provide an informal and flexible approach to meet group learning needs
- The key role for workers in community groups is facilitation
- Groups have their own life cycle
- Groups go through stages of 'Forming', 'Storming', 'Norming' and 'Performing', 'Mourning and Reforming'
- Community groups have a range of tasks that they have to deliver to be effective
- Workers need clarity about their own position in the group
- Freire provides the key methodology to link the personal and group development tasks
- There are critical questions community workers need to keep in mind to ensure good practice with groups

Further Reading

Skills in Neighbourhood Work, by Henderson and Thomas give a very thorough exploration of the process model of community work (London, Routledge and Kegan Paul 2002).

The discussion of the stages of group development can be found in Tuckman **Developmental sequence in small groups,** Psychological Bulletin, Vol.63. It is also discussed in some detail in Benjamin J, Bessant J, Watts R, (**Making Groups Work. Rethinking Practice**. St. Leonards. Australia. Allen and Unwin. 1997)

Once again the work of Freire is made accessible though the **Training For Transformation** volumes by Hope and Timmel.

9

Practice Perspectives: Participatory Practice

Aims of this chapter

In chapter 7 it was suggested that successful community work is based upon promoting maximum participation. To be successful participatory work needs to follow any one of a number of clearly defined pathways. This chapter follows one particular path. Like all paths though it is possible and often desirable to take short cuts, double back, revisits favourite places and sometimes take a completely different route.

This particular path has a number of well defined stages. Stage 1 is about working with the community to build a shared understanding of locally identified need. Stage 2 is concerned with planning how to take action on the identified needs. Stage 3 involves monitoring and evaluating the action and drawing lessons for revised and future action. Each of these stages has a number of steps that link to a collection of participatory methods. This path has been drawn from a variety of sources. In particular the work of the Community Partnership Center (2000) at the University of Tennessee, the Reflect Mother Manual published by ActionAid, various interpretations and applications of Paulo Freire's work and an immense body of activity and techniques which goes under the name of PRA (participatory rapid appraisal). All of these sources have their own path to success

An overview of PRA and PLA

During the 1980's and 1990's it became increasingly obvious to NGO's operating in Asia and Africa that the standard approaches to development usually failed to work. For example see the overview on the failure of traditional development in Sachs 'The Development Dictionary' (1997), the case study on the failure of large dams by Roy 'The Cost of Living' (1999) and the indictment of expert driven development by Sainath in 'Everybody Loves a Good Drought' (1999)

As a result development practice has moved from the western expert with a top down view to working with people from the bottom up. Rapid Rural Appraisal techniques offered a starting point but it was realised that greater effort and improved techniques were require to both fully involve local people and to be able to draw upon their local experience. The result was a body of skills and techniques called Participative Rapid Appraisal (PRA).

PRA methods have spread rapidly due to their success. By the late 1990's PRA was in use in over 100 countries (including to a limited extent the UK). It is used in the urban as well as rural context and in a range of settings from economic development to environmental sustainability, social programmes. In the UK it has been used in anti-poverty work, promoting health and well-being, urban development, urban literacy, gender, race and agriculture. It is the favoured technique of many NGO's and extensively used by national agencies, consultants and Universities.

PRA has been criticised by many development workers and academics as been too focused on needs identification, with often little say on how on the resulting action. Sometimes participative methods have been used to identify need, but the local community have been excluded when it comes to taking action and developing / owning new resources. Participatory Learning for Action (PLA) helps to solve this by ensuring there is both a focus on taking action and learning from the experience.

Carolyn Jones (1996) suggests the following changes in approach have taken place.

1970's model

The table below illustrates the traditional approach to development, based around external expert knowledge and the assumption that local communities have little of value to offer.

Experts know the solutions	*Communities* do not know the solution
Communities are the problem	*Experts* are the solution

1990's model

In contrast the 1990's model gives value to the local community for both identifying needs as well as containing resources and potential for the solution to local problems. This is not to say expert knowledge is not valuable. Rather it is about ensuring expert knowledge is used to the best advantage alongside the community and their contribution.

Communities know the solution	Experts do not know the solution
External influences are the problem	*Communities* are the solution

This shift in perception of how to do development involves a number of changes for workers. If we think of participation in terms of Arnstein's Ladder, the level of participation has to move from the lower rungs of informing or consultation to some meaningful level of participation. This involves resource holders ceding a significant degree of power to local communities to define the agenda and control resources. In effect local people become *subjects* in control of local development, not *objects* to be organised by external agencies.

According to Jones, for this to happen workers need to adapt their thinking and approach and ask themselves the following questions:

- whose reality counts
- whose knowledge counts
- whose criteria - whose values
- whose appraisal
- whose analysis
- whose plans
- whose monitoring and evaluation

The answer to these questions should lead to a more community centred approach and, essentially a change in the methods used by workers.

From *dominance*	to	*facilitation*
closed approach	to	*open* approach
tedium	to	*fun*
individual views	to	*group* discussions
verbal	to	*visual*
absolutes	to	*comparing*
averages	to	*diversity*

Jones suggests therefore, that success in participation is dependent upon workers respecting the community in which they work. This needs to be reflected through action and attitudes and the basic application of principles and practices of participation outlined above.

Participation is about striking a balance. Local people do have detailed local knowledge that experts cannot ever obtain effectively. They are able to determine their own needs that more often reflect Maslow's Hierarchy than expert driven agendas. With support and training they can deliver many of the required local solutions for themselves. This is of crucial importance for a community empowerment strategy which we have argued is the central process of development. Reliance on experts for development can only lead to disempowerment as local people learn the message that they cannot do things for themselves.

However, external expertise is still required. Local knowledge skills and resources often need external support to developed and applied, in Freire's term people also often need support to move from a naïve reactive position to critical consciousness which underpins effective community action. Experts also have technical knowledge and resources that can be invaluable if deployed properly within the community.

Although increasing common both in the developing world and North America participative methods based around PRA and PLA are poorly developed in the UK. As we have said the identification of community needs in the UK is mostly undertaken through social planning methods. In this method professional workers identify needs according to their agency criteria, usually based on statistical information (normative and /or comparative needs in Bradshaw's terms).

Often this statement of needs is put out for consultation amongst other workers and the community. This is often through a series of focus groups based on invited community activists and 'community conferences'. How much influence the community has on influencing the production of the needs audit, or changing the social plan is often limited. Usually, what is happening is some form of consultation based upon the product of top down planning, rather than genuine participative practice.

A model of participatory practice

The diagram in appendix 2 offers a model flow chart approach to developing participatory practice. This micro model fits into the early stages of the macro model of community development illustrated in appendix 1. In reality the work is seldom simple enough to allow the process to unfold in an orderly linear fashion. However, it is helpful to view the diagram as an ideal approach to practice with each sub stage following on logically from the previous activity. It is also a reminder that practice has to be based on carefully defined needs. And that if needs are identified in the right way a significant local interest and organisation can be put in place for the action phase. Too often community groups, and indeed workers, rush into action before the objective of the work is fully explored.

The rest of this chapter discussed this model in more detail and offers examples of how it might look in practice.

Stage 1 - Building a shared understanding of locally defined need

Create snapshot of the community

How do we start to understand the needs of a community? The way we answer this question can shape the future development of our work and the degree of success that may be achieved. Traditionally, external experts have profiled communities and using their technical knowledge with agency priorities decided what action should take place. Local people and groups are then organised to this end. Participatory practice rejects this approach. Not only does the expert approach often fail to correctly identify real local need, it also fails to engage local people as the agenda is correctly perceived to be controlled by an external agency. The starting point must be the exploration of people's own needs, desires and visions that are developed as a reflection on their life and experience.

The easiest way to begin to understand community needs is through a 'listening survey'. This is a very simple approach where the worker just listens to everyday conversations. This may be in shops, in the street at a bus stop, in a café or pub or at the School gates. What is it that people talk about that gives a clue to local concerns and issues? For this approach to work it is important to adopt the Zen approach of 'expecting nothing'. That is to be open to anything and any interpretation and not to approach with a mind fixed on particular sets of issues or an attachment to a specific course of action.

Many organisations dislike such an approach for a number of reasons. It can take a long time when there may be political or funding pressures to show quick results. It is too simple and devalues expert knowledge (although expert knowledge can be utilised at a later stage to help explore the issues and plan action). Wandering the streets listening to people does not look like work. Also there is a notion that community work only takes place in designated space and time; for example at a committee meeting, in a community centre, at a focus group or at a worker led event. But to achieve success the community work process needs to become an integrated part of the informal networks and interactions of a community.

What the worker is searching for is a 'generative theme' that captures the current and deeply felt concerns of a significant part of the community. This can be difficult to achieve, as people's feelings may be contradictory and not clearly expressed. To hone down a generative theme the worker needs to begin to engage people in conversation and explore the following open questions:

- why is this issue important
- do other people think it is important
- who doesn't think it important

- why do they think that
- is it really a problem

The final question is really important because effective organisation can only take place on 'hot issues' where people are fearful or angry and want something done. It may take some discussion on the generative theme for people to come to a clearer understanding of their feeling and desires on a particular issue. But without strong feelings there will not be a commitment to engage in the work required for change to take place. There are far too many examples of community workers struggling to find local people to sit on steering groups or committees to take forward pieces of work that are important only in the mind of the community worker or an agency plan. Often local people are blamed for their apathy when the real culprit is the failure of the community worker to effectively understand and engage with genuine issues.

Once the generative theme is identified more structured groupwork is possible to facilitate people through the reflection and vision phase that in turn lead to planning and action.

More on Freire

As we have discussed above, the work of Paulo Freire provides a model for community groups to explore the nature of their community: to develop a critical consciousness, and to move through a vision – reflection – planning – action cycle. How exactly is this achieved?

From the listening survey and general knowledge of the community a group of interested people can be brought together. Using the generative theme the facilitator prepares a selection of 'codes' to stimulate group discussion. Traditionally codes are photographs or pictures that display a typical situation that is familiar to the group. Although, codes can also be poems, short stories, role-plays or songs. It is for the facilitator to judge the most useful approach.

Group participants are asked open questions on the image. For example, what is happening here, why is this happening, how do you think the people concerned are feeling, have you ever experienced this, how did it feel to you? Usually the discussion moves through six stages:

- description of the what is in the code
- first analysis of what the code is about
- how the people / activity in the code relates to the participants lives
- deeper analysis of what this means and self reflection
- what people might want to do as a result of this discussion
- starting to plan the next action

Through applying this method people can explore their own and collective experiences through the safety of discussing the code. Doing so opens up new insights and understanding that can contribute significantly to personal empowerment, capacity building and an increased understanding both of local ills and possible solutions.

Analysis and profiling of the community

It is likely that the group exploring the generative theme will be small. Once the group is ready to move forward it is time for more people to become involved, although the overall numbers may still be quite small. The new members are most likely to come from the existing family / neighbour / social contacts of the current group. It is becoming common to call this new grouping a learning team. This is a useful label as it clearly identifies the task; that what is required is more information about a situation and what may be done about it. The action team phase comes later once the group is sufficiently equipped with the essential knowledge to move forward.

The group may identify a wide variety of knowledge to be obtained depending on the question under consideration. For example:

- more detailed local knowledge
- technical knowledge on say, housing, environment, transport, employment
- funding sources

- policies of major external agencies, government organisations, quangos
- experience of similar groups in neighbouring communities or internationally via the internet
- possible support in the local political arena
- potential opposition in the local political area
- other friends and allies

There is a range of participative methods available to help build this pattern of knowledge. The most common methods include:

- neighbourhood maps
- life maps
- issue maps
- resource maps
- power maps
- storytelling
- tree of life

These methods are not self-contained as information collection usually involves combinations of these approaches. No one method of information collection can meet all needs. It is important to select the type of information collection that meets the group's needs and is practicable given the time and resources they have. It is also essential to collect information in participative ways. This means involving local people as collectors as well as the subjects of the information. Anyone undertaking information collection should receive basic training and support. Working on the tasks in small groups is also more effective and enjoyable. The resource section below references useful handbooks that can help develop apply these methods. Drysdale and Purcell (2001) provide the following illustrations.

Neighbourhood maps - A good starting activity is to invite people to draw or create personal maps of their communities, or their lives (when working with communities of interest). This has the benefit of helping people identify what are the important areas of their lives, what might be the potential problems or concerns. Who is important to them and what kind of support/threat might be expected from them. This exercise can be undertaken with a wide variety of groups from school children to elders. Maps can be drawn indoors, but it can be most effective if it is compiled by a group of people walking through their community.

Having created the map, participants can be asked to discuss:

- What they see as difficulties for them?
- Where are they located in the map?
- Do they feel that their needs are met within the area?
- What are the gaps?
- What agencies are involved in the area- which are helpful which are not?

Life Maps - these can take two forms, a description of how people came to be in their current position, or a network diagram that helps people identify what difficulties and issues are in their lives. This exercise is best done with individuals, and then snowballed into general themes. Individual maps may need to remain confidential.

Issue Maps - can be made for crime spots, caring need timetables, gaps in child care provision (area or times), access to shops, leisure facilities,

Resource Maps - can be made of physical resources within an area. They can also map the specialist knowledge and skills of organizations, workers and community organizations.

Power Maps - can also be used to see who holds power; over the use of resources, ownership of land and facilities as well as the informal power relationships within a community,

The Use of Maps - by identifying the current situation and what changes they would want to make people can begin to understand that their situations are influenced by external agencies, institutional and structural oppression such as poverty, poor educational opportunities, housing allocation policies. To achieve this people need to think about the various agencies (or individuals) who are in the area and what their relationships are to them. They also need to think about the relationships between these agencies.

These maps can be presented in a variety of forms, for example:

- Through photographs – Digital cameras are an invaluable tool because they allow instant replay for discussion. The images can also be easily and cheaply be used for posters, displays, and other forms of computer production.
- Drawings – Can be very powerful for expressing feeling. They also overcome people's inhibitions about literacy. Also an essential approach when working with young children.
- Diagrams – Useful to make links between diverse elements. For examples flow charts to show how decisions are made.
- Montage – Using images from newspapers and magazines as well as photographs and drawing produced locally.

Storytelling is another activity that can get people talking about their lives, their needs and their dreams. Storytelling can also be about the area that people live in, the situation that people share e.g. nursery schools, older persons' accommodation, disability or poverty.

There are a number of ways to encourage this to happen:

- choose soap characters who remind people of themselves
- pictures, music or other creative art they think says something about their own experiences
- asking people to remember street games and stories that say something about their lives.
- making up stories about people like themselves.
- telling their own story of e.g. oppression, stress, happiness.

People need to feel comfortable, so they should only be encouraged to share as much as they feel comfortable to speak about.

They should not feel coerced into participating. These stories can then be translated into plays, drawings, human sculptures, models made from rubbish etc. You need to have some knowledge of what people will take the risk to try. Most people will have a go if the facilitator is encouraging, sets it up as being a fun activity and is patient.

Tree of Life is another possible technique. In this method people are asked to draw the tree of their own life, in which:

- The roots are the family and the influences that have shaped their life.
- The trunk is the structure of their life today, their family, job, community or organisations which are important to them.
- The leaves are their information sources, newspapers, community radio stations, friends and contacts.
- The buds are the hopes, dreams and aspirations
- The fruits are their achievements.

At this stage the group may need to talk to other stakeholders, agencies or politicians. If so, such approaches need to be made thoughtfully as the first contact with these bodies may frame any future working relationship. It is helpful therefore to have a clearer understanding of how the wider world works. The following section on the civic index may be helpful.

Civic Index

This is a method from the USA that explores the health of local civic society. Such an approach can be useful as part of building a profile of the community and identifying critical issues for future work. The civic index takes as its starting point the social model of health developed by the World Health Organisation. This model sees good health being based upon lifestyle, behaviour and environment. Medical services are deemed to be of only minor importance in promoting health.

The social model of health, although developed for individuals, can be applied to an analysis of the community. Doing so shifts the emphasis form the structures of government to what people actually do and the environment within which these activities take place. The idea of the civic index comes from the National Civic League in the USA (www.ncl.org). The NCL has identified seven patterns of a healthy community; that is a community which:

- practices on-going dialogue
- generates leadership everywhere and at all levels
- shapes its future
- embraces diversity
- knows itself
- connects people and resources
- creates a sense of community

The Community Partnership Center at the University of Tennessee have expanded these points into a checklist for characteristics of a healthy / unhealthy community:

Healthy Community	Unhealthy Community
Optimism	Cynicism
Focus on unification	Focus on division
Consensus building	Polarisation
We're in this together	Not in my back yard
Solving problems	Holding grudges
Interdependence	Parochialism
Win – win solutions	Win - lose solutions
Trust	Questioning motives
Politics of substance	Politics of personality
Diversity	Exclusion
Challenge ideas	Challenge people
Problem solvers	Blockers and bankers
Taking personal responsibility	Other persons responsibility
Listening	Attacking
Focus on the future	Focus on the past
Sharing power	Hoarding power
We can do it	Nothing works

Amended from Community Partnership Center (2000)

According to NCL success in developing a health community depends upon the creation of a civic infrastructure that brings together a number of activities and processes including:

- vision
- governance
- bridging diversity
- reaching consensus
- sharing information
- educating citizens
- building leadership
- learning from experience

These items are similar to the ideas explored in our discussion of social capital and the community empowerment model. Although, in this case they are focussed directly on how decision making and governing the community takes place. Such an analysis can be scaled up to explore the activities of national government, or scaled down to analyse local government or even activities within a specific community.

As usual with a participatory approach this analysis can be approach through a problem posing technique. Key questions to ask include:

1. What is our desired future / vision of community
   o new roles for citizens
   o new roles for local government
   o new roles for voluntary and community organisations
   o new roles for business

2. How do we work together as a community
   o how to bridge diversity
   o how to share information
   o how to reach consensus

3. Are we strengthening our ability to solve problems
   o do we educate citizens to meet community challenges
   o are we building community leadership

o how are we learning from our experiences

These and other questions can be posed in small groups, community organisations, at day workshops and community conferences. They can prove to be effective in resolving differences and building consensus. Alternatively, the questions can be asked by a campaigning group to explore what is wrong with an existing structure and explore campaign objectives. Organisations can also pose these questions about themselves as part of an internal assessment exercise.

Traditional research methods

Often participative methods can raise questions that can best be answered through applying some form of traditional research methods. The following methods can therefore be seen as useful tools to support participative work they should not generally be used as a substitute for it in the community work context. For traditional methods to be applied in a participative manner it is essential that local people are fully involved in identifying the research questions, deciding on the approach, undertaking the fieldwork and analysing the results.

Basically, there are three basic options for collecting information:

- observation
- asking questions
- using existing records

In practice these methods are seldom mutually exclusive. In fact the most effective approaches to data collection involve a combination of approaches. Each method has its own advantages and disadvantages, settings where it will work well and those where its use would not be appropriate. For example, records can only be consulted where they both exist and are accessible, asking questions is a direct approach to finding information but is inappropriate when it would be seen to be intrusive.

Observation - The advantage of observation is that information is obtained directly by the researcher, who is observing what is taking place before them. Other people's opinions and their misreporting are therefore filtered out of the process. It also allows the researcher to see what is happening in its context; who is there, what they do and don't do, how people behave, non verbal behaviour, body language, etc.

However, there are limitations to observation. How many things are happening at once, does the researcher miss key events because they were concentrating on something else, how can all this information be recorded in real time? More importantly, what are the biases of the researcher? What do they select out or prioritise? Is this done consciously or unconsciously? For example, when recording it is often easier to record inferred attitudes or motives than actual behaviour. Light hearted banter in a group may be misinterpreted at interpersonal conflict, off hand comments may be taken as signs of inherent gender or racial attitudes. Video can be used to record events but this either just a general shot of the event or uses selective viewing. It can be helpful but is not a panacea for accurate recording.

Indeed, the presence of the researcher at the event may alter what is said and done, this is known as the 'Hawthorne effect'. If the researcher is an active participant in the event this effect can be reduced. However, by participating it becomes correspondingly more difficult to observe and accurately record. An alternative is it to observe people without their knowledge and consent by using tape recorder or video cameras. Such action raises moral questions. In a large public event this may be acceptable, but is problematic in smaller community group settings. Often the researcher is allowed to view non contentious events but is excluded from the real action. Overall, observations can provide a vital basis for development of hypotheses. These hypotheses can them be further explored by using other methods.

Asking Questions - As you would expect the best way to find out information is to ask questions. But it is not that simple. There is a distinction between written and verbal questions. Written questions are usually in the form of a questionnaire, and they raise a host of difficulties. How many questions can be included in the questionnaire before it becomes boring? How you can be sure what you mean by the question is clearly understood. If the answer is not clear there is probably no way to use follow up questions. You might be asking totally the wrong questions and completely missing the point and inhibiting people from saying the important things, and you may never know.

The advantage of questionnaire is they can distributed to a large number of people. They can be posted out, left in community centres, handed out in the street. Unfortunately, such methods have a low response rate, often below 10%. How do you know if those who replied are representative or not?

Verbal questions give the researcher much more control. Questions made be asked of individuals, in a group setting or randomly in the street. If the question is not clear you explain what is meant, and if the answer is vague you can ask supplementary questions. However, the interviewer then becomes a key player in the process; how the questioned is asked can have significant impact on the nature and length of the reply.

Questions can be fixed where the researcher simply reads out a sentence. This allows for uniform questioning by a number of people. However, it can be limiting in that it prevents the researcher using their initiative to explore answers to gain real insight into what people think. Alternatively, the questions can be more informal to allow flexibility, but this requires more skill on the part of the researcher to work effectively. Questions can be closed, as in 'do you agree – yes or no'. Or open questions, such as 'tell me what you think about or why did this happen'. Again open questions get you more information if the researcher is skilled enough to manage the interview. Closed questions are easier to record; simply add up the yes and no answers. Open questions provide more information but this creates problems on how it might be characterised.

In community work setting it is essential to know the quality of the experience. This means that open questions are often required to help people to explore their feeling and attitudes. Open questions can be 'direct questions' which ask about the current situation. For example, 'do you think the project meets the needs of lone parents'? Alternatively they can be 'projective questions' which explore attitudes to possible developments. For example, 'how would you feel if the project started to work with asylum seekers'?

A useful approach in asking questions in a group setting is nominal group technique. The value of this approach is that supports individuals to express their ideas and at the same time assists the group to reach a consensus. It also avoids the domination of the meeting by the most assertive and vocal members. This simple technique has many variations. One approach starts by individuals writing down their answers to set questions on post-its. These answers are then put on a wall for everyone to see. The facilitator, making sure that everyone agrees with the selection, then groups the responses. The grouping can be voted on to identify priorities and/or further discussion takes place and the process repeated.

Written and verbal questions are clearly essential for research as well as any participative approaches. There are a number of good practice rules that should be followed:

- be clear and avoid bias
- use familiar words, phases and style
- use simple words and simple straightforward sentences
- be specific - without too much elaborate detail
- ask concise questions that cannot result in ambiguous answers
- be precise and not vague
- keep it short
- avoid bias and leading questions
- do not make presumptions.

Using Existing Records - Very often the information you need already exists. For example there could be census data, minutes of meetings of community organisations and public bodies, newspaper and other media reports of events. It may be however, that the records are incorrect or biased and researchers often need to cross check the reliability of records. There is also a danger that researchers change their questions to fit the information that is easily available. This can be avoided by ensuring you are clear on the specific information you need before looking at records.

A basic part of good research is 'triangulation', This is where several sources of information are used to cross check each other. In this way mistakes from faulty records, poor questioning or biased observation can be seen and discounted. The varied the sources of information used, the more accurate the results.

What sort of results can traditional research methods usefully produce for community development? As an example, Barr,

Hashagen and Purcell (1996) suggest the following types of questions may be useful to ask to gain an understanding of an area.

History - how has the area or interest community come to be as it is? What historical events colour perceptions that people have of themselves and their neighbourhood / interest group? This information is often important in appreciating the degree of difficulty that may be involved in achieving change. Here there is likely to be an emphasis on consulting existing records and informal interviewing of key informants.

Environment - how is space used or abused? Not only physical layout but occupancy density and condition of environment, including housing, roads and public space, are critical? Who is responsible for what aspects of the environment? In this context observation is likely to be a particularly important tool.

The residents - how many are there, where do they come from, how long have they been there, what do they do, how poor / affluent are they, what conditions do they live in, what are their values and traditions, what are their demographic characteristics, what services do they use, how far do they perceive themselves as sharing common interests and so on? It should be noted that there are likely to be identifiable sub groups within any population. Their relationships may be a source of tension. Much data will already be available from a variety of sources to supply this information. It is likely to need to be supplemented by observation and by questioning.

Organisations - There will usually be a wide range of organisations functioning in a neighbourhood or in relation to particular interest communities. These include commercial organisations, public sector agencies of local and central government, religious bodies, voluntary agencies as well as organisations created and owned by the community itself. Some will be located in the area while others will service it from outside. Who are they, what do they do, what resources do they have, and what influence do they have on neighbourhood affairs? Such organisations control resources that are potentially of vital importance in the achievement of change. Questioning will be a primary means of establishing who is involved but the exploration of their role is likely to be facilitated as much by access to agency documentation and observations of interactions with the community.

Communications - this dimension is particularly important to the consideration of process. The researcher needs to know how information is passed on both formally and informally. The latter is often most significant but hardest to discover - who are the opinion leaders, what are the key networks in operation in the community, how are they sustained? How effective is communication between local community interests and external agencies? A combination of informal questioning and observation is likely to be relevant for this purpose.

Power and leadership - it is crucial to know who has power and how it is used. This relates both to the external organisations operating in the community and to the community itself. It requires understanding the role of politicians, local and central government officers of all kinds, religious leaders, business and commercial leaders as well as understanding the politics and power struggles within the community and its internal organisations. Records of events (particularly in local media), informal questioning and observation are all likely to be of importance.

Stage 2 - Planning how to take action on identified needs

Developing working groups

If a participatory approach has been used to collecting information about, and analysing the community there will be plenty of people ready to take action for change. However, the temptation to rush into unplanned activism has to be avoided; as does the other impulse, for 'experienced' or professional people to take control, at the expense of excluding other local people. The critical tasks of action planning and evaluating achievements have to be done, but this is achievable in an open and participatory environment.

The smaller groups that explored the issues in stage 1 will provide the core of the working groups to take action. But these groups must be based on openness and a willingness to actively include all interested parties. The bigger the group, the more powerful and influential it will be. In chapter 8 we explored the issues relating to working with groups. These principles have to be applied consistently throughout the action and evaluation stages.

Perhaps the easiest and most common way forward in developing working groups is for the people involved in profiling the community to hold a public meeting to propose the formation of an action group. Following the principles of good participatory practice can ensure the success of the public meeting. Rather than simply relying on leaflets to advertise the meeting local people can use word or mouth, house meetings, the media, local displays and events to create local interest and boost attendance.

The group that is created following the meeting has to develop its own method of working. As we discussed in chapter 8 this has to be done carefully so that group structure and operation meets the needs of work, rather than vice versa. The starting point has to be *'what is the best way to manage our tasks'* not *'lets elect a committee to decide how to manage the tasks'*. A committee structure may be the best solution but it should never be chosen simply by default.

Meeting the Planners

For most, although not all, community work there comes a point when it is necessary to work with external agencies and government bodies to take the work forward jointly or apply for funding. What is important is that local community organisation is clear about its objectives, how it wants to proceed, is strong enough to be able to make its case and negotiate effectively and is prepared for the negotiation.

It has to be recognised that external agencies; Health Boards, local government departments, local enterprise companies, and miscellaneous quangos all have their own legitimate areas of responsibility, expertise and priorities. Successful negotiation requires a range of understanding on the part of the community organisation. This includes an understanding of the nature of participation and power as explored in chapter 7 and sense of how it works locally. The civic index analysis can be helpful here.

Negotiations should be approached on win – win basis from which everyone gets something they want. What is important is that the community organisation knows its bottom line; the things that cannot be given away or compromised.

Negotiations need to be handled carefully. The days when agencies considered they were doing a community organisation a favour by simply talking to them are, hopefully, long gone. However, it is still not uncommon for community organisations to be diverted from their goal through being offered money for projects that may be key for the agency but not the community; for example offering a housing campaign group funding for a tenant's hall, with the result that the community group ends up concentrating on social activities at the expense of housing improvements.

Many agencies now realise that it is in their own interest to work in a genuine collaborative way with community organisations. This requires the giving up of some power if the relationship is to be genuine participation rather than a token gesture. The powerful, organised and media savvy the community organisation the more likely it is to negotiate a suitable relationship. Sometimes this is not possible and the alternative to giving in, p is campaigning. We explore campaigning options in the next chapter.

Action Planning

Success in taking action depends upon careful planning. To borrow a slogan from business:

Remember the 6 P's

Perfect Prior Planning Prevents Poor Performance

This is just as true for community work. There is no point rushing off without being absolutely clear about what is to be done and why it is to be done this way. Much community work is justified on the grounds that being busy is the same as being effective. Such an approach is often called mindless activism and should be avoided. It is seldom possible to have both maximum quantity of work with maximum quality. The production of quality work requires time and careful planning.

It is useful to remember the concept of *opportunity costs*. That is to take an action is to exclude an alternative action. Nothing should be done unless it is clear that this is the best option and alternatives have been considered. This is not to say that the community group should become bogged down and indecisive. Decisions need to be made and the work progressed as quickly as possible. The key to success is to make the best decision in a planned way.

Let us explore an example of action planning. Suppose the community has identified the needs of lone parents as an issue. The detailed work above will have refined the issue in a number of ways. An example could be the need for local accessible and affordable child care, opportunities for education for lone parents, social support systems, and local community safety issues. Each one of these sub issues need to be linked to specific objectives that are achievable.

According to Jane Clark (1997) objectives need to be:

- realistic
- clear
- specific
- timed
- as concrete as possible
- measurable
- achievable

As we are talking about community work the objectives also need to relate directly to the five key aspects of community empowerment from the community development model (personal empowerment, positive action, developing community organisations, power relationships and participation, and leadership), outputs and the quality of life outcomes that we discussed in chapter 7. If we explore with local people the issue needs of lone parents against these headings we may get objectives something like the following:

Personal empowerment – Explore how the work may change peoples lives. Examples could be:

- Informal educational opportunities for leisure activities

- Informal and formal education opportunities for employment related skills and qualification
- Informal approaches to building the confidence of lone parents

Positive action - Explore how the work will target disadvantaged people. Examples may be:

- Prioritisation of access to educational opportunities for lone parents
- Prioritisation of access to child care for children of lone parent
- Group work with lone parents to explore their self image and vision of a better life

Development of Community Organisations - Explore how the work may build and support community organizations. Examples could be:

- Establishing a lone parent support group
- Establishing an after school club
- Linking lone parents to groups and organisations outside the community

Power Relationships and Participation - Explore how the work may change policies, and services. Examples may be:

- Linking lone parents to structures within the community —e.g. fora and partnerships
- Assisting lone parents to understand how to access resources
- Assisting lone parents how to change relevant policies and procedures

Leadership- Explore how leadership will be developed through the work. Examples may be:

- Local people taking responsibility for running the services

- Local people learning the skills and knowledge to make the correct decisions
- Clear and accountable processes for decision making

The above lists are refined and achievable sets of objectives. However, they may still represent a workload in excess of what the organisation can achieve. If so, the organisation may need to prioritise working on the objectives or phase them over a number of years.

The next step is to be clear on the following questions. *What do these objectives look like when specified in detail* and *what are the likely effects of the work*? Put another way we are asking about **outputs** and ***quality of life outcomes***. The objective is what you intend to do; the output is what you have actually delivered. An output is something that the project has direct responsibility and control in delivering. The project can therefore be credited with success if the output is achieved and has to take responsibility if it is not. In contrast an outcome is something that happens as a result of the outputs of the project but which is subject to a number of factors outside the control of the project. Sometimes outcomes are called impacts.

For example, an output in this example may the direct provision of training to a group of lone parents by a local community organisation. Whether this provision is actually delivered and its quality is clearly the responsibility of the organisation. What happens as a result of this training in an outcome. In the case of our example lone parents obtaining work or going onto further education. Clearly this is outside the control of the community organisation even though it may influence what happens. Funding bodies often make outcomes of the work a criterion of success. It is better for groups receiving funding to try and ensure they are judged on what they actually control, that is the output of their work.

In both cases it is important that the change is measured otherwise it is impossible to really know what is being achieved, what works and what does not. For this measurement of change to happen it is important to know what the situation was like before the work started. This is called in the jargon, establishing the *baseline*, and is based on collecting relevant information. The same information is collected periodically and is known as monitoring. It is collected again at the end of a piece of work. This final comparison of information gathered at the beginning to that at the end is part of the evaluation process.

How do we know what information to collect? In our example we have identified as an objective the provision of informal and formal education opportunities for lone parents. We need now to identify *indicators* that will tell us if this has been successfully achieved. Indicators can be *qualitative*, that is based on peoples feeling and understanding. Or indicators may be *quantitative* and based on statistics. Many funded community activities are measured solely in quantitative terms. The concern being the number of people involved rather than the quality and usefulness of their experience. Good practice requires a sensible mixture of qualitative and quantitative indicators. In our example of we may use the feedback of course students as a qualitative indicator and the number who completed the course as a quantitative indicator

In most cases it is not necessary to have many indicators. What is important is that the indicators used tell us something critical about the work. Very often this information is readily available in existing statistics or can be easily collected through interviews, focus groups, 'vox pops', observations and questionnaires. It is good practice to use a variety of different kinds of information to give a broad understanding of the nature of the work.

Following through our example we can now construct a workable plan. The following table puts together the above components using a selection of our objectives and the related outputs and outcomes. As can be seen from the table the clarity of purpose that this action planning process creates allows reliable estimates to be made of how long pieces of work will take, the sequence of events, whose responsibility it is for their completion, resources required and any critical factors that may impede success.

Objectives	Output / Outcome	By Whom	When	Indicator	Resources Required	Critical Factors
Establishing a lone parent support group	1 Making contact with lone parents	Community worker	Sept and Oct 06	List of people contacted	Workers time 10 days	Identification of interested people
	2 Exploring needs of these lone parents	Community worker and other lone parents	Nov Dec 06	Completed meetings	Worker time Meeting Space Refreshment	Meeting planning and preparation
	3. Formation of a lone parents support group	Community worker and other lone parents	Dec 06	Formation of group	Worker time Meeting room Admin support	Adequate interest and preparation
Linking lone parents to groups / organisations outside the community	1 Provision of joint activities by lone parent support group	Community worker and other lone parents	April 07	Range of new provision	Volunteers Question'res Admin support	Ability of group
	2 Linking new lone parents group to programme providers	Community Worker	Feb 07	Meeting taking place	Worker time	Response of providers Support to lone parents
	3 Increased opportunities available to lone parents from programme providers	Programme providers	Sept 07	Improved provision	From programme providers	Monitor planned changes

Stage 3 - Monitoring and evaluation and lessons for the future

Participatory monitoring and evaluation

We now have a planning model that links the following aspects of practice:

Aims *to*
   Objectives *to*
      Output / Outcomes *to*
         Indicators *to*
            Information Collection

Evaluation is the final stage in this process. We need to know how successful we have been, or otherwise, know what aspects of our plan have succeeded and which failed, and to be able to review the planning process. We can also reflect upon the whole process of the work and learn appropriate lessons on how to move forward.

For many people evaluation is threatening as its makes failure and its reasons clear. Far better, some people claim, is to avoid these exposures and make general (and unsubstantiated) claims about your performance by hiding behind the myth that community work cannot be evaluated. However, we must confront our anxieties here. If we cannot effectively demonstrates successes, why will funding bodies continue to give us money. More importantly, why should local people support what we do, and how do we know that we are doing the best we can for the community.

It is commonly thought that evaluation is a highly technical process than can only be properly undertaken by external experts. This is not the case. Outside expertise is useful in evaluation in reviewing the information collected to give an 'objective' view and to ask the difficult questions. However, local people can undertake the majority of evaluation tasks. Sometimes training on data collection techniques, interviewing or questionnaire design may be required, but this is just part of the normal local capacity building process. What is important is that all stakeholders in the evaluation (workers, funders, service users, local people) are confident in the evaluation plan and how it is to be undertaken. The difference between a traditional external evaluation and a participative evaluation is not the rigour of the process but the direct involvement of local people in, and the demystification of, the process.

Evaluations can become a participative exercise through using a problem posing method everyone concerned. The following illustrates the process using our lone parent example.

Why evaluate? – This question needs to be discussed first. Everyone involved has to identify why they want and evaluation to take place and what for them are the key issues. A wide variety of ideas and needs are likely to be produced which all have to be incorporated in the evaluation.

What needs to be evaluated? - For practical reasons it is impossible to evaluate everything. Only evaluate what has been identified as the key issues. But keep in mind that it may be impossible to evaluate some aspects due to difficulties in collecting information.

Who is involved? – Everyone with a direct interest in the work should be involved in its evaluation. In the example above of lone parents this may include:

- Lone parents groups
- Other lone parents in the area
- Community workers
- Project management
- Funding organisations
- Other directly related organisations

Has the work changed people's lives? – This question relates directly to the planned objectives built around personal empowerment, positive action, building community organisations, power and participation, improvements in the quality of life and sustainability. The evaluation needs evidence to show changes according to the agreed selection of outputs and outcomes. Using the example above we can ask if, a lone parent group been established, how many people attend, do they attend regularly and what do they say they gain from participating. Notice that these basic questions should cover both the qualitative and quantitative aspects of evaluation.

Has the work included disadvantaged people? – In some ways this question revisits the positive action point identified above. However, it is worth including separately to ensure that minority groups or hard to contact people have been included in the work. Often we content ourselves with working with easy to reach people. It may be that there are many lone parents who are not part of the group and who either do not know about or who are not confident enough to attend. The evaluation should explore what has been done to assist in this area.

Is the work relevant for local people? – This again checks how the piece of work was identified and how important it is currently for the community. Asking this question ensures that the organisation has to look outside of itself and its usual group members for a wider view on community need.

When to evaluate – Once we have answered the above questions we simply select the appropriate objectives, outputs, outcomes and indicators from the action plan. Collect the agreed information and we will know what has and has not been achieved. This exercise needs to take place at least three times. Firstly, when the action plan has been agreed but before the work starts to identify the baseline situation. Secondly, at regular points to check if the work is proceeding to plan and to identify any changes that may be necessary. This mid point exercise is called monitoring and should take place at regular intervals. So over a three year project monitoring may take place after 9 months, 18 months and 27 months. The final exercise is the full evaluation. This compares the situation at the time of the baseline to the final position. The monitoring exercises help to track the changes and how they took place.

How can we make this information available and useful? - Evaluation reports can be used for a variety of purposes. For example to:

- take stock of the current situation
- see if the work is being effective

- help plan changes and future development in the work
- report back to funders
- report back to the wider community
- provide evidence for further funding
- promote the work of the organisation in the media
- inform possible changes in local government services and policies.

It is important to make the information available in the most accessible and appropriate way. The report to a funding body should normally be detailed with financial and statistical appendices. As the basis of a report to the wider group, community or AGM, a short abstract would be more effective along with posters, displays and perhaps a short video or PowerPoint presentation that included photographs. For a press release personal quotes and photographs can be used. Like all participative work imaginative and accessible ways to put your ideas across should be employed.

Summary

In this chapter we have covered the following points:

- Traditional top down and expert driven approaches to development have not been successful
- Participatory approaches, especially PRA and PLA, from the developing world provide a more effective model of practice
- These approaches match well with Freirian methods of finding the generative theme and exploring the meaning of codes
- PRA, PLA and Freirian practice have generated a wide range of tried and test participative techniques that can be applied across settings and contexts
- It is essential to take the time to identify local needs from the perspective of local people
- Success in community work is based upon correctly identifying need and exploring the related essential knowledge before embarking on the action phase

- Action needs to be carefully planned, monitored and evaluated
- Negotiate with external agencies from a carefully developed and powerful position
- External experts have an important role in supporting this process
- The continuing direct involvement of local people, and their control of the process, is intrinsic to this method

Further Reading

The practical guides for participatory practice listed at the end of the resource section provide a wide range of proven methods.

The Eldis web site at www.eldis.org/ has extensive links to papers and projects relating to participatory practice

10

Practice Perspectives: Campaigning

Gentlemen, he said,
I don't need your organization, I've shined your shoes,
I've moved your mountains and marked your cards
But Eden is burning, either brace yourself for elimination
Or else your hearts must have the courage for the
changing of the guards.   Bob Dylan

Aims of the Chapter

This chapter looks the process of organising a campaign. This includes consideration of how to start and build an organisation, the use of the media and the basic techniques of taking non violent direct action.

Why Campaign

With the current pressure to work with stakeholders and to enter into partnerships, the idea of campaigning has almost begun to feel outdated and illegitimate. After all we are all working together as partners now. However, there are times when local needs are ignored, powerful organisations run over local views and interests and the intolerable is about to happen. The choices then are simple. Either roll over and accept it, or campaign. As Frederick Douglass the 19th century anti slavery campaigner wrote:

> "If there is no struggle there is no progress. Those who profess to favour freedom and yet depreciate agitation...want crops without ploughing up the ground, they want rain without thunder and lightening. They want the ocean without the awful roar of its many waters.... Power

concedes nothing without a demand. It never did and it never will."

In fact campaigning happens all the time. Social change from women gaining the vote to the democratisation of Northern Ireland has come about largely through organised protest. The chapter on the secret history of protest illustrates this macro change process as well as some of the micro changes in communities. We have to remember that non violent direct action is a basic democratic right. This chapter explores the how to of campaigning.

Starting a Campaign Group

Campaigning groups usually come about as a result of frustration. After years of complaining, letter writing and lobbying local councillors and MP's with no result, frustration builds and local people decide to take action themselves. Alternatively, the group may start suddenly when a new road or quarry is announced that local people believe will have an unacceptable detrimental effect on their quality of life.

Usually campaigning is based upon two core principles and it is important to keep these in mind. Firstly, the purpose of a campaign is to make real improvements in the quality of people's lives. There is no point in running a campaign as a noble but failed gesture. If you do not expect to win there is no point in campaigning.

Secondly, campaigning is all about power. You are building an organisation to make somebody else that already has power do what you want. It is essential therefore that you understand what power the opposition has, and what that power is based upon. Campaigns need to create an organisation that itself is powerful so that it can engage the opposition. For this to be achieved campaigns need to both successfully build their organisational and empower their members to take the appropriate action.

In many ways though, a campaigning group is just like any other community group. They have to be open, democratic and accountable. The differences are that they also have to be very flexible and quick to respond to situations and be inherently creative.

Such requirements clearly mean that the committee driven group that meets monthly is out.

Most campaigning groups are therefore non-hierarchical. Often they are organised into sub groups where responsibility, say for media relation, fundraising and event organising. Each sub group gets on with its job and is accountable back to the membership through campaign meetings. Such a structure allows creativity and innovation. The learning circle approach discussed in chapter 8 can also be useful in assisting people to research and explore the technical issues relating to many campaigns. For example, understanding relevant legislation or health issues linked to pollution.

Campaign meetings should take place when required with flexible agendas that allow the members to focus on the critical subjects at that time. There needs to be an overall structure to facilitate this and a mechanism to record decisions, track money and chair meetings. These tasks can rotate, although it is sensible to let people who have the skills take the jobs. However, in many such organisations keen, but inexperienced members shadow experienced workers, to learn the required skills.

As the membership grows the new procedure need to be adopted to ensure everyone has voice. One approach is the 'talking stick' method where an object (stick, stone, or even a microphone) circulates through the meeting. Only the person holding the object can speak. This restricts a few individuals for dominating the meeting.

Campaigning groups need to take a decision on how far their protests should go. Will they stay within the boundary of conventional protest: demonstrations, mass lobbying, media events. Or will they embark on non violent direct action where people physically confront the issue. This may be for example through a vigil, members chaining themselves to building or trees to block demolition, or occupying a building. Either way, the success of the campaign will depend upon effective organisation and the thoughtful application of strategy and tactics. We mention the classic strategy of Sun Tzu and the community organising work of Saul Alinsky in chapter 7. Their writings should be studied as a primer for campaigning techniques.

Building the Organisation

As Alinsky pointed out the campaigns are only won by effective organisation, and the way to build an organisation is to campaign around the issue. Organisation can be built through a variety of methods: leaflets, posters, stickers, petitions, postcards, stalls, door knocking, route walks, house meetings, mailing lists and phone trees public meetings, social events, newsletters, and the Internet

Leaflets are the most common way of distributing basic information about a campaign. In one sense they are ineffective. The number of people who become actively involved through reading a leaflet is very small. Their main value is that they create a strong impression that things are happening. For this to work the leaflet has to be professional, after all they are in competition with every other advertisement for people attention. The environmental campaigning group Road Alert suggests that effective leaflets should follow the following guidelines.

- Computers produce bold, legible designs, but these will look less friendly than (well) hand- produced ones. Avoid messy, badly-drawn designs.

- Unless you're advertising an event, avoid putting details on the leaflet that will soon make it out-of-date. Ensure all vital information is included, especially a contact address, email and phone number.

- Keep the design simple, as it is likely to be photocopied, and thus distorted, many times.

- Always bear in mind the audience, and write to change other peoples' opinions, not to confirm your own.

- Resist the temptation to use jargon, exercise your personal hobby horse, or write leaflets while influenced by mind-altering substances...

- Unless the design is untraceable to your campaign, don't incite anything illegal.

- Check the draft leaflet with a few others before you finally copy it. Also, test them on people not connected with the campaign.
- File paper originals and disk copies, so you can easily produce more and update them if required.

Linked to a leaflet campaign is the use of posters, small stickers and handing out postcards for people to fill in or petitions to sign. Setting up a stall in a shopping area or other popular public space attracts attention. It also creates the opportunity to talk to people, which is the only really effective way to involve others in taking action. Be prepared though, for people who disagree with you who want to talk (argue) as well.

If the issue clearly effects a geographical location then door knocking can be very effective. Usually the local community is the last to know what is happening and a significant number of people are likely to be interested in what you have to say. Again the key to success is to be friendly and reasonable. If it is relevant, for example campaigning against a road, then a route walk with media coverage can be a powerful event and a further opportunity to talk to local people and hand out information.

Once significant contact has been made with local people a good organisational tactic is the house meeting. This is a North American technique that is both effective and simple. A campaign member asks an interested local resident to invite five or so, friends, neighbours or relatives to a meeting in their house. The campaign issues are discussed and local people's interests and concerned are explored. The meeting ends by each person being asked to organise their own house meeting, and so on. Very quickly existing local networks are used to have the issue discussed throughout the community. This network can be the basis for a targeted mailing list. In addition each house person can be organised on a telephone tree. This is where the campaign can phone selected people, who then in turn phone others. In this way information can be distributed very quickly throughout the community.

The traditional public meeting can also be used effectively for campaigning. For a public meeting to work a large turnout of local people is required. This is more likely to happen if the above work of talking to people and discussing the issue with them has taken place. A further aid to making public meetings work is to attach it to a social event where people can informally meet each other, share food and have fun. Alinksy reminds us that a good action is where people feel comfortable and enjoy themselves. Successful social events also provide the opportunity for fund raising.

Finally a good well written and properly printed newsletter keeps people informed of what is happening and what is about to happen. In the same vein the Internet is now an indispensable tool for campaigning. Emails are the easiest way to keep people informed and a professionally looking web site gives a global face to your campaign. Currently around one in three house holds have access to the Internet and the figure is increasing rapidly. Internet skills are common in the community and finding competent people to run a web site is not that difficult.

Using the Media

As Paul Routledge pointed out above, and as experience campaigners have known for years, the battle is won or lost in media space. The effective use of the media is therefore crucial to both build support and pressure the opposition. You may wonder why the media would be interested in your cause. Well, if you have a genuine issue and can organise creatively around it, the media will come and play.

The key to involving the media is to use effective press releases. The press release should be written in a way that will appeal to the audience of the publication. This means different version for local newspapers, national tabloids and broadsheets, local radio and TV. There are a number of 'rules' around press releases. Conforming to the rules makes you look competent and organised. Road Alert summarise the following as key to an effective press release:

- Mark NEWS RELEASE clearly at the top - plus your campaign name, phone number, email and logo.

- Next, put date of issue and mark "FOR IMMEDIATE RELEASE" unless it is embargoed (that is you do not want it used until a particular date and time). When publicising an event, make sure the press release is out well in advance.

- Use a snappy headline.

- Include a summary of the main facts in the first paragraph, including WHAT is happening, WHERE, WHY, WHEN and by WHOM. It needs to immediately grab an Editor's attention or will be binned.

- The press release should be short, factual and well-written. Avoid opinionated rants and jargon.

- Use short paragraphs and simple sentences. Keep to one or at most two pages.

- Use a quote by an identified person to tell your side of the story. Use pseudonyms if you do not want your name in the paper.

- Write ENDS at the foot of the press release.

Also make sure there is a named person and preferably a mobile phone number on the release who is briefed and available to respond to calls. It can also very useful to include photographs with the press release. It is not that difficult to get yourself on local radio and even TV. Be prepared for this and role play getting your message over in two minutes or less. Always be charming and friendly. There is nothing more counter productive than appearing aggressive. The people to front the group for the media should be those who come over best. It is ability here that is important not status. Once you have made contact with journalists you need to foster the relationship and continually feed them information. Having a professional journalist supporting your campaign can be a cause winning asset.

Taking Action

If the group decides on taking direct action it has to be carefully planned and organised. The purpose of the action has to clear and its impact in the media carefully analysed. There is little point doing something that will alienate potential support. Whatever action you take it has to appear a reasonable response to the situation.

Ideally, good relationships with the police will be in place to minimise the possibility of arrests. But just in case everyone should know their rights and be committed to peaceful action whatever the provocation. Friendly lawyers should be available just in case it goes wrong. Video recording of the action can also restrict overreaction by the opposition and provide evidence for the defence in court should the worst happen.

Road Alert has identified the following checklist for preparing a direct action event. In their case the action were focussed on road development, however the principles apply generally to other situations.

Checklist for Organising an Action

1. Choose a name, date and broad focus as far in advance as possible (at least a month).

2. Start networking now!

3. Fundraise.

4. Ask people from other towns and cities to organise and advertise transport to the action.

5. Organise accommodation, food, toilets and entertainment.

6. Prepare Legal Support, Action Observers and contact a solicitor.

7. Consider whether to invite media, and if so, send out a press release.

8. If intending to stop work, know what work is happening where, and get to know work patterns.

9. Ensure you have a realistic and strong focus for the day.

10. Form an elementary plan, including decoys and back up plan. Build in a large element of flexibility so that people coming in can have an input.

11. Acquire necessary equipment and tools, including communications.

12. Think about transport needs on the day - walking, bikes, hire vans and public transport are all options.

13. Draft accurate maps of the area, including more detailed ones of the target sites.

14. Make sure you have a team of people to fill all the important roles on the day - drivers, legal support team, media spokespeople, site guides for each affinity group, camp sitters, cooks, office staffers, route monitors and people to clear up afterwards.

15. Hold briefings and training sessions preferably the day before.

16. Get an early night the night before an action. Wake people up in plenty of time and have breakfast prepared.

Campaigning can take a long time. They are usually very stressful on participants, but they are also transformative. Most long term campaigners come through the experience as stronger more confident, knowledgeable skilled and aware. Friendships are made and people move on to share their new expertise with others.

Summary

In this chapter we have suggested:

- It is a basic right to resort to non violent direct action campaigning when required
- Campaigning groups need to be creative and flexible if they are to succeed
- The larger and stronger the organisation the more chance of success
- Creative approaches need to be used to build an organisation

- There is *no* substitute for talking with local people about the issues.
- The campaign my be won or lost depending on how well the group uses the media
- Actions taken as part of the campaign need to be carefully planned and realised
- Actions should be used to build public support not antagonise it
- Campaigning is a challenging but transformative experience.

Further Reading

The classic texts for direct action campaigning are the Saul Alinsky books: **Reveille for Radicals** (New York, Vintage Books a 1969) and Rules **for Radicals** (New York, Random House 1971).

In the UK context both Michale Latimer and Road Alert offer detailed practical guides to campaigning: **The Campaign Handbook** (Directory of Social Change 200) and **Road Raging,** on the Internet at: http://www.eco-action.org/rr/index.html, respectively.

A thorough explanation of campaigning methods as practices in the USA is contained in **Organizing for Social Change** by Bobo, Kendall and Max (Santa Ana, Seven Locks Press, 1996)

Underpinning all this is the classic text by SunTzu on the art of war. This is available on the Internet at www.sonshi.com

Appendix 1 – Community Development Model (Purcell 2004)

Inputs
from external agencies: resources and policies

Inputs
from resources within the community

Reflection Vision Planning Action Cycle
+
Building Learning Orgs

Community Empowerment Process
- Personal Empowerment
- Positive Action
- Buildings Collective Organisations
- Power Relationships and Participation
- Leadership

Capital Outputs
Social
Economic
Human

Specific Outputs
Buildings
Activities
Etc.

***Sustainable* Quality of Life Outcomes**
- Economic
- Environmental
- Social

Underpinned by development values and human rights

Appendix 2 - Model of Participatory Practice

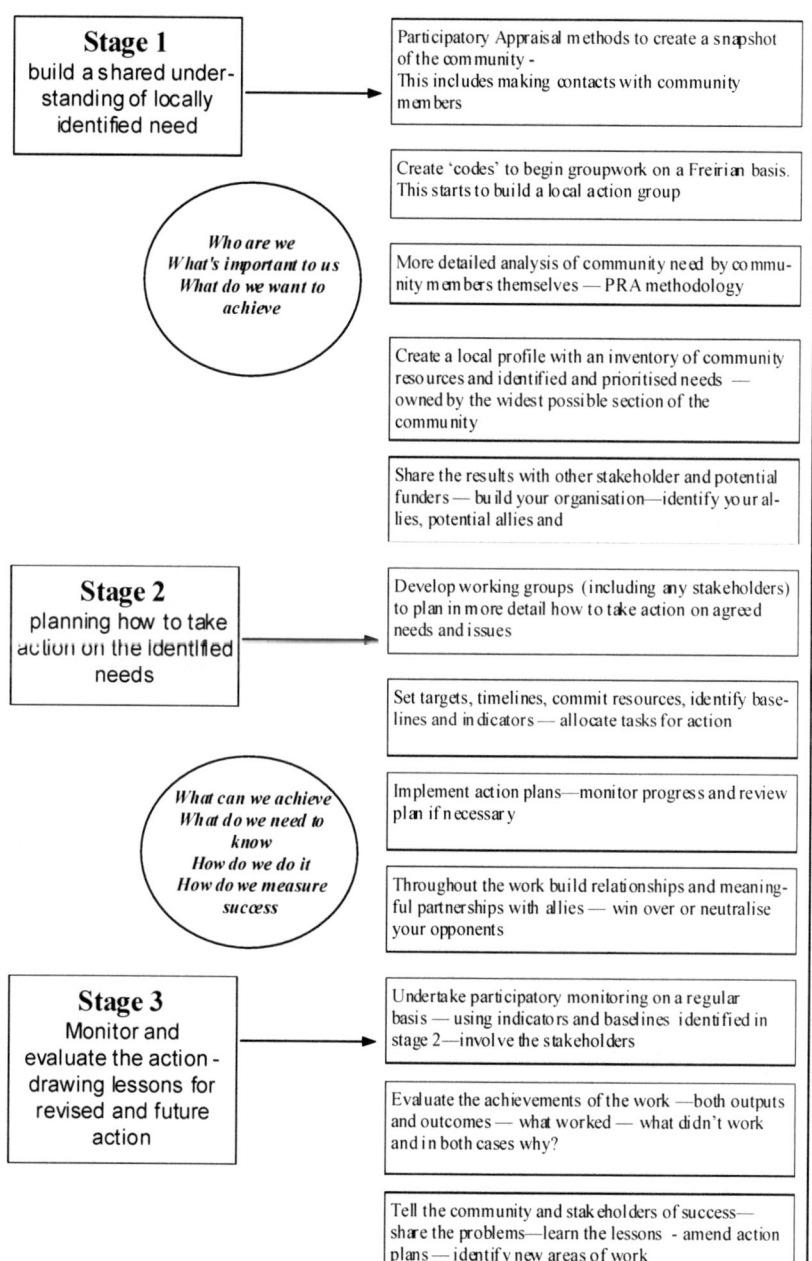

Appendix 3 – Millennium Development Goals

Goal	Current Position	Expected date of achievement
1. Eradicate extreme poverty and hunger *Target for 2015: Halve the proportion of people living on less than a dollar a day and those who suffer from hunger.*	More than a billion people still live on less than US$1 a day: sub-Saharan Africa, Latin America and the Caribbean, and parts of Europe and Central Asia are falling short of the poverty target.	The target has largely been met in East Asia and the Pacific, but Sub-Saharan Africa, Latin America and the Caribbean, and parts of Europe and Central Asia are falling short.
2. Achieve universal primary education *Target for 2015: Ensure that all boys and girls complete primary school*	As many as 113 million children do not attend school, but the target is within reach. India, for example, should have 95 percent of its children in school by 2005.	Many regions1 are on track to achieve the target before 2015, but lower levels of achievement and progress persist in sub-Saharan Africa, Western Asia and Southern Asia.
3. Promote gender equality and empower women *Targets for 2005 and 2015: Eliminate gender disparities in primary and secondary education preferably by 2005, and at all levels by 2015.*	Two-thirds of illiterates are women, and the rate of employment among women is two-thirds that of men. The proportion of seats in parliaments held by women is increasing, reaching about one third in Argentina, Mozambique and South Africa.	In developing countries, gender gaps still exist in enrolment at all levels of education.

4. Reduce child mortality *Target for 2015: Reduce by two thirds the mortality rate among children under five*	Every year nearly 11 million young children die before their fifth birthday, mainly from preventable illnesses, but that number is down from 15 million in 1980.	In developing countries on average, more than 100 children die before age 5, for every 1,000 born.
5. Improve maternal health *Target for 2015: Reduce by three-quarters the ratio of women dying in childbirth.*	In the developing world, the risk of dying in childbirth is one in 48, but virtually all countries now have safe motherhood programmes.	Based on best estimates for 1995, maternal mortality is far higher in all developing regions, compared to developed, and fifty times higher in sub-Saharan Africa.
6. Combat HIV/AIDS, malaria and other diseases *Target for 2015: Halt and begin to reverse the spread of HIV/AIDS and the incidence of malaria and other major diseases*	Forty million people are living with HIV, including five million newly infected in 2001. Countries like Brazil, Senegal, Thailand and Uganda have shown that the spread of HIV can be stemmed.	HIV prevalence rates are still increasing for men and women in the developing world. The rate is seven times higher in developing countries than developed countries for women, and almost three times higher for men.
7. Ensure environmental sustainability *Targets:*	More than one billion people lack access to safe drinking water and more than two billion lack sanitation.	Worldwide emissions of CO_2 — the largest single source of greenhouse gas emissions from human

• Integrate the principles of sustainable development into country policies and programmes and reverse the loss of environmental resources. • By 2015, reduce by half the proportion of people without access to safe drinking water. • By 2020 achieve significant improvement in the lives of at least 100 million slum dwellers	During the 1990s, however, nearly one billion people gained access to safe water and the same number to sanitation.	activities — hardly changed on a per capita basis.
8. Develop a global partnership for development		*Net official development assistance — as a percentage of donor countries' gross national income (GNI) — has decreased over the last decade and is at an all-time low, and net ODA to least developed countries has decreased even more.*

(Source UNDP)

Appendix 4 – Models of Poverty

Political Dimension	Conservative	Third Way / New Labour	Radical / Revolution'y	Radical / Revolution'y
Type of activity	*Welfare*	*Development*	*Liberation*	*Transformatn*
Causes of the problem	Circumstances beyond the control of local people Bad luck National disasters	Lack of Education Lack of resources causing low standard of living Lack of opportunities	Exploitation Domination Oppression Oppression Alienation	Inadequate structures and values
Goals	To relieve immediate suffering	Develop self reliance Equal opportunities	Challenge and overcome exploitative structures	Build alternative economic, political, legal and educational structures
Service programes	Care of the disabled Child care Clinics, famine relief	Income producing activities Savings / redit Affirmative action	Trade Unions Political parties Movements Conscientisatn programmes	Co-operatives, workers councils, new forms of education and management
Types of change	*Function and non-conflictual*	*Function and non-conflictual*	*Structural and conflictual*	*Structural and conflictual*
Type of leadership	Strong reliance on authority	Consultative	Shared by delegation of authority from base up. Strong discipline	Animation, enabling, participatory, shared responsibility
Inspiration	Help the Poor Charity	Help People to help themselves	Vision	Making things new

Adapted from Training for Transformation, Hope and Timmel 1991

Appendix 5 – Components of Community Empowerment

1. Personal Empowerment *means working to develop:*	2. Positive Action *means working to develop:*
<ul><li>Informal skill and knowledge derived from community activity</li><li>Non formal training and education opportunity related to the purpose of the group / community development and its effect on individuals and groups</li><li>Formal training and education opportunity related to the purpose of the group / community development and its effect on individuals and groups</li><li>Conscious belief in the possibility of change; personal – group – community</li><li>Capacity for effective action as individuals and in community groups</li><li>Growth of leadership within the community</li><li>Understanding of how to use power for the benefits of the community</li></ul>	<ul><li>Acceptance that the principles of social justice and collective support should underpin community activity</li><li>Understanding of needs in relation to discrimination</li><li>Equal opportunities policies</li><li>Equal opportunities practice</li><li>Affirmation and assertion of own cultural heritage and identity</li><li>Affirmation of other cultures</li></ul>

3. Development of Community Organisations *means working to develop:*	4 Power Relationships and Participation *means working to develop:*
• Investigation and monitoring of community needs • Increased activity in community organisations • Increased use of services provided by community organisations • Support networks between people in the community • Support networks between community organisations • Links between community organisations and other agencies / bodies • Structures to sustain long term action	• Strong democratic community organisations • Openness and accountability of community organisations • Understanding of policy frameworks and political systems • Effective influence by community organisations on public policy and practice • Capacity to participate effectively in the political process

5. **Leadership** *means working to develop*

- Accountability to local constituency
- Autonomy of the organisation
- Strategic thinking to make things happen
- Transformatory work based on needs and values
- Creating a learning driven organisation

(Adapted from Barr, Hashagen, Purcell 1996, Purcell 2004)

RESOURCES

Internet Resources

This is a collection of useful web sites. The addresses were correct at time of going to press.

Action Sites

Adbusters Innovative site turning advertising and consumerism against itself http://www.adbusters.org/

Culture Jamming Creative play on the 'Empire of Signs' http://www.abrupt.org/CJ/CJ.html

Direct Action Links Brings you the latest news from actions, demos and events, along with background features and campaigning resources. http://www.urban75.com/Action/index.html

Free Burma Coalition The campaign to free Burma from military rule http://www.freeburmacoalition.org/

GreenNet Collection of sites for peace, human rights and environmental action http://www.gn.apc.org/index.html

Live 8 Campaign against debt in the developing world http://www.live8live.com/

McSpotlight The classic anti McDonalds campaign site http://www.mcspotlight.org/

No Logo anti globalisation resources http://www.nologo.org/

Reclaim the Streets Opposition to globalisation and the reclaiming of public space http://www.reclaimthestreets.net/

Relief Web Latest news of relief mission across the world http://www.reliefweb.int/w/rwb.nsf

Undercurrents UK based alternative video based news
http://www.undercurrents.org/

Library Resources

INFED Archive of informal education
http://www.infed.org/

Search the Social Sciences (SOSIG) Search page of the Social Science Information Gateway, a useful source for academic information http://www.sosig.ac.uk/

Search for Community Development Resources Extensive links to UK Government bodies, voluntary agencies, policy bodies, etc
http://www.gla.ac.uk/Acad/AdultEd/Personnel/rodp/resources.htm

Wikipedia participatory encyclopaedia

http://en.wikipedia.org/wiki/Main_Page

Media Sites

Anatomy of Power Critical thinkers from Tom Paine to Marx to Postmodernists
http://www.davidsmail.freeuk.com/anpower.htm

Bureau of Public Secrets Off the wall collection of radical texts http://www.bopsecrets.org/

Noam Chomsky Archive The collected works of Noam, radical reworking of American imperialism and media
http://www.zmag.org/chomsky/

Economist The world according to the capitalist orthodoxy of globalisation http://www.economist.com

History of Ideas Collection of Marxist material
http://www.dcu.ie/~comms/philosophy/ph-texts.htm

Marxism on Line Internet resources to Marxist writers and history http://www.marxists.org/

Postmodernism Library Selection of resources by postmodernist writers http://www.euro.net/mark-space/Postmodern.html

Red Pepper UK left of centre magazine
http://www.redpepper.org.uk/

John Pilger Articles Archive and video material of the crusading journalist http://pilger.carlton.com/

ZMAG On line magazine with alternative views from the USA http://www.zmag.org/ZNETTOPnoanimation.html

Resource Sites

Changelinks New Zealand based site with substantial information for development and change activities
http://nrm.massey.ac.nz/changelinks/

Civic Society links Links to a range or organisations involved in promoting aspects of civic society
http://www.civicus.org/new/default.asp?skip2=yes

Community Toolbox USA based site with a wide range of practical tools for community health and development work
http://www.communitytoolbox.org/

Eldis Participation Resource site The international resource site for development information
http://www.eldis.org/

Human Development Reports he United Nations Development Programme reports on the current state of the world. http://hdr.undp.org/

Human Rights Home page for the UN High Commission for Human Rights, explores rights issues on a global basis
http://www.unhchr.ch/

Lifelong Learning The papers from the Open University Colloquium on Lifelong learning
http://www.open.ac.uk/lifelong-learning/index.html

Oneworld Portal for NGO's and development issues
http://www.oneworld.net/

PovertyNet World Bank resources site for poverty issues and development
http://www.worldbank.org/poverty/index.htm

RegenNet The UK information site for regeneration partnerships http://www.regen.net/

PRACTICAL GUIDES FOR PARTICIPATORY PRACTICE

The Reflect Mother Manual from ACTIONAID.

This manual uses a Freirian approach and the application of learning circles. Used extensively in Africa and Asia the main focus is on literacy work. However, the method and exercises can be adapted for a variety of ends.

Available from: ACTIONAID, Hamlyn House, Archway, London N19 5PG, 020 281 4101

Training for Transformation

A participative handbook for community workers in 4 volumes. Developed in, and written for, work in Southern Africa. These volumes provide an integrated and wide ranging practical approach to Freirian work

Available from Intermediate Technology publications, 103/103 Southampton Row, London, WC1B 4HH,

Living Adult Education: Freire in Scotland

Written by Gerri and Colin Kirkwood, this is the story of the creation of a Freirian inspired project in an inner city area. Gives lots of detail and significant insight in how to do it.

Limited availability through Amazon.

From the Roots Up: Strengthening Organisational capacity through guided self assessment

A very practical handbook for capacity building with lots of useful exercises and activities.

Available from World Neighbors, 4127 NW 122nd Street, Oklahoma City, Oklahoma, USA http://www.wn.org

Fun with 21: a source book for workshop facilitators

Written by Robert Chambers this is a source book of 21 sets of 21 ways to approach participatory events. On the net in pdf format, it can be downloaded and copied. In keeping with the ethos of participation comments on the methods are invited.

http://www.ids.ac.uk/ids/particip/research/pra/fun21.pdf

Bibliography

Abel-Smith, B. Townsend, P. 1965, *The Poor and the Poorest*, London: Bell
Abercrombie, N. 1980 *The Dominant Ideology Thesis*, London, George Allen and Unwin
Archer, A. Cottingham, S. 1996, *The Reflect Mother Manual*. Actionaid: London
Active Communities Unit, 1999, *Report of the Policy Action Team on Community Self Help,* London: Home Office
Ahmed, W. and Atkin, K., 1996, *Race and Community Care*, London: Routledge
Aigner, S. Butler, Flora C. Tirmizi, S. Wilcox, C. 1999, Dynamics to Sustain Community Development in Persistently Poor Rural Areas, in *Community Development Journal* 34.1
Alcock, P. 1996, *Social Policy in Britain: Themes and Issues*, Basingstoke: Macmillan
Alexander Report, 1975, *Adult Education and the Challenge of Change,* London: HMSO
Alinsky, S. 1969, *Reveille for Radicals*, New York: Vintage Books
Alinsky, S. 1971, *Rules for Radicals*, New York: Random House
Althusser, L. 1977, *Lenin and Philosophy and Other Essays,* New Left Books
Anderson, E. 1995 Street Etiquette and Street Wisdom, in *Metropolis: Center and Symbol of our times,* P Kasinitz (ed) New York: New York UP
Arnstein, S. 1969, A Ladder if Citizen Participation, in *Journal of the American Institute of Planners*, 35.4
Association of Metropolitan Authorities, 1989, *Community Development: the Local Authority Role*, London: AMA
Atampugre, N. 1998, Colonial and Contemporary Approaches to Community Development, in *Community Development Journal* 33.4
Aynton-Shenker, D. 1995, *The Challenge of Human Rights and Cultural Diversity*, United Nations Department of Public Information
Baldwin, S. 1993, *The Myth of Community Care, An Alternative Neighbourhood Model of Care*, London: Chapman and Hall
Banks, S. 1993, Community Youth Work in Butcher, Glen, Henderson and Smith, *Community and Public Policy*, London: Pluto Press
Barber, B. 1984, *Strong Democracy*
Barber, B. 1995, *Jihad Versus McWorld*, New York: Times Books

Barclay, P. 1982, *Social Workers their Role and Tasks (The Barclay Report)*, London: Bedford Square Press
Barker, H. 1986, Recapturing Sisterhood: A Critical Look at Process in Feminist Organising and Community Work, *Critical Social Policy* 16
Baron, S. Field, J. Schuller, T. 2000, *Social Capital: Critical Perspectives*, Oxford: Oxford University Press
Barr, A. 1991, *Practicing Community Development*, London: CDF
Barr, A. Drysdale, J. Henderson, P. 1997, *Towards Caring Communities*, Brighton: Pavilion
Barr, A. Drysdale, J. Purcell, R. Ross, C. 1995, *Strong Communities, Effective Government*, Vol 1 Summary of Practice Vol 2 Case studies, Glasgow: SCDC
Barr, A. Hamilton, R. Purcell, R. 1996, *Learning for Change*, London: CDF
Barr, A. Hashegan, S. Purcell, R., 1996, *Evaluation and Monitoring in Community Development*, Northern Ireland Voluntary Activities Unit, NI DHSS
Barry, M. 1998, Social Exclusion and Social Work, in Barry, M. and Hallet, C. *Social Exclusion and Social Work*, Dorset, Russel House Publishing
Barry, N. 1979, *Hayek's Social and Economic Philosophy*, Basingstoke: Macmillan
Batten, T. 1967, *The Non Directive Approach in Group and Community Work*, Oxford: Oxford University Press
Baudrillard, J. 1989, *America*, Blackwell Verso
Baudrillard, J. 1994, *In the Shadow of the Silent Majorities*, AK Press
Bauman, Z. 1998, From Pilgrim to Tourist - or a short history of Identity, in Hall, S. and du Gay, P. *Questions of Cultural Identity*, London: Sage
Becker, S. 1991, *Windows of Opportunity: Public Policy and the Poor*, London: CPAG
Benjamin, J. Bessant, J. Watts, R., 1997, *Making Groups Work. Rethinking Practice*, Allen and Unwin.
Beresford, P. Croft, S. 1993, *Citizen Involvement*, Basingstoke: Macmillan
Blackburn, J. Holland, J. 1998, *Who Changes? institutionalizing participation in development*, London: Intermediate Technology Publications
Blagg, H. Derricourt, N. 1982, Why we need to reconstruct a theory of the state, in Craig, G. *Community Work and the State*, London: Routledge and Kegan Paul
Blair, T. 1997, *Speech 2 June 1997 at the Aylesbury Estate*, Social Inclusion Unit
Blair, T. 1998, *The Third Way: New Politics for the New Century*, London: Fabian Society

Blair, T. 1999, *Speech January 1999 at NVCO on the Active Community* www.ccp.ca/information/documents/gd29.htm
Bobo, K. Kendall, J. Max, S. 1996, *Organizing for Social Change: a manual for activists,* Santa Ana: Seven Locks Press
Bolman, L. and Deal, T. 2003 *Reframing Organizations: Artistry, Choice, and Leadership,* Jossey Bass Wiley
Bottomley, V. 1996, *Building Communities: Community Development, Participation and Partnership,* Department of National Heritage
Bourdieu, P. 1985, The Forms of Capital, in Richardson, J. *Handbook of Theory of research for the Sociology of Education,* Greenwood Press
Bradshaw, J. 1972, The Concept of Social Need, *New Society,* 30 March
Brahan et al, 1994, *Racism and Anti Racism,* Buckingham: OUP
Brickell, P. 2000, *People Before Structures,* Demos
Bridges, W. 1974, *Helping People Develop Their Communities,* Lexington: University of Kentucky
Bryant, B. Bryant, R. 1982, *Change and Conflict - a study of community work in Glasgow,* Aberdeen: Aberdeen University Press
Bryson, V. *Feminist Political Theory,* Basingstoke: Macmillan
Buchanan, M. 2000, *Ubiquity,* London: Weidenfeld & Nicolson
Buckland, J. 1998, Social Capital and Sustainability of NGO Intermediated Development Projects in Bangladesh, in *Community Development Journal,* 33.3
Burden, T. 1998, *Social Policy and Welfare: a clear guide,* London: Pluto Press
Burton-Jones, A. 1999, *Knowledge Capitalism: Business, work and learning in the new economy,* Oxford, Oxford University Press
Butcher, H. 1993, *Community and Public Policy,* London: Pluto Press
Butcher, Collis, Glen, Sills, 1980, *Community Groups in Action,* London: RKP
Butler, B. 1996, The Tree, the Tower and the Shamen: the material culture of resistance of the M11 link road protest of Wanstead and Leytonstone, London, *Journal of Material Culture,* 1.3
Butler and Whitlam, 1989, *Feminist Group Work; Self Identity and Change,* London: Sage
Cabinet Office, 2000, *National Strategy for Neighborhood Renewal: a framework for consultation,* London
Cant, R. Kelly, E. 1995, *Roads to Racial Equality,* Edinburgh: SCVO
Castells, M. 1977, *The Urban Question,* London: Edward Arnold
Castells, M. 1983, *The City and The Grassroots,* London: Edward Arnold
Castells, M (et al) 1999 *Critical Education in the Information Age,* Oxford: Rowman and Littlefield
CCETSW, 1991, *Anti Racist Social Work Education,* London, CCETSW
CDP Inter-Project Editorial Team, 1974, *Interproject Report,* London: CDP IIU

CDP Inter-Project Editorial Team, 1976, *Whatever Happened to Council Housing,* London: CDP IIU
CDP Inter-Project Editorial Team, 1977a, *The Costs of Industrial Change,* London: CDP IIU
CDP Inter-Project Editorial Team, 1977b, *Gilding the Ghetto,* London: CDP IIU
Channan et al, 1989, *Affirming Flame,* London: CDF
Chaudhry, F. 1996, *Race and Poverty in Strathclyde,* Glasgow: Poverty Alliance
Checkoway, B. 1995, Six Strategies of Community Change, in *Community Development Journal,* 30.1
Cleaver, H. 1997, Socialism, in Sachs, W. *The Development Dictionary,* London: Zed Books
Coates, K. Silburn, R. 1970, *Poverty the Forgotten Englishman,* Harmondsworth: Penguin
Cockburn, C. 1978, *The Local State,* London: Pluto Press
Cohen, A. 1982: A Polyethnic London carnival as a contested cultural performance. *Ethnic and Racial Studies* 5, pp 23-41.
Cohen, A. 1993, *Masquerade Politics: explorations in the structure of urban cultural movements,* Oxford, Berg
Cohen, A. 2000, *The Symbolic Construction of Society,* London, Routledge
Coit, K. 1978, Local Action, Not Citizen participation in Tabb & Sawers, Marxism and the Metropolis, Oxford University Press
Coles, B. 1995, *Youth and Social Policy,* London: UCL Press
Collins, T. (2002) Community Development and State Building, in *Community Development Journal,* 37.1
Community Development Foundation, (2004) *Survey of Community Development Workers in the UK,* London, CDF
Cooke & Shaw 1996, *Radical Community Work: perspectives from practice in Scotlad,* Edinburgh: Moray House Publications
Command 3854, 1998, *Working Together for a Healthier Scotland: A consultation document,* The Stationary Office
Command 4048, 1998, *Opportunity Scotland: a paper on life long learning,* The Stationary Office.
Community Partnership Center, 2000, *Promoting Participation in Community Development,* Knoxville: University of Tennessee
Community Workers Co-operative, 1997, *Strategies to Encourage participation,* Community Workers Co-operative
Craig, G. Derricourt, N. Loney, M. 1982, *Community Work and the State,* London: RKP
Craig, G. Mayo, M. 1995a, *Community Empowerment,* London, Zed Books,
Craig, G, Mayo, M. 1995b, Rediscovering Community Development, in *Community Development Journal,* 30.2

Craig, G. Mayo, M. 1998, Community Development in a Global Context, in *Community Development Journal*, 33.1
Crook. Pakulski. Waters. 1993, *Postmodernization: change in advanced society,* London: SAGE
Crummy, H. 1992, *Let the People Sing (Story of Craigmillar),* London: CDF
Cuba and Cocking. 1994, *How to Write About the Social Sciences,* London: Harper Collins
Daly, M. 1991, *Gyn/Ecology,* London: Womens Press (originally published 1979)
Danziger, N. 1997, *Danzigers Brtiain,* London: Flamingo,
Davis, A. *Women, Race and Class,* London: Womens Press
Davis, C. 1993, *Women and Violence at Home,* NFHA
Davis, M. 1998, *The Ecology of Fear: Los Angeles and the Imagination of Disaster,* New York: Henry Holt
Davis, M. 2002, *Dead Cities and Other Tales,* New York: The New Press
Dawkins, R. 1989, *The Selfish Gene,* Oxford, Oxford Paperbacks
De Beauvoir, S. 1983, *The Second Sex,* Harmondsworth: Penguin (originally published 1949)
de Sassure, F.1974 *Course in General Linguistics,* Fontana
Demery, L. Walton, M. 1998, *Are Poverty Reduction and Other 21st Century Social Goals Attainable,* Washington: The World Bank,
Democratic Leadership Council, 1996, *The New Progressive Declaration: a political philosophy for the information age,* Washington: Democratic Leadership Council
Derrida, J. 1976 *Of Grammatology,* trans Gayatri Spivak, Baltimore, John Hopkins University Press
DETR, 1999, *National Need and Deprivation, in Regeneration Programmes – The Way Forward,* Department of Environment, Transport and the Regions
DfEE, 1998, *The Learning Age; a renaissance for a New Britain,* Green Paper, London, HMSO
Dhesi, A. 2000, Social Capital and Community Development, in *Community Development Journal,* 35 No 3
Diamond, J. Nelson, A. 1993, Community Work: Post Local Socialism, in *Community Development Journal,* 28.1
Directorate General 22 (DGXXII), 1995, *Teaching and Learning; towards the learning society,* www.cec.lu/en/comm/dg22/dg22.html
Dobson, A. 1990, *Green Politics,* UC Press
Dobson, A. 1991, *The Green Reader,* Andre Deutsch
Dominelli, L. Mcleod, L. 1989, *Feminist Social Work,* Basingstoke: Macmillan
Dominelli, L. 1990, *Women and Community Action,* Birmingham: Venture Press

Donnison and Middleton, 1987, *Regenerating the Inner City: Glasgow's Experience,* London: RKP
Douglas, T. 1983, *Groups: understanding people gathered together,* London: Routledge.
Drakulic, S. 1996, *Café Europa: life after communism,* London: Abacus
Driver and Martell 1998, *New Labour: politics after Thatcherism,* Polity Press
Drucker, P. 1994, The Age of Social Tranformation, in *Atlantic Monthly,* 11
Drysdale, J. Purcell, R. 1999, Breaking the Culture of Silence: groupwork and community development, in *Groupwork* 1999 11.3
Drysdale, J. Purcell, R., 2000, *Reclaiming the Agenda; participation in practice,* Bradford: CWTC
Duneier, M. 2001 *Sidewalk,* New York: Farrar, Straus and Giroux
Dunleavy, P. 1980 *Urban Political Analysis,* Basingstoke: Macmillan
Dworkin, A. 1981, *Pornography. Men Possessing Women,* London: Womens Press
Eade, D. 1997, *Capacity Building: an approach to people centered development* Oxford: Oxfam
Ellis, J. 1989, *Breaking New Ground: Community Development with Asian Communities,* London: CPF
Equal Opportunities Commission, 1983, Women and Men in Britain, London: EOC
Estrella, M. Gaventa, J. 2000, Who Counts Reality: Participatory Monitoring and Evaluation, A Literature Review, Sussex, *ILDS Working paper 70* also at http://www.ids.ac.uk/ids/publicat/wp/Wp70.pdf
Etzioni, A. 1995, *The Spirit of Community,* London: Fontana
Evans, E. 1992, Liberation Theology, Empowerment Theory and Social Work Practice with the Oppressed, in *International Social Work,* 35
Field, J. 2003 *Social Capital,* London, Routledge
Fine & Macbeth, 1992, *Playing with Fire - training for the creative use of conflict,* Youth Work Press
Flecknoe & Mclellan, 1992, *Neighbourhood Community Development,* Bluebell
Foley, G. 1999, *Learning in Social Action,* London: Zed Books
Forrest, D. 1999, Education and Empowerment: Towards Untested Feasibility, in *Community Development Journal,* 34.2
Foucault, M. 1972, *The Archaeology of Knowledge,* London: Tavistock
Foucault, M., 1984, *The Foucault Reader,* Harmonsdworth: Penguin
Freire, P. 1972, *Pedagogy of the Oppressed,* Harmondsworth: Penguin
Freire, P. 1993, *Pedagogy of the City,* New York: Continuum
Friedland, R. 1992, *Power and Crisis in the City,* Basingstoke: Macmillan
Fritz, C, 1982, *Because I Speak Cockney, They Think I'm Stupid,* Newcastle: Association of Community workers.

Fukuyama, F. 1992, *The End of History and the Last Man,* New York: Free Press
Gaffikin, F. Morrissey, M. 1999, *City Visions: imagining place, enfranchising people,* London: Pluto Press
Galbraith, J. 1994, *The World Economy Since the Wars,* London: Sincair-Stevenson
Galloway, V. 1999 'Building a pedagogy of hope: the experience of the Adult Learning Project', in Crowther, J. Martin, I., Shaw, M. (eds.) *Popular Education and Social Movements in Scotland Today,* Leicester: NIACE, 226 – 239.
Gamble, A. 1994, *The Free Economy and the Strong State,* Basingstoke: Macmillan
Geddes, M. 1997, *Partnership against poverty and exclusion?* Bristol: The Policy Press
Gelpi, E. 1979, *A Future for Lifelong Education,* Manchester: DAHE University of Manchester
Giddens, A. 1990, *The Consequences of Modernity,* Cambridge, Polity
Giddens, A. 1999, *LSE Lecture series*
Glasgow Women's Study Group, 1983, *Uncharted Lives,* Pressgang
Glendinning & Millar, 1992, *Women and Poverty in Britain in the 1990's,* Harvester Wheatsheaf
Goffman, E, 1973, *Relations in Public,* New York: Harper and Row
Goldberg, B. 1996, *Why Schools Fail,* Cato Institute
Gorz, A. 1982, *Farewell to the Working Class: An Essay in Post Industrial Socialism,* London: Pluto Press
Gounis K. 1992. Temporality and the domestication of homelessness. in Rutz HJ, ed. *The Politics of Time.* Washington, DC: American. Anthropological Association
Gramsci, A. 1971, *Selections from the Prison Notebook,* ed by Hoare, Q. and Smith, G. London, Lawrence and Wishart
Gray, A. McGuigan, J. 1997, *Studying Culture: an introductory reader,* London: Arnold
Green, J. Chapman, A. 1992, The British Community Development Project: Lessons for Today, in *Community Development Journal,* 27.3
Gray, J. 1996, *After Social Democracy,* London: Demos
Greene, R. 1998, *The 48 Laws of Power,* London: Profile Books
Gulbenkian Committee, 1968, *Community Work and Social Change,* Harlow: Longman
Gugler, J. 1996, *The Urban Transformation of the Developing World,* Oxford: Oxford University Press
Gupta, A., & Ferguson, J. 1992 Space, identity, and the politics of difference. *Cultural Anthropology,* 7, 1: 6–23.
Habermas, J. 1974, *Theory and Society,* London: Heinemann
Hall, S. 1991, Brave New World, in *Socialist Review* 21

Hall, S. du Gay, P. 1998, *Questions of Cultural Identity,* London: Sage
Hallet, C. 1987, *Critical Issues in Participation,* Newcastle: ACW
Halsey. Lauder. Brown. Wells. 1997, *Education: culture, economy, society,* Oxford
Hampton, W. 1991, *Local Government and Urban Politics,* Harlow: Longman
Hanmer, J. Maynard, M. 1987, *Women, Violence and Social Control,* Basingstoke: Macmillan
Harris, M. 1966, *Town and Country in Brazil,* New York: Columbia University Press
Harris, V. 2000, *ACW Skills Manual,* Newcastle: ACW
Harrison, P. 1985, *Inside the Inner City,* Harmondsworth: Pelican
Harvey, D. 1997, *The Condition of Post Modernity,* Blackwell
Hawtin. Hughes. Percey-Smith. 1994, *Community Profiles - auditing social needs,* Buckingham: OUP
Hayek, F. 1960, *The Constitution of Liberty,* London: Routledge and Keagan Paul
Henderson, P. 1993, *Rural Action,* London: CDF
Henderson, P. Thomas, D. 2002, *Skills in Neighbourhood Work,* London: Routledge and Kegan Paul
Hildebrand, M. Grindle, M. 1994, *Building Sustainable Capacity: challenges for the public sector,* Harvard Institute for International Development
Hill, M. O'Neill, J. 1990, *Underclass Behaviours in the United States: measurements and analysis of determinants,* City University of New York
Hintjens, H. 1998, Community Development in the Third World: Continuity and Change, in *Community Development Journal,* 33.4
Hobbs, T. 1969, Leviathan, Menston: Scholar Press
Hobsbawm, E. 1994, *Age of Extremes, History 1914-1991,* London: Michael Jospeh
Hogget, P. 1997, *Contested Communities: experiences, struggles, policies,* Bristol: The Policy Press
hooks, b. 1990, *Yearnings: Race, Gender, and Cultural Politics,* Boston: South End Press
Hoopes, J. 1991, Peirce *on Signs: writings on semiotics,* Chapel Hill, University of North Carolina Press
Hope, A. Timmel, S. 1995, *Training for Transformation Vols 1,2,3,* Zinbabwe: Mambo Press
Hope, A. Timmel, S. 1999, *Training for Transformation Vol 4,* London: Intermediate Technology Publications
Hopper, K. 1991. Symptoms, survival and the redefinition of public space. Urban *Anthropology* 20:155-75
Horkheimer & Adorno, 1973, *Dialectic of Enlightenment,* London: Allen Lane

Hughes, J. Carmichael, P. 1998, Building Partnerships in Urban Regeneration, in *Community Development Journal,* 33.3
Hutton, W. 1995, *The State We're In,* London, Johnathon Cape
Hutzon & Liddiard, 1994, *Youth Homelessness - The Construction of a Social Issue,* Basingstoke: Macmillan
Ibrahim, A. 1996, *The Asian Renaissance,* Kuala Lumpur: Times Books
Illich, I. 1971, *Deschooling Society,* London: Writers and Readers Publishing Co-operative
Illich, I. 1973, *After Deschooling What?* London: Writers and Readers Publishing Co-operative
Illich, I. Verne, E. 1976, *Imprisoned in the Global Classroom?* London: Writers and Readers Publishing Co-operative
Illich, I. 1990, *Tools for Conviviality,* London: Marion Boyars
Illich, I. 1997, Needs in Sachs, W. *The Development Dictionary,* London: Zed Books
Jackson, P.A. 1988: Street life: the politics of carnival. *Environment and Planning D: Society and Space* 6, pp213-27.
Jacobs, J. 1972, *The Death and Life of Great American Cities,* Harmondsworth: Penguin
Jacobs, S. Popple, K. 1994, *Community Work in the 1990's,* Nottingham: Spokesman
Jarvis, P. 1995, *Adult and Continuing Education,* London: Routledge and Kegan Paul
Jeffs & Smith. 1987, *Youth Work,* Basingstoke: Macmillan
Jeffs & Smith. 1988, *Welfare and Youth Work Practice,* Basingstoke: Macmillan
Jeffs & Smith. 1990, *Using Informal Education,* Buckingham: Open University Press
Jameson, F. 1984, Postmodernism: or the cultural logic of late capitalism, *New Left Review* 146
Jones, C. 1996, *PRA in Central Asia: Coping With Change*, Brighton: IDS Sussex University,
Kaplan, R. 1994, The Coming Anarchy, *Atlantic Monthly*
Kaplan, R. 1997, *The Ends of the Earth*, Papermac
Kaplan, R. 1998, *An Empire Wilderness,* New York, Random House,
Kasinitz, P. 1995, Metropolis*: Center and Symbol of our times,* New York: New York UP
Kelleher and Whelan. 1992, *Dublin Communities in Action,* Dublin: Combat Poverty Agency
Kelly, A. Sewell, S. 1989, *With Heads, Hearts and Hands, Dimensions of Community Building,* Brisbane: Boolarong Press
Kelly, K. 1996, The Economics of Ideas, in *Wired* 4.06
Kenny, S. 1994, *Developing Communities for the Future: Community Development in Australia,* Thomson Nelson

Kenyes, J. 1936, *General Theory of Employment, Interest and Money,* Macmillan

Keough, N. 1998, Participatory Development Principles and Practice, in *Community Development Journal,* 33.3

Kirkwood and Kirkwood. 1990, *Living Adult Education; Freire in Scotland,* Buckingham: Open University Press

Klein, N. 2000, *No Logo,* London: Flamingo

Le Grand, J. 1982, *The Strategy of Equality,* London: Allen & Unwin

Leggatt, J. 1999, *The Carbon War,* Harmondsworth: Allen Lane The Pengiun Press,

Lanagan & Day. 1993, *Women, Oppression and Social Work,* London: Routledge and Kegan Paul

Lattimer, M. 2000, *The Campaigning Handbook,* London: Directory of Social Change

Lenin, V. 1960, *Collected Works,* London: Lawrence and Wishart

Li, X. 1998, Postmodernism and Universal Human Rights: why theory and reality don't mix in *Free Inquiry,* 18.4

Liberty. 1994, *Defending Diversity and Dissent; what's wrong with the criminal justice and public order bill,* London: Liberty

Liebow, E. 1967, *Talley's Corner Washington DC: A Study of Negro Streetcorner Men,* London: Routledge and Kegan Paul

Lightfoot, J. 1992, *Involving Young People in their Communities,* London: CDF

Locke, J. 1977, *Essay Concerning Human Understanding,* Glasgow: Collins

London Edingburgh Weekend Return Group. 1980, *In and Against the State,* London: Pluto Press

Loney, M. 1985, *Communities Against Government: The British Community Development Project 1968-78,* London: Heineman

Loney, M. 1995, *The State of the Market; Politics and Welfare in Contemporary Britain,* Buckingham: Open University

Lovell A. 1992. Seizing the moment: power, contingency, and the temporality in street life, in Rutz H. J. (ed) *The Politics of Time,* Washington, DC: American. Anthropological Association

Lovett, T. 1975, *Adult Education, Community Development and Working Class,* London: Ward Lock

Lovett, T. 1988, *Radical Approaches to Adult Education,* London: Routledge and Kegan Paul

Lowe, S. 1986, *Urban Social Movements,* Basingstoke: Macmillan

Low, S. 1996 The Anthropology of Cities: Imagining and Theorizing the City, in *Annual Review of Anthropology,* 25: 383-409

Lyotard, J F. 1984, *The Postmodern Condition,* Minneapolis: University of Minnesota Press

McKay, G. 1996, *Senseless Acts of Beauty: cultures of resistance since the sixties,* London: Verso
Mann, M. 1987, Ruling Class Strategies and Citizenship, *Sociology* 21
Marcuse, H. 1964, *One Dimensional Man: Studies in the Ideology of Advanced Industrial Society,* London: Routledge and Kegan Paul
Marris, P. 1987, *Meaning and Action: Community Planning and Conceptions of Change,* London: RKP
Martin, D-C. 2001 Politics behind the mask: studying contemporary carnivals in political perspective, theoretical and methodological suggestions, *Research in Question* 2
Marx, K. 1984, *Basic Writings on Politics and Philosophy - Marx and Engles,* London: Fontana
Maslow, A. 1943, A Theory of Human Motivation, *General Psychological Review* 50.
Max-Neef, M. 1989, Human Scale Developments: An Option for the future in *Development Dialogue* 1
Mayo, M. 1977, *Women in the Community,* London: RKP
Mayo, M. 1994, *Communities and Caring,* Basingstoke: Macmillan
Mayo, M. 1997, *Imagining Tomorrow, adult education for transformation,* Leicester: NIACE,
Mayo, P. 1999, *Gramsci, Freire and Adult Education,* London: Zed Books,
Macdonald, R. 1997, *Youth, the Underclass and Social Exclusion,* London: Routledge and Kegan Paul
McLellan, D. 1987, *Karl Marx: His Life and Thought,* Basingstoke: Macmillan
Middleton, N. 1994, *Kalashnikovs and Zombie Cucumbers: travels in Mozambique,* London: Phoenix
Mies, M. Vandana, S. 1993, *Ecofeminism,* London: Zed Books
Miller, C. Bryant, R. 1990, Community Work in the UK: Reflection on the 1980's in *Community Development Journal,* 25.4
Millet, K. 1977, Sexual Politics, London: Virago
Mills, C Wright. 1959, *The Sociological Imagination,* Harmondsworth: Pelican
Milne, S. 1995, *The Enemy Within,* London: Pan
Mitchell, J. Oakley, A. (eds.), 1986, *What is Feminism?* Oxford: Blackwell,
Monbiot, G. 2000, *Captive State: the corporate takeover of Britain,* Basingstoke: MacMillan
Morgan, P. 1994, *A Framework for Capacity Building – What Why and How,*
Mullender & Ward. 1991, *Self Directed Groupwork: users take action for empowerment,* Whiting and Birch
Munn and Drever. 1990, *Using Questionnaires in Small Scale Research,* SCRE

Murphy, M. 2002 Social Partnership - is it the only game in town, *Community Development Journal*, 37.1
NCVO. 1994, *Supporting Environmental Action*, Warburton
Newham Monitoring Project. 1991, *Forging a Black Community - Asian and Afro Carribean struggles in Newham*, NMP/CARF
Nietzsche, F. 1968, *The Will to Power*, New York
Nelson & Wright. 1997, *Power and Participatory Development*, ITP
New Internationalist. 1999, *The World Guide - Millenium Edition*, Oxford: New Internationalist
Ng, R. 1988, *The Politics of Community Services: Immigrant Women, Class and State*, Toronto: Garamond Press
Niebanck, P. 1999, Community Development Training: An Industry Discovering Itself, *Community Development Journal*, 34.1
Norberg-Hodge, H, 1991, *Ancient Futures – Learning from Ladakh*, Rider
O'Donovan, O. 2000, Theorising the Interactive State; reflections on a popular participatory initiative in Ireland, *Community Development Journal*, 35.3
OECD. 1996, *The Knowledge Based Economy*, Paris, OECD
Ohio State University. 1999, *Fact Sheet: community development* www.ag.ohio-state.edu/~ohioline/cd-fact/1700.html
Ohmae, K. 1996, *The End of the Nation State*, London: HarperCollins
Ohri, A. Manning, B. Curno, P. 1982, *Community Work and Racism*, London: RKP
Oliver, M. 1990, *Politics of Disablement*, Basingstoke: Macmillan Education
O'Malley, J. 1977, *The Politics of Community Action*, Nottingham: Spokesman
Oppenheim & Harker. 1996, *Poverty the Facts*, London: Child Poverty Action Group,
Paine, T. 1791, *The Rights of Man*
Park, R. 1925, *The City*, Chicago: University of Chicago Press
Patel, S. 1997, *From the slums of Bombay to the housing estates of Britain*, CIVA,
Pearce, J. 1993, *At the Heart of the Community Economy*, Gulbenkian Foundation
Percy-Smith, J. 2000, *Policy Responses to Social Exclusion*, Buckingham: OU Press
Peters, M. 2002, Education Policy in the Age of Knowledge Capitalism, Keynote address to the *World Comparative Education Forum*, Beijing
Pilger, J. 1992, *Distant Voices*, London: Vinatge
Pilger, J. 1996, *Heroes*, London: Pan
Pilger, J. 1998, *Hidden Agendas*, London: Vintage
Pit & Keane. 1984, *Community Organising? You've never really tried it! J & P Consultancy*, Birmingham

Popple, K. 1996, *Analysing Community Work,* Buckingham: OUP
Portes, A. 1998, Social Capital: its origins and application in modern sociology, *Annual Review of Social Sciences* 24
Powell, J. 1996, *Derrida for Beginners,* Writers and Readers
Powell, J. 1998, *Postmodernism for Beginners,* Writers and Readers
Purcell, R. 1998, *The Art of Community: a strategic view of community work, community organising and campaigning,*
http://www.gla.ac.uk/Acad/AdultEd/Personnel/rodp/elec/art.htm
Purcell, R. Brown, S. 1996, *New Directions: A Study of Scottish Community Organisations,* Glasgow: SCDC,
Purcell, R. 2003, Empowering Communities Through Knowledge Driven Practice, *InsideOut Biennial Conference, Charting uncertainty; change, community and citizenship,* Brisbane, http://www.uq.edu.au/insideout/pdfs/rodpurcell.pdf
Purcell, R. 2004, Towards a Redefinition of Community Development, in *Community Development, Human Rights and the Grassroots (Conference Proceedings),* Melbourne: Deakin University
Purcell, R. 2005 Lifelong Learning in the Community: social action, in Sutherland, P. and Crowther, J. (eds) *Lifelong Learning,* Routledge
Putnam, R. 1996, Who Killed Civic America, *Prospect,* March
Radford, J. 1970, 'From King Hill to the Squatting Association' in Lapping, A. (ed.) *Community Action* (Fabian Tract 400) London: Fabian Society.
Rist , G. 1997, *History of Development,* London: Zed Books
Road Alert, *Road Raging,* http://www.eco-action.org/rr/index.html
Robertson, D. 1992, *Choices for Tenants,* Edinburgh: SCVO
Rotenberg, R, McDonogh G.W. 1993. *The Cultural Meaning of Urban Space,* Westport, CT: Bergin & Garvey
Rotenberg, R. 1995. *Landscape and Power in Metropolitan Vienna.* Baltimore: Johns Hopkins Press
Routledge, P. 1996, The Third Space as Critical Engagement, *Antipode* 28.4
Routledge, P. 1997, The Imagineering of Resistance: Pollok Free State and the practice of postmodern politics, *Transaction of the Institute of British Geographers*
Rowbotham, S. 1970, *Hidden from History,* London: Pluto Press
Rowbotham, S. 1983, *Dreams and Dilemmas,* London: Virago
Rowbotham, S. 1979, *The Past is Before Us: Feminism in Action Since the 1960's,* Harmondsworth: Penguin
Rowbotham, S. 1992, *Women and Movement : Feminism and Social Action,* London:. Routledge
Roy, A. 1999, *The Cost of Living,* London: Flamingo
Roszak, T. 1970, *The Making of a Counter Culture: reflections on a technocratic society and its youthful opposition,* London

Rutz, H. J. (ed) 1992, *The Politics of Time,* Washington, DC: American. Anthropological Association
Sachs, W. 1997, *The Development Dictionary,* London: Zed Books
Sadie, S. editor, 1980: *The new Grove dictionary of music and musicians,* London: Macmillan
Sainath, P. 1999, *Everybody Loves a Good Drought,* London: Headline Books
Sardar, Z. 1997, *Postmodernism and the Other,* London: Pluto Press
Saunders. (ed), 1998, *Action for Health,* London: CDF
Schuller, T. Field, J. 1998, Social Capital, Human capital and the Learning Society, *International Journal of University Adult Education,*
Scottish Executive. 1999, *Inclusive Communities: report of the strategy action team,* Edinburgh
Scottish Executive. 2000, *Social Justice; a Scotland where everyone matters,* Edinburgh
Scottish Office. 1999, *Promoting Social Inclusion; The Strategic Framework,* Edinburgh
Senge. P. 1993, *The Fifth Discipline: art and practice of learning organisations,* Random House
Shaw, R. 1996, *The Activists Handbook,* University of California
Shor, I. Freire, P. 1987, *A Pedagogy for Liberation,* Westport: Bergin and Garvey
Seebohm Report. 1968, *Local Authority and Allied Personal Social Services,* London: HMSO
Shutt, H. 1998, *The Trouble with Capitalism,* London: Zed Books
Sivanandan, A. 1990, *Communities of Resistance; Writing on Black Struggles for Socialism,* London: Virago
Skinner, S. 1997, *Building Community Strengths,* London: CDF
Slocum, R. Wichart, L. Rocheleau, D. and Thomas-Slayter, B. 1998, *Power, Process and Participation – Tools for Change,* London: Intermediate Technology,
Smith, A. 1976, *The Wealth of Nations,* Oxford: Clarendon Press
Smith, B. 1998, Participation without Power: Subterfuge or Development, *Community Development Journal,* 33 No 3
Smithies, J. Webster, G. 1987, Feminist Organising in Community Work, *Critical Social Policy,* 17
Strinati, D. 1995, *An Introduction to Theories of Popular Culture,* London: Routledge and Kegan Paul
Storey, J. 1997, *Introduction to Cultural Theory and Popular Culture,* Prentice Hall,
Sun Tzu, *Art of War,* on the Internet at: http://www.sonshi.com/
Tanner, M. 1996, *The End of Welfare: fighting poverty in the civil society,* Cato Institute

Taylor, J. 1998, Transformation and Development: A South African Perspective, *Community Development Journal*, 33.4
Taylor, M. Langan, J. and Hogget, P. 1995, *Encouraging Diversity in Voluntary and Private Organisations in Community Care.*
Taylor. Marais. Kaplan. 1997, *Action Learning for Development*, Juta - South Africa
Taylor, M. 2003, *Public Policy in the Community*, Basingstoke: Palgrave
Teather, E K. 2001, Time out and worlds apart; tradition and modernity meet in the time space of the gravesweeping festivals of Hong Kong, *Singapore Journal of Tropical geography*, 22(2), pp 156-172
Thomas, D. 1983, *The Making of Community Work*, London: George Allen and Unwin
Thompson, E P. 1978, *The Making of the English Working Class*, Harmondsworth: Pengiun
Thompson, N. 1998, *Promoting Equality*, Basingstoke: Macmillan
Tight, M. 1983, *Adult Learning and Education*, London: Croom Helm
Tomlinson, J. 1991, *Cultural Imperialism*, London: Pinter
Tonnies, F. 1957, *Community and Society: Gemeinschaft und Gesellschaft* translated and edited by Charles P. Loomis, The Michigan State University Press.
Touraine, A. 1981, *The Voice and the Eye. An analysis of Social Movements*, Cambridge: Cambridge University Press.
Tuckman, B. 1965, Developmental sequence in small groups, *Psychological Bulletin*, 63
UNED. 2001, *Earth Summit 2002: briefing paper*, http://www.nssd.net/References/Links/es2002bp.pdf
United Nations Development Programme. 1996, *Global Report on Human Settlements*, New York, UNDP
United Nations Development Programme. 1997, *Capacity Development: technical advisory paper 2*, New York, UNDP
United Nations Development Programme. 1998, *Empowering People: A Guide to Participation*, http://www.undp.org/csopp/paguide.htm
United Nations Development Programme. 1998, *Human Development and Human Rights: report of the Oslo symposium*, New York, UNDP
United Nations Development Programme. 1999, **Human Development Index 1999**, New York, UNDP
United Nations Development Programme. 2000, *Human Development Report 2000*, New York, UNDP
United Nations Development Programme. 2004, *Cultural liberty in today's diverse world, in Human Development Report 2004*, New York, UNDP
Van Koningssbruggen, P. 1997 *Trinidad carnival: a question of national identity*, London, Caribbean
Van Rees, W. *Survey of Contemporary Community Development in Europe*, European Bureau for Social Development

Vandana, S. 1989, *Staying Alive: Women, Ecology and Development,* London: Zed Books
Visvanathan, N. 1996, *Women and Gender Development Reader,* London: Zed Books
Waddington, P. 1983, Looking Ahead – Community Work in the 1980's in Thomas D, (ed.) *Community Work in the Eighties,* London: NISW
Walter, S. 1997, *Globalization, Adult Education and Training,* NIACE
Wang, C. (1998) 'Photovoice: involving homeless men and women of Washtenaw County, Michigan', in *Health Education and Behaviour,* 25, (1) 9-10.
Waterman, S. Carnivals for Elites? The cultural politics of arts festivals, *Progress in Human Geography* 22.1 pp 54-74
Wazaki, H. 1993 The Urban Festival and Social Identity, in *Humanizing the City? Social Contexts of Urban Life at the turn of the Millennium.* A Cohen (ed) Edinburgh, Edinburgh UP
Western, J. 1992: *A Passage to England. Minneapolis,* MN: University of Minnesota Press.
Whitmore, B. Wilson, M. 2000, *Social Development in the Era of Globalism,* Fernwood
Whyte, W. 1993, *Street Corner Society: the social structure of an Italian slum,* Chicago: University of Chicago Press
Wilcox, D. 1995, *The Guide to Effective Participation,* York: Joseph Rowntree Foundation
Williams, F. 1993, *Social Policy - A Critical Introduction,* Oxford: Polity Press
Williams, R. 1989, *Resources of Hope,* Verso
Wilson, J. and Kelling, G. 1982, Broken Windows, *The Atlantic Monthly,* March 1982
Wolfensberger, W. 1972, *The Principle of Normalization in Human Services,* Toronto: National Insitiute on Mental Retardation
Wollstonecraft, M. 1992, *A Vindication of the Rights of Women,* Harmondsworth: Penguin, (originally published in 1793).
Working Group of the WTO. 1999, *A Citizens Guide to the World Trade Organisation,* New York: Apex Press
Wright, J. Green, M. Warren, L., 1994, *An Assessment of Crime in Maryland Today,* Maryland State Conference of Branches, NAACP
World Bank. 1996, *Poverty Reduction and the World Bank: progress and challenges in the 1990's,* Washington: World Bank
World Neighbors. 2000, From the Roots Up, Oklahoma: World Neighbours
Yurval, D. 1992, Fundamenatalism, Multiculturalism and Women in Britain in Donald and Rattansi (eds) *Race Culture and Difference,* London: Sage/Open University Press

Summary Index

Alinsky, Saul 25, 199, 201, 206-7
Baudrillard, Jean 144-146
Blair, Tony 100-101, 107, 211
Brown, Gordon 103
Capitalism 119-124
Castells 171-173
Chaos Theory 147-148
Communitarianism 134-136
Community
- definitions of 170-171
- capacity building 208-211

Community development projects (CDP's) 17-19
Community Work
- colonial history 15
- critical questions for workers 229-231
- current trends 33-36
- definitions 6
- empowerment 190, 257-258, 283-4
- groups 217-219, 222-223
- groupwork model 224-229
- models 186-192, appendix 1
- non directive approach 16
- organising 198-205
- theories of the state 154-157
- values 44-45

Conservative Government 95-98
Criminal justice Act 30
Culture 137-140
Democracy 59
Derrida, Jacques 148-149

Easterhouse 78-79
Equality 46-51
- see poverty
Feminism 124-128
- and community development 19
Foucault, Michel 146-147
Freire
- community work practice 159-162
- examples of practice 12-13
Gramsci, Antonio 157-159, 199
Gulbenkian Foundation 16
Globalisation 30-32, 69-76
- IMF 71
- transnational corporations 70, 73
- WTO 7
Greenpeace 33
Identity 147
Illich, Ivan 133-134
Information Age 76-78
Lao Tzu 14
Leadership 203-205, 213-215, 258
Learning Circles 219-221
Libertarianism 128-134
Lifelong Learning 104
Hayek 129
Marxism 116-119
Memes 32
Millennium Development Goals 63
-summary appendix 3
Modernism see Postmodernism
Needs 51-53
- identifying 253-260
New Labour 98-103, 105-110
New Right 128-131
Participation 192-198

- Civic Index 245-248
- model of practice 238-245, append 2
- monitoring and evaluation 261-264
Postmodernism (and Modernism) 140-153, 162-164
Power 205-207
Poverty 78
- absolute and relative 79
- income inequality 80-82
- models 282
PRA 234-238
Protest (secret history of) 26-33
Reclaim the Streets 32
Research methods 248- 253
Rights 53-58
- UN declaration 54, 78
Seebohm Report 17
Social capital 211-213
Social Entrepreneurship 36-40
Social Inclusion 106-110
Social Movements 29, 137-140
- see Castells

Social Planning 34-36
Socialism 113-115
Stakeholding 102
Sustainability 85-89, 191
- Rio 85
Third Way 98-100
Traditional development 64
- oil crisis 66, 114
- international debt 67
United Nations Development Project 73-76
- capacity building 208-211
- sustainability 85-89
Urbanisation 82-84
- The Street 173-178
- Festivals 179-184
Women (as development) 84
- see Feminism
World Bank 71
Zambia 63-64
Zapatista 68

Lightning Source UK Ltd.
Milton Keynes UK
12 March 2010

151321UK00001B/36/A